9 Gold Bullets

By Christopher G. Moore

Novels in the Vincent Calvino P.I. series

Spirit House
Asia Hand
Zero Hour in Phnom Penh
Comfort Zone
The Big Weird
Cold Hit
Minor Wife
Pattaya 24/7
The Risk of Infidelity Index
Paying Back Jack
The Corruptionist
9 Gold Bullets

Other novels

A Killing Smile
A Bewitching Smile
A Haunting Smile
His Lordship's Arsenal
Tokyo Joe
Red Sky Falling
God of Darkness
Chairs
Waiting for the Lady
Gambling on Magic

Non-fiction

Heart Talk
The Vincent Calvino Reader's Guide
The Cultural Detective

9 Gold Bullets

A VINCENT CALVINO P.I. NOVEL

CHRISTOPHER G. MOORE

Heaven Lake Press

Distributed in Thailand by:
Asia Document Bureau Ltd.
P.O. Box 1029
Nana Post Office
Bangkok 10112 Thailand
Fax: (662) 260-4578
Web site: http://www.heavenlakepress.com
email: editorial@heavenlakepress.com

Heaven Lake Press paperback edition 2011

Jacket design: K. Jiamsomboon
Author's photograph: Mick Elmore © 2009

ISBN 978-616-90393-7-2

For Peter Dennis and Milan Popelka

It takes two to make an accident.
The Great Gatsby

Part 1

The Downtown Halloween Bachelor

ONE

"I'm wearing a werewolf mask," said Josh Levy.

LATE OCTOBER. COOL, still air, no wind, as Calvino
waited on the Lower East Side. Another half hour before the
sun would set. Not day and not night. A dead in-between
time, with the traffic picking up volume, but also a time for
the Halloween diehards to don their masks. As he waited,
Calvino looked up and down the street, noting the kinds of
masks the revelers were wearing. The Thais have a saying—
sai na kak. In English it means wearing a mask, but what
it really means is that behind the smile might be a ticking
bomb. True intentions are hidden beneath the disarming
smile, and you have to search for clues or risk being caught
wrong-footed. This perspective makes Thais suspicious, on
edge around strangers. You'll see them looking around the
office, club or dinner table, sizing people up as if it were
Halloween every day of the year.

The street on the Lower East Side could have passed as a
crime scene, one ripped out of a Hollywood movie trailer—
one of the Rip Van Winkle stories where a guy wakes up
after twenty years and looks around and tries to make sense
of the situation, masks and all. *Sai na kak*, thought Calvino.
He found himself thinking in Thai.

Vincent Calvino stood on the street corner, looking over
the crowd for a werewolf mask. Halloween flooded the streets

with straight-to-video horror movie-like extras dressed as ghouls, vampires, pirates and witches. He approached a guy in a werewolf mask.

"Josh?" he asked.

"Fuck off," said the wrong werewolf.

Another man walked by wearing a werewolf mask without giving Calvino a second look. Manhattan seemed to be overrun by the wrong kind of werewolf, he thought. None of them were his man. In this reality show of a movie, the murderers and villains dressed up in masks to look like muggers, bank robbers, thugs and wise guys—or dressed as monks and priests and combat wounded military personnel—to stroll anonymously alongside dead-eyed goblins. Watching for that werewolf on Halloween in New York, it occurred to Calvino that this was the perfect night to kill someone and get away with murder.

On Wednesday the threatening calls to Josh started, calls about a set of coins he'd brought back from Thailand. Josh had been cool, with no emotion in his voice. But what Calvino heard on the phone half an hour ago was a different voice, the tone colored by the emotional frequency of someone who'd been hurt. It was a sound most cops, investigators and emergency workers recognized—it came from the fear-and-pain-contracted voice box of a victim.

"You okay?" Calvino had asked him.

"Nothing I can't handle," Josh had said.

Calvino hadn't pressed him. Victims could also be brave, he'd thought.

Josh had said, "You got time to meet before the party?"

Calvino glanced at his watch. It was quarter to six in the evening. The party wasn't going to start until eight.

"Okay, corner of Astor and Saint Marks," Calvino said.

"I'll be there in fifteen minutes."

"Yeah." That hadn't seemed like enough time.

"I'm wearing a werewolf mask."

4

"You're serious."

"I'm not certain . . ." Swallowing, in a whispered tone he'd continued, "Someone might be following me."

"Another werewolf?" Calvino asked.

"Russians."

Josh ended the call with Calvino faster than a bar *ying* disappearing into the shower.

Calvino remembered a couple of Russians who stood out in his memory like skullcaps in Utah. The main Russian was Andrei, a genius mathematician and self-made man, Josh's client, or ex-client, as Josh had gone to work for him. And Andrei's sidekick, a Russian businessman named Maxim who lived in Pattaya, Thailand. A couple of months earlier, Calvino met Maxim in Bangkok. Maxim had hated Calvino the minute he'd laid eyes on him. The way the Russians operated in Thailand reminded Calvino of an old law—there's no shame in whoring; the only shame is in not getting enough money for it.

Whatever it was, it couldn't wait until after Josh's bachelor party at Sammy's. And it concerned Russians. Josh was in a hurry. Fifteen minutes should have put him at the corner at six o'clock. Josh's billing cycle was based on fifteen-minute intervals, the smallest atomic measure of a lawyer's time. Josh should have been on time. Calvino imagined Josh hanging somewhere nearby, looking over his shoulder, darting from doorway to doorway like a character in a bad movie, edging his way to Astor and Saint Marks on Halloween night. Even as a kid, Josh Levy had had a flair for the dramatic moment. The real drama had started once he'd resigned from the law firm and signed on with Andrei.

Calvino had come to New York for a couple of reasons. Josh had asked him to be the best man at his wedding. Many years before, Josh had been best man at Calvino's wedding. That marriage hadn't worked out. It wasn't anyone's fault.

5

The divorce some twenty years ago was a distant memory, but the failure hadn't deterred Josh Levy from asking Vincent Calvino to be his best man. But there was second reason—it had to do with a leather pouch holding rare Thai coins that Josh had brought back to New York for his Russian boss, Andrei.

The fucking coins, Calvino had thought as Josh's call ended. Calvino had walked through the small lobby of the co-op building, a two-minute walk from the corner of Astor and Saint Marks. He'd been thinking about the way Josh had shuddered when he'd said the word "Russians." If Josh Levy had ever been scared before, Calvino couldn't remember it.

Calvino posted himself on the corner, pacing back and forth, hands inside the pockets of his leather jacket. Looking down the street, he expected Josh to come from Astor Place. He watched as the crowd crossed on Astor. Some wore Halloween masks—the cheap ones. They were young, too, off to a party as a clown or a ghoul; small crowds of students in a collective party mode. No one looked like a Russian. He would recognize Andrei or Maxim but couldn't imagine them walking along Astor. As for other Russians, they came in different heads, body types and hair colors.

Calvino carried a bag. Inside it was a pirate's mask he'd bought for a hundred dollars on West 4th. It was only the early hours of Halloween, and this was insane. He'd tried phoning Josh but his cell phone was off. With the crowds there would be no way to tell whether Josh was being followed. Or, if so, how many were tailing him. Professionals worked in teams; that's why they rarely lost a target. More masked people walked past Calvino. No werewolves. It wasn't the night of All Souls; it was the night of inhabiting a soul that belonged to someone else.

He tried Josh's number again but his cell phone was still switched off.

A parade of young university-aged women dressed in black tights, jackets and hats walked past him. None of them made eye contact. No smile, no nothing but the treadmill walk-past at high-medium speed. It was still early, and those not in costume were shopping for costumes, running around in sweatshirts, jeans and running shoes, the fashion on the Lower East Side. An old Jewish woman with red hair and gold bangles on her wrists, clutching shopping bags, gabbed with her friends on either side as they walked, crowding everyone to the margin of the sidewalk as they headed toward Cooper Union. She looked vaguely Russian. The kind of person he'd detail for a surveillance job on the Lower East Side.

More candidates streamed past—a hunchback, a dwarf, a woman with deformed arms and flipper-like hands. People with big hair yapped into their cell phones, smiley faced, zonked in some headspace other than the street, showing their teeth as they laughed. Every second person carried a backpack. North Point. They looked like travelers in Bangkok or Katmandu, young men and women geared up for trekking on urban streets.

At Cooper and Astor, in the deli opposite Cooper Union, Calvino bought a coffee and went back out to the corner. He thought he saw a werewolf mask and almost spilled his coffee trying to get a closer look. A white woman elbowed him out of the way as she passed; she wore black head to toe except for green sandals and white feet and red-painted toenails. A fashion ninja with hidden powers and ninja stars up her sleeves. Men with tall black hats wore earrings and smelled of perfume. A bag lady had a ski jacket slung over her shoulders like a 1940s movie star; she was Asian, seventy-ish, with blurry eyes and a slack mouth that looked like it had spit out a couple of sets of false teeth.

A bony finger poked him in the back. Josh Levy came up behind him as Calvino stood drinking his coffee and looking at the ninja woman.

7

"It's me," said Josh. "Don't turn around."

Calvino turned around.

"Josh, what the fuck is going on?"

The werewolf mask was one of those five hundred dollar molded plastic ones with real fur, brown, rubbery warts on one cheek, fangs, and sculpted, arched eyebrows. Calvino stared at the mask and shook his head.

"Vinny, I need to talk."

"Let's go back to my apartment," said Calvino.

Josh shook his head, looked over his shoulder, and then looked back.

"No. Some place public is better. I'm not ready to get in another elevator."

"There's a hamburger joint on 2nd Avenue."

They started to walk down Saint Marks.

"Is that where they grabbed you? An elevator?"

Josh nodded and lowered his head. A sob came out. Calvino put an arm around him. They continued down Saint Marks to a restaurant on the corner of 2nd Avenue. The joint advertised the best burgers in New York. They went inside and took a table away from the door. Josh sat with his back to the door. He removed his mask and put it on the table. Calvino wished he'd left the mask on. Josh had been beaten up. His face was bruised under the right eye. The swelling had turned a cruel smudge of black and his eye was nearly closed. His lower lip was cut, swollen fat like a slug, and his right ear had puffed up like a big mushroom.

"What happened?"

"Two of them jumped me."

"They mugged you?"

Josh shook his head. "Nothing that simple."

"Who were they?"

"They didn't give me their names."

"When?"

8

He sighed, his head falling as he rubbed his jaw. "Two hours ago."

"They didn't happen to be Russians?" asked Calvino.

"They spoke Russian. I've picked up some of the language working with Andrei."

"What'd they want?"

Josh sighed, shaking his head, eyes still full of fear. It was the one thing a man couldn't hide. The eyes never lied.

"Three of the gold bullets were fakes. They think I have them."

"Why would they think that? Josh, there's something you're not telling me."

The fear in his eyes almost made them glow.

"I didn't want to get you involved."

"That hasn't worked out, has it?"

He looked around to see if anyone was listening. Calvino had never seen Josh Levy rattled like this, pitching back and forth in his seat, monsters eating his brain as he stared out through battered eyes.

From the beginning Calvino had had a bad feeling about the Thai coins—bullets, as they are known. A strange choice, to name a coin—one without a head or tail—after a slug that loaded into a firing chamber.

The waitress came to the table with menus. She looked at Calvino.

"I'll have a beer," said Calvino. "And my friend will have a ..."

"A coffee."

"Bring him a whiskey, too."

"Honey, you should get some ice on that eye," she said, clicking her tongue.

After she'd left, Josh leaned forward on his elbows.

"A couple of days ago, I was told that I'd better come up with the genuine bullets. Or I'd have a problem."

Calvino stared at his friend. The bashed face, the nose a little lopsided, suggested this was the category of problem the Russians assumed could be resolved by using violence.

"You didn't say anything."

"I thought I had everything under control."

"Big mistake."

"What am I supposed to do? I gave Andrei the coins from Bangkok. I'm no expert. I was doing him a favor. A fucking small favor. Delivery boy wasn't part of my job."

"Coins for his grandson," said Calvino.

That was Josh's line in Bangkok. His new boss asked him to take back some coins for Andrei's grandson, who collected them.

The waitress returned with ice inside a plastic bag that had been rolled in a towel. It was on the tray with the beer, whiskey and coffee.

"Honey, put this on your eye." She handed him the towel.

"Thanks," he said.

"Fight with the wife?" she asked with a sympathic sigh.

Josh let the remark go.

After she'd left them alone again, Calvino sipped the beer and waited. Josh winced as he pressed the ice pack against his eye and cheek. He couldn't stop the small groans escaping. He tossed back the double shot of whisky, and his body shook like it had been hit by a jolt of electricity. He managed a small smile.

"If I don't produce the real coins they'll kill me next time," he said.

He paused, staring at Calvino.

"Do you have them?" asked Calvino.

Josh shook his head. "I don't. I'm sorry, Vinny. I should have listened when you said don't bring them back. I'm so fucking stupid. And now you're involved. Sorry, Vinny. Really, I mean it."

" 'Involved?' What the fuck does that mean?"

"I had to tell the guys who were beating me up something. They were going to kill me."

Calvino waited until Josh stopped blubbering into the cold pack.

"What did you tell them, Josh?"

"That you had the missing bullet coins. And I'd get them from you."

"And they promised to let you go?"

Josh nodded.

"What else did you tell them?"

"I said there'd been a mix-up. It was a misunderstanding. That I'd get them the coins. I'm asking you to help me out, Vinny."

"You told them that I have the coins. Do you believe I have them?"

Josh shrugged, and slowly his shoulders slumped back in defeat. He leaned back in his chair.

"Things are confused," said Josh, straightening his tie and moving his jaw with his hand, the kind of movement to test whether the muscles and bones are functioning.

"Josh, this isn't gonna work."

"They were going to kill me, Vinny."

"You figured sending them after me would buy you some time."

"Whoa," Josh said, lowering the ice pack. The right side of his face half-frozen, he reached over and patted Calvino's arm. "Andrei will fix it."

"You could've told them Ben Harris had the coins," said Calvino.

"I tried that but it didn't work. They'd already talked to Ben."

"This is like a game of 'tag.' Ben tags you, then you tag me and somehow Andrei is supposed to make the Russians go away? Why didn't you tag him?"

"Andrei trusts me," said Josh, as if he actually believed something that insanely improbable. "He knows I didn't do anything wrong."

Josh had been a lawyer long enough to know that not doing anything wrong was irrelevant when a deal fell apart and someone had to pay the freight. Being in the vicinity of the disappointment was the close cousin of doing something wrong. Mud splashed and everyone got dirty.

"Josh, cancel the bachelor party tonight. Put the wedding on hold. Get out of town until you figure out what happened. You're like a lightning rod on a barn in a thunderstorm."

Josh frowned. He'd been a big shot lawyer in a high-profile Manhattan law firm. Lawyers of that class were wired to solve problems, not run from them. No one had ever suggested he go into hiding like a common criminal on the run. Josh looked offended, as if the insinuation hurt more than the beating. But the last thing he needed was to alienate Vincent Calvino. There were alternatives. He took a deep breath and dug deep down, drawing upon years of practice and negotiation. Calvino had to produce those three gold bullet coins.

Neither would go first. Calvino tried to pull Josh into the open. Josh refused, just as he had with the Russians, and tried to nudge Calvino inside his circle of confidence.

"Vinny, with the Russians you can't ever show them you're afraid."

"Are you giving me advice, or are you talking to yourself?"

"I need to clear this. Tonight. Let me do it my way."

"What happens when these Russians find out you lied to them?"

"But I didn't lie. I'm hiring you to find the four-, two- and one-gram bullets."

"How much time did you tell them I needed?"

"I said a week."

"What did they say?"

"Forty-eight hours. I can negotiate more time. Not that it matters. What we've got is a fuck-up. A misunderstanding. And I've got a call in to Andrei."

"Why isn't he answering the phone?" asked Calvino.

"He does that sometimes. He goes into isolation working on some long equation."

"The genius needs peace and quiet like the rest of us," said Calvino.

"You don't like him."

"I don't know him. Maxim, his friend, I didn't much like him."

"Andrei's coming to my party," said Josh. "Andrei knows me. He knows I'm professional, and that's why he hired me. Why would I cheat his grandson? It's absurd."

Calvino looked at the busted face. Josh was sticking to the story that the coins were for Andrei's grandson. Josh Levy's delusions were becoming progressively more complex and difficult to clean up.

"You're mad at me."

Calvino sipped his coffee.

"Don't take this personally, Josh. But I told you not to get involved with the coins. I said it in Bangkok. Stay away from them. You knew better. You didn't listen. Now you've got a problem. You've bought yourself some time. Nothing more. Once they find out that you bullshitted them, they'll be back."

Josh's eyes widened. He thought about the two men who had escorted him from an elevator, bundled him into a car, drove him to Brooklyn, beat him up, and dumped him at a station for the F train.

"You'll help me out on this?" said Josh.

"Why not go around the corner and buy three Thai bullets?"

Josh raised his hands like a football referee for a time out. "After the party, we'll laugh about it."

"And that's how you see the problem ending? The two of us slapping each other on the back and laughing about what happened to you?"

"Like old times."

Some Russians had threatened to kill Josh but in his mind it turned out to be a mistake and in the end everyone hugs and makes up. Calvino examined the damage the goons had inflicted on Josh's face: It was professional. It was done as a job. There was nothing to make up; only something they wanted. Corporate lawyers weren't trained for physical beatings. To Josh's credit, he'd taken a fair amount of punishment before dropping Calvino's name as a golden parachute. The Russians had either bought Josh's story or they had orders to work him over until he coughed up of someone who had information about the apparent switch of the gold bullets—a strange name for handmade Thai coins fashioned from gold into a form like a prima ballerina, her knees tucked under her chin, and her bottom half, firm and tight, facing out, waiting to inspire a passing Siamese craftsman.

Josh slipped a twenty-dollar bill under his coffee cup. He pulled the werewolf mask over his head. "I'll see you at the party. Eight."

"How many Russians grabbed you?" Calvino smiled, realizing that he was now talking to a werewolf.

"Three," said Josh. "Strong, young and mean." His voice was muffled under the mask.

"Where are you going? To join a pack of werewolves?" asked Calvino.

Josh's cell phone rang as he stood up. He half-turned and put the phone against the rubber mask. The werewolf head nodded. Calvino guessed from the way Josh's body slumped as he sat back down that Josh's face registered fear.

"It's one of them. He wants to talk to you."

Josh handed Calvino the phone.

"Levy says you have what we want."

"Depends what you want," said Calvino.

"Do you have the coins?"

Calvino stared at Josh behind the werewolf mask. It was as if his friend had stopped breathing.

"I don't know you. And I have a rule not to do business over the phone with strangers with funny accents."

There was a pause at the other end.

"We also have a rule. It calls for extreme measures. We apply that rule when someone fails to give us what belongs to us."

Standoff.

Josh Levy removed the mask and whispered to Calvino. "Tell them you'll cooperate. Please tell them that."

"Maxim is the man you need to talk to," said Calvino. "Levy doesn't have them. You can go ahead and kill him. But he can't give you what he doesn't have."

Calvino handed the phone back to Josh.

"This is your problem, Josh," said Calvino, thinking it might be a good idea to borrow one of his cousin's handguns for a couple of days. "You work for Andrei. You've got to figure no Russian is going to push you into a corner without him on side. That means you're gonna have to work it out with Andrei."

"I helped you out once, right?" Josh said. "Your back was against the wall. You had the Chinese looking to put a bullet in your head. Your law firm had dumped you like a load of dirt. Your wife had moved out. You had no one. Did I say, 'Vinny, it's your problem, don't involve me, because I've got better things to do than get in the line of fire with a bunch of Chinese gangsters?'"

Calvino took the phone back. "There's been a misunderstanding. Josh will work it out with Andrei," said Calvino.

The Russian must have been listening to Josh's little speech, grinning and drinking a glass of vodka, admiring his tattoos in a mirror. Only the Russian spoke perfect English; no hint of an accent, making it impossible for Calvino to retain the gangster Russian image. It faded out as the Russian said, "Then we understand each other."

"What's your name?"

"Sparrow."

"Sparrow, he'll need some time."

"You know where they are. Fetch them."

"Phone Maxim. He fetches for Andrei."

"You have them, asshole."

Calvino wanted to reach through the phone and grab the Russian by the throat.

"I don't fucking know where they are, or I would get them. In America only dogs fetch."

"There is no negotiation," said Sparrow.

Calvino rolled his eyes at Josh and covered the phone with the palm of his hand. "Who the fuck is this guy, Sparrow?"

Josh Levy shrugged. "I don't know."

The absence of information shot right through every part of the case. It was the kind of light-fingered conduct that had got men killed ever since gold took on value. Sparrow wanted the real coins returned.

The Russian waited on the other end and as Calvino put the phone to his ear he said, "Mr. Calvino, bring me the coins in three days. If you can't add, don't ask your friend; you can ask me. That's seventy-two hours."

"What if Maxim has them in Thailand?"

"Then *you* would have a problem."

"Why would I have a problem?"

"Like your friend, you ask too many questions. Questions waste time. Goodbye, Mr. Calvino."

Calvino handed Josh Levy the phone. The waitress came to the table.

"Can I get you two gentlemen anything else?"

"Three gold bullets," said Calvino.

"Excuse me?" she said, and had no interest in waiting for an answer. "My shift ends in ten minutes. Do you mind paying the bill?"

Calvino pointed at the twenty-dollar bill under Josh's cup. "Keep the change."

The waitress picked up the cash and left.

"They want the three bullets in three days."

"And if they don't get them?"

Calvino turned his hand into a gun and dropped his thumb three times. "They send three bullets our way."

Josh looked relieved. "That's what I've been trying to tell you, Vinny. These guys will kill us if we don't deliver what they want."

The Russian had done a great job on Josh, thought Calvino. Or he was playing a brilliant game of three-card monte. Calvino got up from his chair, and leaning over the table said, "It's time we had a little talk with Mr. Andrei."

"I told you. He's the one who can straighten all of this out."

Andrei wasn't Calvino's first choice as the guy who could straighten out Josh's problem, seeing that he had a dog in the race. The Russians stuck together like refrigerator repairmen attending a Las Vegas convention.

Outside the restaurant Josh, with his werewolf mask over his head, waved down a taxi and got in the back. The driver didn't even blink as a werewolf in a tailored suit closed the door and gave the address. Like it was something he did every day. Calvino watched the cab spider up 2nd Avenue. He walked back to the apartment of his cousin Nero, who owned real estate on the Lower East Side, Brooklyn and Queens and had given him the place to use while he was in New York.

"If you'd stayed in New York instead of pissing off to Taiwan, you could've bought property too, Vinny."

"Thailand. Not Taiwan."

"Taiwan, Thailand, what's the fucking difference? You weren't here."

TWO

Mafia building on the Lower East Side—Halloween night

Chekhov's rule for guns

CALVINO WALKED AROUND the corner to Astor Place and into Nero's apartment building. It was one of those buildings that never had a robbery, home invasion or mugging. Criminals, even the worst junkies, had enough brains to leave it alone. The second night in the apartment Calvino found the hiding place in the wall of the walk-in closet. Inside the mailbox-sized opening were a couple of 9mm handguns—a Glock 17 and a Browning Hi-Power—plus several boxes of ammo. Enough firepower to keep any real estate owner secure in his bed. Nero had always been a gun freak, an NRA member with badges, billed cap and magazines with covers of Dick Cheney and Charlton Heston. Nero had a paid-up life membership at a shooting range in Jersey.

Colonel Pratt, who was Calvino's long-time "get out of jail" friend in Thailand, had left his unpacked suitcases in the second bedroom. Over the years, Pratt had played that card to help Calvino. But, in America, Pratt was playing a different game with different rules. He had gone to the Thai Embassy in Washington, D.C. for further briefings and orders. Calvino thought about calling the Colonel, but figured it would be better to brief him in person. A phone call with this news would only upset him.

Calvino walked into the closet of Nero's bedroom, switched on the light, removed the wall panel and wrapped his hands around the holstered Glock 17. He pulled it out of the belt holster and removed the clip. One 9mm round was chambered. That was Nero's style. "Never saw any point in a gun that isn't ready to use." Nero's mantra was engraved in Calvino's mind like the date inside a wedding band. It was the same kind of vow, made with the same kind of commitment.

Calvino examined the magazine from the Glock 17 and ejected nine rounds. Again that number had come up—nine—finding him like a bad penny. He slid the rounds back into the magazine and slapped it into the base of the handgun. Turning the Glock around, Calvino recalled Anton Chekhov's rule for guns. A rule invented by a playwright—and a Russian. Russians, like bad pennies, seemed to return to the owner no matter how far they'd been thrown. Onstage, expectations are everything; showing a gun means using a gun before the final curtain. But it doesn't necessarily follow in real life, Calvino thought. On the other hand, maybe Chekhov, being a good Russian, had stuffed that message in a bottle and everyone simply believed it to be true.

Calvino rested the Glock on the bed. He checked the clip on the holster. It was the kind of holster he could wear inside his blue jeans with a clip that slipped over the belt. He fastened the clip to his belt, reached down, picked up the Glock and holstered it. Pulling his sweater down over the holster, he looked around the room before switching off the light, closing the door and walking into the kitchen, where he opened a bottle of Johnnie Walker Black and poured himself a double shot.

He took the glass back to the living room and turned on the TV; a baseball game delayed by rain was a sorry thing to watch. The Yankees were in Philadelphia, waiting for the weather to clear to start game three of the World Series against the Phillies. The bookmakers favored the Yankees; he favored the Yankees. No one had put odds on when the rain would stop. Why would anyone have a bachelor party when the Yankees were playing, and they could sit at home and watch the World Series? Calvino wouldn't expect the Russians to get it, but Josh Levy loved baseball, or at least he had thirty years ago. He'd fallen hard in love if he thought a bachelor party on a game night was the right thing to do to your friends.

On TV the camera scanned the Citizen's Bank Park and found people trying to keep their Halloween costumes dry. The announcer said it was only the second time a World Series had been played on Halloween night, proving that anything that happened once could happen again. Calvino watched a man in a Terminator mask. He pulled down his sweater and concentrated on the ball game. He leaned back, put his legs up on the coffee table, hooked one ankle over the other and sipped the whiskey.

The rain kept falling. He told himself it didn't matter; he wouldn't be able to keep his mind on the game anyway. The TV screen filled with slanting rain. In the void was the empty playing field. Calvino closed his eyes and saw a fastball moving straight toward Josh Levy's bruised face—no longer the face of a lawyer inside the ring of power and privilege, but the face of a frightened and uncertain boy wearing a mask. Josh had one thing going for him. He knew that Calvino would help him. Just like in the old days, when Josh found himself in trouble he turned to Calvino, who always dragged him out of his latest circle of fire.

As Calvino finished the whiskey, the Yankees were still in the dugout, waiting. He aimed the remote, and killed the picture of rain. Calvino pulled his leather jacket off the back of a chair and slipped it on. He had a bad feeling about the trouble Josh was in, and packing one of Nero's guns was a travel insurance policy, good for one journey through Russian territory. He zipped up the jacket. Fishing out the life-sized pirate mask from the shopping bag, he put it on, adjusting the holes for his eyes and nostrils. His head felt like someone had put a can of Sterno inside the mask. He took a couple of steps down the corridor and stared at himself into a mirror. The pirate's jaw-line and eyes vaguely resembled John Travolta. The rubber cheeks were riddled with deep acne scars. A pox of twisted tissue ran along the side of one nostril. The high, thick cheekbones were modeled on Cro-Magnon man. Over the eyes hung big, bushy black eyebrows, and the jaw dropped to expose a row of long, yellowish teeth below a broken potato nose. Pirate, longshoreman or one of the old Bowery drunks who used to live around the corner—the mask sent a different message to anyone who looked at him. The expensive leather jacket was made to match.

He took a good long look at himself. Tough as a Russian named Sparrow, he thought to himself. But the man who looked back at him in the mirror wasn't the same one who'd left New York twenty years ago. It wasn't anyone he knew.

THREE

Chrystie Street, Lower East Side—Halloween night, 8:00 p.m.

"Hey, is it fucking John Travolta?"

CALVINO CROSSED HOUSTON to Chrystie Street. The crowd had thinned out; everyone was inside watching the World Series. Sweat rolled down the back of his neck. He adjusted the pirate mask but it was like a furnace with no thermostat control. His hands were numb with cold, but it wasn't actually that cold. He thought this must be what menopause was like. He couldn't remember the last time he'd felt so hot and cold at the same time. It had been inside a short-time hotel that he didn't want to remember.

A hammer in the back of his head kept hitting the same nail—he'd let himself get involved in someone else's messed-up life. He didn't want any more involvements. Wives, ex-wives, girlfriends, lovers, short-times, your children, her children, both your children together, aging parents, uncles and aunts, cousins, neighbors and classmates—enough entanglements to inflict serious rope burn as you tried to wiggle free.

There was a much larger truth—those dozens of entanglements circulated like a living virus through an overnight train. He should have thanked Josh for reminding him that life was an endless cycle of dealing with a person who wanted to take a big bite out of your apple. In this case some Russians had sunk their teeth in, juice running down the corners of their mouths. And Josh had told them Calvino was holding the apple. It wasn't the kind of message he was happy for Josh to deliver. Sure, he owed him from the old days, and Calvino had no problem paying back that debt. Walking on the Lower East Side, jumping at shadows and worrying about Russian thugs, it crossed his mind that Josh had loaded a large balloon payment onto that old personal debt.

The trip to New York had started out as one thing and turned into something entirely different. Josh's busted up face was a reminder not to get between money and power. Someone wanted in a bad way the complete set of nine gold bullet coins. This wasn't any set of coins—they connected two of the last great absolute rulers. That was enough to make them valuable. Men killed for symbols and icons. Nine gold bullets represented the kind of treasure larger than a man; they belonged to history, a country and its people. Ever since the Thai icons had gone missing, the panic had set in. No one was sharing information. No one trusted anyone.

Calvino had already been involved before he set foot in New York. It wasn't a holiday. It wasn't nostalgia. Calvino hadn't come to stand up at Josh's wedding, to watch the World Series, to see old friends and relatives or to relive the past like on an old TV show. He had come back because he had no choice. The missing Thai treasure had given him no choice but to return to New York.

The purpose of the trip hadn't worked out so far. Probably, it had never been realistic to think that it would. Not with Colonel Pratt tagging along to keep an eye on him. Calvino had got himself involved. He'd backed into the situation. He should have looked in the rear-view mirror. He should have seen it coming in Bangkok. But magical thinking about Josh and the old days in New York had blinded him, made him forget that it's just a matter of time before involvements accumulate and people with connections, power and guns hunt down an involved man.

Sometimes a man had no good choices, just a couple of bad ones, and what mattered was figuring out which was less bad and going with it. A prison sentence from the authorities or a death sentence from Russians thugs. Americans had no problem making that decision. They carried guns, hoping to be an exception to Chekhov and his goddamn gun rule.

Walking along Chrystie Street cleared his mind. Calvino had a good idea that Josh knew he had the missing gold bullet coins—but Josh couldn't bring himself to admit it. What was stopping him? That was what Calvino wanted to know. Or who was stopping him? Josh was either bluffing or he really didn't know about how Calvino fit into the deal. It was a double bluff—or was one bluffing and no one calling the other's hand?

"You're going to be my best man, Vinny. That's something. All these years, and what do we do? We go back to our roots. We were kids together, chased the same girls, hung out," Josh had said.

The last time Calvino had seen the gold bullets was in Bangkok. Josh had laid them out on a table in his hotel room like the winner of a game. He smiled like a cat with a rat in its mouth. He had no idea whether this was Czar Nicholas II's set of nine gold bullets or one of many look-alike sets. This one passed between two great kings at a historic moment and, once that had happened, politics took over, making them gold relics, sacred objects from semi-divine reigns.

Later, Calvino told Colonel Pratt about seeing a set of nine bullets. The Colonel had quoted Shakespeare's Julius Caesar: "Let me tell you, Cassius, you yourself are much condemned to have an itching palm; to sell and mart your offices for gold to undeservers."

Colonel Pratt never trusted either the Russians or Josh. He said sooner or later an itchy palm would turn up on the hands of one of them. He'd been right.

The Russians had worked Josh over until he gave up Calvino as the one with the itchy palm. Josh escaped with a few bruises, cuts and a black eye, shaken to the core, sitting in a hamburger joint on 2nd Avenue, whimpering like a whipped dog. Calvino would have to tell the Colonel what had happened. He shivered in the cold.

A little cold wasn't something that had ever bothered Calvino growing up in New York. October used to be a piece of cake—shirtsleeve weather—yet there he was on Chrystie Street, shivering like a drug addict in withdrawal.

Calvino passed a UPS truck unloading at a warehouse— the doors open, inside palettes stacked with boxes of fruit and plastic juice bottles. His New York street edge had gone dull. That knife wasn't cutting through the night. May be it was cold. But Calvino knew it was more than the weather. He hurried past a couple of showrooms filled with kitchen supplies and appliances, hands in his pockets, looking into the windows of interior design places, shops selling chairs, aprons, waiter vests, scales, blenders, trays, large chrome slicers and sake cups imported from Japan. Selling everything but a pair of fucking gloves.

And then he turned and stood at the top of several steps that led down to Sammy's Restaurant.

FOUR

"Accident." The word worked itself around the table like the mantra of a street hooker looking for a place to shelter for the night.

CALVINO WALKED IN wearing the pirate mask; he was the last guest to arrive. Half a dozen other men sat around at a big wooden table listening to the announcer kill time as the rain continued in Philly. Sammy's had the air of post-war Eastern European secret meeting place where some one vouched for you to get in. Like an old Transylvania speakeasy, it was down a narrow flight of stairs from the street through a door that opened on to a large room that had not been renovated in thirty years. The men who ran Sammy's looked like close kin pulled from a gypsy band. Men whose ancestors lived near the Cave with Bone, men who took bets over the phone, a cigarette hanging from their wet lips, as they cooked large steaks. Josh was the only other guy wearing a Halloween mask. Wires snaked from beneath the mask to his BlackBerry. Tracy Chapman's "Fast Car"—"I want a ticket to anywhere . . . Me myself, I got nothing to lose"—flowed through the earpieces, soothing him. He was covering his wounds, playing for time. Wired for sound at his own bachelor party was weird enough for others to notice.

"What's the score," one of the waiters asked him, pencil behind his ear.

Josh pulled out one of the earpieces.

"I said you must be a New Yorker, you're getting married tomorrow and you're listening to a baseball game."

Josh was listening to music, but he thought it better to go with the flow. "Yankees are gonna win this one," he said. He put the earpiece back in.

It was a strange table, given the nature of the event; it was Josh Levy's bachelor party, and he wasn't showing his face. There was something slightly Freudian about wearing a werewolf mask on Halloween night to one's own bachelor party. But Freud had no more to do with the masked men than Chekhov had to do with the Glock 17 tucked inside Calvino's belt. Calvino thought about removing his mask. He decided to keep it on. As he eased himself into a chair, he got his first question.

"What are you?" asked one of the guests.

"A Somali pirate," said Calvino, removing the mask.

"This is Vinny, my best man," said Josh.

"The guy from Thailand," said Ben Harris, seated across the table.

Calvino raised his hand like a student in the back of the class. "You're confusing being from New York with someone who lives in the city."

"Another lawyer," said the guest with a large forehead, dimpled chin and small eyes. He looked like an intelligent rodent.

"And you're . . . ?" asked Calvino, taking off the mask and wiping the sweat off his face with a napkin.

"Ingram. Software designer."

"Which one is your new boss?" Calvino whispered to Josh.

Josh nodded at the distinguished looking man who sat between Ingram and Harris. Andrei reached for the vodka. The bottle, served inside a block of ice, had a strange, otherworldly appearance. A waiter hovering behind sprang into action, taking the block of ice and pouring. He filled Andrei's glass to the rim, and when he looked up, he caught Calvino's eye.

"Calvino? Haven't seen you around for a while," said the waiter.

"Twenty years is more than a while," said Calvino.

The waiter walked around the table and hugged him.

A couple of the waiters looked familiar in the way an old neighbor you hadn't seen in years looked like someone you once knew. Sammy's waiters still wore the same blue shirts with "Sammy" on the back, seemingly scribbled by a child in a failed handwriting assignment or by someone whose native language was written in an exotic script like Chinese, Japanese or Thai.

The waiter stared at him, smiling, shaking his head.

"Banica," Calvino said.

"You remember," he said, kissing Calvino on the forehead. He had the same general outline, but age had taken a claw and run deep furrows and ridges along his eyes and mouth. The wrinkles left him with the perpetual surprise look of a man who had no idea how he had survived the Cold War. That was what twenty years did to a man who waited tables every night—it gave him gunshot wide-open eyes flecked with sadness and regret.

"I not see you in a long time. But you look the same."

He filled Calvino's glass.

"Same, same, but different," said Calvino, raising his glass. "Here's to you, Banica."

After the waiter left, Calvino said, "Romanians never forget a regular customer."

"A toast to regular customer, Vincent Calvino. My best man from Thailand," said Josh, having removed his werewolf mask. "What's with my face, I heard someone say. I had a little accident. Nothing serious. It serves me right. My mind's been in the clouds and I wasn't watching. Next thing I smash into a pole. Fucking accident. Getting married is dangerous to a man's health."

"Accident." Josh's face made a couple of the men wince. Nothing about it looked like an accident with a pole. Knuckles marks left a graffiti on Josh's skin in rainbow colors of violence—purples and blacks with hints of yellows and greenish hues.

The iced vodka loosened up the men at the table. They waited for baseball and food. It didn't take them long before they drifted back to the game. A couple of waiters delivered steaks with bones, the common club that later evolved into baseball bats and boomerangs; a large hunk of flesh was curled up at one end.

Eight massive steaks came along with more bottles of vodka, the labels blurry inside the slabs of ice. The diners could have been primitive hunters sharing a woolly mammoth. Ingram, the software guy, gazed at the steak the way a child stared in horror at a plate of stacked with asparagus. Conversations fragmented into groups of two or three as the men attacked the meat and liquor. Eight white men with expensive haircuts, tailored shirts and Italian shoes. They could have been stockbrokers, bankers, or doctors, and they had the distinctive look of men who had never done hard manual work or, with the exception of Josh, been in a fight. Not a callus or mark on them. Nails cut, polished, and clean. As worldly as they appeared to be, they were as cloistered as medieval monks. Same kind of work—putting words on paper, words that had power and authority and carried down the corridors of power. They sat listlessly around the table waiting for the Yankees to score. The waiters flapped around the room, pouring vodka and delivering steaks. Boredom, tension, and booze drifted through Sammy's like a Roman legion's camp on the eve of battle.

"Josh doesn't look so good," Harris whispered. Calvino thought he was trying to make conversation. Harris looked more like an abbot than an ordinary drone monk, stuck in a cubicle writing the text of Mark and Matthew.

"People getting married or buried never look good," said Calvino, cutting into the steak.

Harris laughed. "Josh said that you had strong views."

"Josh said you had some strong opinions on billing," said Calvino. "Like steak. You eat it or put in on your face to stop the swelling."

"You could kill someone with this bone," said Williams.

Harris fingered the whiskers on his *Planet of the Apes* mask. "Marriage and partnerships are risky. Accidents ready to happen, right?"

Calvino's law—it's generally a mistake to trade bar fines for the full board and lodging package arrangement.

"Depends. They're both based on exclusivity and enthusiasm," said Calvino.

"She's into only you and she loves it."

Whatever "it" is, thought Calvino. "Until entropy overtakes 'like' and breaks it into boredom."

"Got it," said Harris. "Apathy is the deal breaker."

Harris nodded, his eyes shining as if he saw something in Calvino he'd missed before. "In essence, you're saying marriages and partnerships are accidents waiting to happen? Someone always gets hurt?"

"Everyone has a blind side."

Everyone around the table looked at Josh's face. It looked like a spring-loaded object had smashed into his face, a fist attached to powerful arm.

"Were you blindsided, Josh?" asked Harris.

"I was careless," said Josh.

"That's not like the Josh Levy I know," said Harris. "Careful, careful always. No accidents on his watch."

Andrei had been listening and hovering, waiting for an entry point like a bullet in slow motion.

" 'Many years ago my friend from university in England had an accident on the motorway outside London. His face hit the windscreen. The doctors removed most of the glass but some pieces were lodged below the eye, and to remove them by surgery would have risked injury to the nerves. The medical judgment was to leave the glass inside my friend's face. A month ago, I saw him at lunch. He took out a Ziploc bag and handed it to me. 'Andrei,' he said, 'look inside. What do you see?' I see a shard of glass, I told him. 'Look closely,' he said. 'What does it look like?' I removed the glass from the Ziploc and examined it closely. 'Tolstoy,' I said. 'It looks like him.' My friend smiled and nodded. It was the perfectly formed shape of a human head. He had shown it to other people. They had guessed it looked like Jesus or Marx or Hillary Clinton, all depending on their education, nationality, gender, and age. My friend had been carrying this object around inside his flesh for more than twenty years. A small piece of glass from an accident. It had taken more than two decades to work its way to the surface.

"As my friend spoke, he stroked a small reddish scar five centimeters below his right eye. I asked him what he thought about the emergence of the tiny glass head. He said it was a lesson about life. With every accident there is a hidden anti-accident. You must be patient and wait, and one day, as if by miracle, the anti-accident reveals itself. He held up the Ziploc and said, 'Now the accident and anti-accident have merged. But no one can tell me the name of the glass that came from my body.' I said to him, 'That is fine, my friend. When we are young, a couple of decades meant nothing. But as we grew older, we could no longer wait for destiny. When the accident occurs, we demand the anti-accident appear and restore the balance.' This is my formula."

Calvino looked up from his plate. "Tolstoy. I prefer Derek Jeter."

The others at the table laughed, except for Josh, who stared at the long bone on his plate.

Harris carved a piece of steak and pushed it in his mouth.

"I am not familiar with his work," said Andrei.

"He's team captain. Plays shortstop. Jeter was born about the time Josh and I were graduating from law school. He's got all the women and money. We're a bunch of schmucks who can't remember a formula and never read Tolstoy. But we're Americans who have been blindsided by optimism, belief in progress, getting to the top. We can't give up on the idea that we will sooner or later hit a grand slam out of the stadium. Even werewolves know that's bullshit, isn't that right, Josh?"

Josh's face turned a hue of salmon pink as if he'd easily been netted in midair. He couldn't believe his best man was talking like this in front of his boss.

"We were talking about accidents," said Josh. He leaned over to Calvino, "Are you drunk? This is my fucking boss you're talking to."

Calvino shrugged and looked over at Andrei, who was about to say something.

"I was talking about letting our imagination, dreams, and desires project themselves on to a piece of glass," said Andrei. "Glass from a serious accident."

Calvino paused, chewing his steak. "If he'd showed me that piece of glass, you know who I'd have guessed?"

Andrei showed no emotion like a professional card player.

"Nicholas II," said Calvino.

Andrei smiled. "You understand my formula, Vincent. Did you study mathematics at university?"

"The only math that I ever remembered is that you can never beat the house odds. Oh, and I forgot. Jeter's career batting average is .317. Tolstoy, what was his average?"

"A valuable lesson in determining an average is to decide what game you are playing," said Andrei.

"Andrei, on this Halloween night, there's only one game. Baseball. The World Series."

"Sports, like other games, are about winners and losers," said Andrei. "In my business we predict the likelihood of winning."

"That's what bookies do," said Calvino.

"You are right. We make the odds."

"What are the odds of getting beat up on Halloween night?"

"Quite small, I would have thought."

Calvino nodded. "Yeah, that's what I thought, too."

Andrei was a math genius, or so his Wikipedia entry claimed. Educated at the best schools and institutes in Moscow, Boston, and Oxford. Part of the year he lived on a large yacht moored in Malta. He'd survived two failed assassination attempts. He had made a reputation by writing papers about exotic subjects such as confirmation bias, the Gini coefficient, and game theory. He was an early pioneer in the complex modeling of randomness and chaos. But he'd made his money by inventing an algorithm for factoring large numbers—and scaled it to create derivatives in the real estate investment business. His consulting company made a fortune advising Wall Street. Some of his critics said Andrei's invention had caused the implosion of the subprime real estate mortgage market. It wasn't Marx but a Russian mathematician who had brought America to its knees.

Not everyone who had taken a shot at him was Russian. Andrei had collected enemies along the way, as all successful and ambitious men had from the beginning of time do. He had arrived at Sammy's with a couple of tough-looking bodyguards, who were parked at the next table, backs to the wall, with a full view of the front door and the dance floor. The two men in dark suits and wires snaking from their ears to their shirt collars spoke Russian and neither ate nor drank. They watched every person in the restaurant like air traffic controllers, making certain no one came within ten feet of Andrei. Both of the Russians looked as though they'd have trouble passing the Turing test—Calvino thought of them as the kind of men whose intelligence barely passed as human.

After the plates were cleared, Josh stood up and called for everyone's attention.

"Sit down, Josh. You're drunk and getting married," said one of his friends.

"Of course I'm drunk."

"An honest man," said someone else.

"We have a special person with us. Many of you have read about Andrei, who has been compared to Einstein. I have invented a game in his honor," said Josh.

"But we just ate the subprime," said one of the guests.

Everyone laughed. But they weren't laughing at the joke.

Josh hadn't seen it coming as the woman approached him on his blind side.

Dressed as a zombie, she wore an orange mini-skirt, black leather boots and her face was make up to look like it had recently crashed through a windshield. Calvino watched her stagger out of the restroom, lean against the wall before weaving behind the DJ and heading toward their table. Where did this creature come from? he asked himself. Before Josh reacted, she locked her arms around his neck and bent down to kiss him as he struggled to break free.

"Hi lover boy. One last kiss before you turn into a pumpkin," she said.

Josh's friends egged her on, "He's already a pumpkin."

The zombie—she was about six feet tall, blonde, and early 30s—grabbed his necktie and yanked his head down, planting her blood red lips on his, making a loud moaning, smooching noise. She inserted her tongue in his mouth. Calvino winced, turned away.

"Getting married, big boy?" she asked, rolling her tongue back into her mouth.

Men pounded the table and shouted her on. But those were her last words. While she had started out well with her routine, the zombie woman who'd consumed a large quantity of vodka for courage, turned ash white; her eyes rolled up and she vomited barely missing the table but managing a direct hit on Josh's pant leg. After the zombie woman collapsed on the floor, the waiters rushed in with hot towels.

Josh pulled his chair back, disgusted and angry. He stepped around the woman, rubbing a towel against the ugly wet spot on his leg. She rose to her knees and grabbed hold of Josh's leg. He managed to break free and the zombie started to laugh.

"I need some air," Josh said under his breath to Calvino.

"You need a drink," said Ben.

Josh finished his glass and put on his coat. He said nothing as attention was diverted by the zombie hooker with a drinking problem and slipped outside.

"She likes you, Josh," said one of the men. "Hey, where's Josh?"

The zombie sat wobbly in a chair beside the Russian bodyguards. They didn't seem all that happy with the waiters parking her there as if she were another hired hand. One of the bodyguard's whispered something to a waiter, stuffed a hundred in his pocket.

Calvino watched as a couple of the men helped the zombie to her feet, gave her some cash, and helped her to the restroom. By the time they emerged, the zombie smiled, her mess cleaned up by the waiters, and they helped her out the door.

Absent the party boy and zombie, the party fell into a somber mood. Andrei sat at the table, Josh's werewolf mask near his plate. His Russian bodyguards nervously watched as their man turned into a werewolf.

Calvino leaned back toward the two Russians. "Either one of you guys wouldn't happen to know a Russian named Sparrow?"

They stared at him as they'd done with hooker—with contempt and suspicion fused into an unpleasant wariness.

"Bite me," said Calvino, turning back to the main table.

"Where's Josh?" a question asked by a couple of his friends.

"He's still outside," said Calvino.

A few feet away a DJ tried to pick up the pace and mood. He told a couple of lame jokes about Jewish princesses and drunken zombies. No one laughed. In between jokes he spun vinyl records from the '70s. Calvino, tired of watching the door, asked a waiter to go out and look for Josh. When the waiter came back, he pulled a face and shrugged. A moment later Calvino's cell phone rang. The others had grown restless. Calvino talked as all eyes were on him. He nodded as he listened, looking at Andrei. He folded up the phone, slipped it into his pocket, and pushed back his chair.

Ingram piped up. "Vinny, don't tell me our boy is upset about the zombie."

"Elvis has left the building," said the man with an Indian mystic mask.

"Another accident?" asked Harris.

"He's not coming back," said Calvino.

The news got several of the men worked up. No one was happy. "So what do we do now?"

"Go home. The party's over," said Calvino. "The rain's stopped in Philly. He said he's gone home to watch the game. We all should."

"Was that Josh on the phone?" asked Andrei, nodding at his bodyguards. In seconds both bodyguards were standing beside him. Andrei fingered a clown's mask on the table. Big red nose and enlarged mouth shaped in a huge O, with single teardrops under each eye. A sad clown, thought Calvino.

"Josh's got a problem. You're the expert on anti-accidents. Maybe you can help him," said Calvino.

Josh, the man who wanted to be someone, was in bad shape.

"Maybe I can," Andrei said.

The waiter came with the bill, and one of Andrei's bodyguards tried to take it and hand it to Andrei.

"Josh works for me," Andrei said. "I'll take care of this."

It was the way he said it, like he owned Josh.

"No," said Calvino, grabbing the bill, "The best man pays."

Andrei shrugged. "I like a man who looks after his friend," he said.

"Like a boss who looks after his employees," said Calvino.

As the men at the table started to leave, it was the bottom of the second inning in the World Series, but neither the Yankees nor the Phillies had scored a run. On the way out, one of the men slapped Calvino on the back, saying, "Thanks, buddy, for picking up the tab."

Before clearing out, the Josh's colleagues grumbled, cursed, and finally laughed as they recounted the performance of the zombie. Their idea of a joke hadn't worked out, one of them said. "He was stressed out," said another. "You see his face? Something happened and he's not talking about it," said Ingram. No one probed Calvino for details about Josh's call; they were mostly drunk, still laughing about the hooker dressed like zombie, an ear on the baseball game. Sometimes New Yorkers instinctively understood it was better not to ask too many questions. The idea of knowledge setting a man free left out that knowledge could also land him in prison.

Calvino was the last to leave the restaurant. He stood out front looking over the street. He tried Josh's cell phone again; still switched off. He stopped several people and asked if they'd seen a guy getting into a car. He described Josh as a middle-aged Jewish lawyer in a dark suit and with a busted up face. The people Calvino stopped ignored him. One or two said they'd not seen anyone with a busted up face. It was dark and most people wore masks. No one paid him any attention. It was, after all, they reminded him, Halloween and the fucking World Series, and was he hitting them up for money or trying to hurt them or give them a problem?

Calvino looked across the street and saw some teenagers in hooded sweaters and Nikes hanging out, passing a joint between them. They didn't look like they were listening to the baseball game. He walked across the street, hands in his pockets.

"Who are you?" one of them asked Calvino.

"I got a fifty for anyone who can tell me about some men pushing a white man into the back of a car or van.

"You a cop?"

"No, a pirate." He showed them his mask.

One of the young men showed a set of teeth with some diamonds inlaid on a couple of incisors. "You're, funny, man."

"Fifty?" asked another kid.

Calvino pulled a fifty-dollar bill out of his pocket, brushing his jacket back, exposing the top of the Glock. It was still pie in the sky, but he was convinced that a slice of that pie had edged a bit closer—he could almost smell it. Until the kids saw the gun.

"You're not a cop. So what the fuck are you? Some kind of made guy or something?"

"Something."

The kid with the special dental work took the fifty, stuffed it in his pocket, and opened up wide enough for his story to spill out.

A white Caddy had parked outside Sammy's. The kid figured it had been stolen in Camden, New Jersey, where more cars were stolen than sold. The driver wore colors from one of the New Jersey gangs that had been trying to muscle into the Lower East Side. The Caddy was a four-door late model number from the '80s. A gangbanger's car with polished hubcaps and a green miniature pine tree hanging from the rearview mirror, giving off that sickly fake mint smell like an old man's breath. The kid had noted a couple of strange things. Before it had parked, the Caddy had cruised up and down the street, as if the occupants were looking for someone or an address that they couldn't find. The Caddy's driver wore gangbanger colors—he was fat, too old to be in a gang, too white to be a brother. The setup looked like a "false flag operation" that any street kid could see through—an operation run by morons or someone who had no idea about New York and Jersey gangs.

Three big white guys in the Caddy. "Just cruising the neighborhood," said diamond mouth.

The kids said the Caddy driver put a cell phone to his ear as the car pulled in front of Sammy's, at which point they had gotten a better look at the men inside. All of them wore Halloween masks except for the driver, who had taken his off to answer the phone. He was thirty-something or maybe older. In the kids eyes, all old white guys looked somewhere between thirty and fifty. There had been another white guy about the same age, beefier, like a professional football player. He sat in the passenger seat. And the one in the back had a mask with long braided hair like a Viking.

Two of the men had hustled a guy who had come out of Sammy's into the back of the car while the driver waited.

"Did the man resist?"

"You mean put up a fight?"

Calvino nodded, hands in his jacket pockets, moving slowly from foot to foot, trying to stay warm. The teenagers stood like statues. Young and strong and lean, the cold bounced off them, but it drove straight through Calvino's skin like nails from a carpenter's nail gun.

"Nah, but he looked scared."

"It was dark. How could you tell he was scared?"

"I'd be scared if I had a gun stuck in my side."

"You saw a gun."

"Saw it when the driver got out. I said, 'That motherfucker's got a gun.' "

"That's what he said," said the teenager aspiring for a life with better dental work like his friend. "Saw a motherfucking gun." He was looking at Calvino's side with the pocket holster. "Lots of them around tonight." He spat and turned.

"You catch the license number?" asked Calvino.

"Not for fifty I didn't."

Calvino peeled off a hundred from Josh's envelope and handed it to him; the kid just looked at it until Calvino laid down another hundred. Turned out the kid noticed details and understood that on the street there was always a market for the right combination. He had the full license number. Only problem was the risk that the license plates had been stolen from another car. At least it was a lead, and Calvino needed some small handhold to either climb up another notch or climb down and go home. What were the odds of finding the car and Josh? It was the kind of question to ask Andrei, the new Einstein. Or maybe one of his bodyguards, who were wired and talking into their sleeves, and for all Calvino knew had told the men in the white Caddy that Josh was on his way out the door; get out of the car and grab him. However, they would have said that in Russian.

It was a ballsy move, Calvino thought as he stood on the pavement under a street lamp. His phone rang. It was from an unknown number.

"Vinny, it's me, Josh."

"Where the fuck are you?"

"I have no idea. It's the same bunch from earlier this afternoon."

"Last I heard they'd agreed to give me some time," said Calvino.

"That was then."

"What do they want?"

There was a pause. "Same as before. A guarantee the missing merchandise is returned. Don't get the police involved. What did you tell the guys at the restaurant?"

"That you went home."

"They must hate me."

"Josh, what are you talking about? You've been kidnapped, and you're worried about what a table of drunks thought? This has gotta be a joke."

"It's no joke, Vinny."

"You're starting to piss me off." Calvino drew in a breath. "You're saying you can't leave. They won't let you."

"That's what I'm saying."

"You don't sound all that upset."

Josh went quiet.

Calvino pictured a man in his thirties holding a gun at Josh's head. This wasn't something Josh had ever had done before. Mostly that kind of thing made a man crazy with fear. But Josh was calm, at peace, like he was dead inside his own mind. Calvino figured them for the kind of criminals who do whatever it takes to get a job done so they can go on to something else. Judging from the catch in his throat, Josh Levy had come to terms with that reality.

"Please, Vinny. They will kill me. Don't waste time trying to find me. Give them the fucking gold coins. If you don't have them, find them, then. . ."

He started to blubber like a man who'd discovered the lock on the panic room door was broken. With the thought of failure sinking in, his composure had fallen apart. Josh couldn't hold it together; he was sobbing, pleading, begging like a man with a noose around his neck, staring down at the trap door. If it was a performance, it had started earlier. In that case, Josh deserved an Oscar in his supporting role with a zombie.

The difference between real courage and the fake kind was the difference between watching someone shot at on TV and being in the line of fire. Real courage meant that a man no longer gave a fuck whether he lived or died; either way, it didn't matter. The fake kind looked real enough until the moment when everything went sideways and a man had to make a choice. He'd do what he could to stop inevitable from happening or else he'd wise up, turn and run. That was the moment of truth.

On the phone Josh was on his way to becoming one of those guys who didn't come out of the situation in one piece. He was in deep. Someone had made a calculation that Calvino was the man who wouldn't run. Maybe that was the reason they grabbed Josh rather than him.

Calvino understood that as the line went dead. "To live another day"—that was all Josh would be thinking about.

Calvino had a different take on the situation. He'd been minding his own business. He wanted them to believe he had no dog in their race. He would walk away, calling their bluff. Let them chase him back to Bangkok. They would cut Josh loose. Kill him for what? There was no good reason.

Except there was one small detail: Calvino owed Josh a twenty-year-old debt, from a time when Calvino had no friends and the triad had threatened to kill him. It was the kind of obligation that had no statute of limitations and had grown larger with interest. Josh Levy had just delivered up that old IOU, and that suddenly made things very messy.

FIVE

Washington, D.C., Thai Embassy—Saturday, October 31

"We are following up several leads," said Colonel Pratt.

COLONEL PRATT BOARDED the morning train from New York to Washington, D.C. From the station it was a twenty-minute taxi ride to the Four Seasons Hotel on M Street. It was convenient to the Thai Embassy, in Georgetown near the Potomac River. The Four Seasons was around the corner. He'd received a message from the embassy that he would be met at the hotel by an embassy official. They had left out the position of that official. First secretary? How far down the ladder would they go until the official ranked evenly with the Colonel?

The Colonel hadn't expected a woman. Khun Chanya introduced herself as third secretary. She *waied* him. A silver bracelet slid back on her thin wrist, and an emerald ring caught the light as she pressed her palms together. No wedding ring. Chanya looked to be in her mid-thirties and had that modern way of looking you in the eyes along with a faint, knowing smile. Her hair, pulled back, fell in a waterfall of strands down to her shoulders, just missing her pearl earrings. A purple scarf splashed color onto the knee-length dark dress, down the sides of which ran a faint pattern of silver globes. The elegant face, long and narrow, could have broken more than one heart.

After almost four hours on the train, Colonel Pratt was tired. A drink was welcome. He was glad to have a fellow Thai waiting for him. In his mind he'd pictured a man near his own age. Instead he'd found a beautiful woman. He was disappointed in one way but pleased in another. Travel days were mostly wasted. The journey exhausted both time and body. But Chanya lifted his spirits so that he felt refreshed and ready to talk. She had arrived well prepared and greeted him as if he were a member of her family. Her father had served as a junior officer under General Yosaporn. The General had been the Colonel's mentor. That, in his mind, established Chanya as someone he could implicitly trust and confirmed her family and class credentials. For the first time since arriving in America, Colonel Pratt felt he had an ally.

"How is your English?" he asked, as the drinks arrived at their table. He signed his room number to the bill.

"Good enough for a Ph.D. in foreign affairs at Georgetown University."

So it was brains as well as family connections. He reassessed his initial impression. He had tried to remember General Yosaporn mentioning Chanya's father but had drawn a blank. The General had had many junior staff over a long career. He made a mental note to phone the General in Bangkok.

"I went to university in New York," said the Colonel. "But that was many years ago."

"Your English is very good."

It dawned on him that he had switched into English without thinking about it.

"My father says Mr. Calvino helped General Yosaporn with a problem a couple of years ago. He said your friend refused payment. *Jai dii.*"

Not expecting money had won a *farang* the coveted good heart label. She smiled, raising her tall glass of iced tea.

"You can trust a man with a good heart," he said.

"Yes, like the General," she said.

"And like Khun Vincent."

Her eyebrow raised on one side. "That's encouraging to know."

Calvino had helped the General collect back rent. The General had sent him a case of expensive whiskey. The blowback from Calvino's services had brought some personal damages that a case of whiskey couldn't begin to cover. But it was a good thing that Chanya's father had passed along a favorable impression of Calvino. It was a minority view among those in charge of the missing Thai bullet coins case.

Across the room a tall, angular blonde woman, who could have been anywhere between forty and early sixties, sat alone at a table, hands folded around a small black purse, batting heavily eye-shadowed eyes at the Colonel. Chanya caught the routine.

"You are attractive to women," she said.

He fingered his wedding ring.

"That never stops a determined American woman," Chanya said.

He glanced at the blonde, who continued to stare at him. Her skin, stretched taut over large cheekbones, clouded the line between plastic surgery and taxidermy. She had an ageless appearance. Calvino—he thought it was Calvino—had once said certain women could hide their age well; they weren't like a tree that could be cut in half and the rings inside counted. The way skin could be stretched like a drum erased the evidence. He smiled to himself, thinking how he'd been trained to spot a honey trap, but never one baited with such ancient nectar.

"She likely mistakes me for someone else."

"You are a modest man, Colonel, very much like General Yosaporn. I can see why you were close to one another. How can I say this? The General is a gentle, serene man.

47

If only more men were like him, life would be better for everyone."

As he was starting to relax in Chanya's company, another Thai in a dark suit and tie joined their table. Major Tinakorn apologized for being late. His taxi had got lost. Chanya asked how any taxi driver in D.C. could not know where the Four Seasons Hotel was located. The Major explained that the driver was a foreigner. The Colonel laughed. They were all foreigners. Only some foreigners knew more than others.

"Like your friend, Mr. Calvino," said the Major, smiling as he *waied* Chanya and the Colonel. "I thought he would be joining us."

"He had other plans, I'm afraid."

Major Tinakorn's faced clouded. "May I ask what?"

Colonel Pratt swallowed, thinking how to word the situation for official usage. "Khun Vincent, as you know, is best man in Josh Levy's wedding party. He's been asked to officiate at a party for the groom and make a toast. All of the groom's friends will be present."

Chanya felt the tension gathering. The diplomat came out of the beautiful packaging.

"That's why we are here, Khun Tinakorn. To discuss any progress."

She looked at Colonel Pratt and waited a moment, until it was clear he would say nothing. His silence didn't deter her.

"And allow me to report any developments," she continued. "I am certain Mr. Calvino will be able to handle a wedding party without the Colonel's presence."

"Khun Vincent is my responsibility," said the Colonel.

"My brief makes him a joint responsibility," said the Major. A cup of coffee arrived and he took a sip.

"Well, he's in New York. So we will have to make the best of it," Chanya said, brushing a loose strand of hair from her eye.

The Major and Colonel had both arrived on assignment from Bangkok, flashing their diplomatic passports at JFK, proving that passports granting immunity aren't necessarily delivered only to diplomats.

Again Chanya intervened, with an encouraging grin that said, "Aren't we all Thais?"

"Major Tinakorn earlier visited the Smithsonian's special coin collection. They have a good collection of Thai coins," she said.

Colonel Pratt could imagine her making those arrangements—going through the protocol, making certain the person with the right rank would greet and escort the Major.

"Do you have any new information, Colonel?"

The Major's tone was measured, respectful. Colonel Pratt was not only older but had a higher rank. Still, this had to be balanced with the fact that Colonel Pratt was an ordinary policeman, not part of an elite unit. Older officers like him sometimes provided obstacles, and Tinakorn had been warned that the Colonel and Calvino had been close personal friends for many years. And in Thailand no obstacle created a higher wall to scale than the one built from a long-standing friendship.

"We are following up several leads," said Colonel Pratt.

"We?"

"Calvino is from New York. He has contacts that we need."

Tinakorn nodded, shaking his head. "That is a shaky assumption."

"Shaky or not, it is the best we have."

"I understand your name is on the annual reshuffle list. Promotion to deputy commander is a position for a man of firm assumptions, I would have thought."

Tinakorn's smile returned as if he had something more along the upturned corners of his mouth than he wished to reveal. The list had been delayed for months. Political parties had demanded their favorite officers for promotion. Colonel Pratt had no political party behind his appointment to a higher rank, and unlike other officers, he'd made no effort to lobby senior officers. Major Tinakorn had obviously been briefed about the Colonel's prospects, and in the Thai way had made the link between his performance in this case and his prospects for promotion.

"Promotions, like evidence, are more worthy when based on truth and logic," said Colonel Pratt.

"Something we can agree upon," said Major Tinakorn.

Two hundred miles away, Vincent Calvino had an urgent, panicky phone call from Josh Levy. The subject was the same: Thai coins, bullets. Nine of them.

SIX

"No one born in New York is ever someone who used to be from New York."

MONDAY WAS AS clear and cold as deep space. Calvino walked into the coffee shop and caught the whiff of fresh coffee. Colonel Pratt had phoned from the consulate, saying he was running late but would arrive soon. There weren't a lot of people in the coffee shop. Certainly not like the old days when the cops, even on the weekends, having elbowed each other for space at one of the tables, drained their coffee mugs dry as they shoveled down eggs and bacon and steaming hot pancakes.

The coffee shop was across the street from the old police headquarters. Years ago the building had been converted into luxury condos and sold off to people whose crimes had made them mountains of cash. The developers had driven out the cops, just as they'd done with the Italians and the Chinese who had lived in the neighborhood for generations. In the short term crime was a dangerous business; in the long term, with the right set of accountants and lawyers, the waterfalls of money washed out the old timers and the cops.

Calvino sat opposite an ex-homicide cop. He was Russian. His name was Sokolov, but everyone called him by his nickname, Falcon. Falcon had been one bird who was ahead of the curve—maybe so far ahead that he'd lost sight of the forest. He'd joined the NYPD before the big push to hire men born in Haiti, Jamaica, Pakistan, and Russia. The Italians and the Irish were orphans, stragglers who soldiered on but had no future. Falcon, in his mid-forties, should have been a captain by now. Russians had earned a reputation as gangsters, all swagger, steel, and cement, living on the edge, violent and unpredictable. Some of them managed to live up to their reputation. The Chinese equivalent would show respect, and if someone upset them, they'd send the offender a number of warnings. Not the Russians. Turn your back as they're still smiling and one of them runs a blade through your ribs. Dead before you hit the ground.

Falcon, though, violated the general, comfortable image of a Russian. He never swaggered. He gave warnings. He stepped on some big toes from Moscow, and the boots that caught him from behind were on the feet of bigwigs in his own department.

"Politics is the same. Moscow. New York. Police are chess pieces for politicians," he said to Calvino over the blue Formica top table, his hands wrapped around a thick coffee mug. "In your mind you move across the board like a knight. But in reality, you're a pawn sacrificed for the larger game."

Calvino watched him light a cigarette and rub his three-day growth of beard.

"As a private investigator," Falcon continued, "I am now a chess piece for the wealthy people who use politicians to play the capitalist board game. I call that a promotion. But I don't take cases that don't interest me."

"A man's got to like what he does and be good at it," said Calvino. "When I was a kid, I liked the smell of India ink. You know that smell?"

Falcon nodded with a crooked smile of recognition.

Calvino sipped the coffee put on the table in front of him while Falcon's memory worked out the fragrance details of India ink.

"Not even writers remember that smell anymore," said Calvino. "They all use computers. A good investigator never forgets a scent, a glance, or a habit. It's what makes a skilled hunter. Nero tells me you're a hunter. A good one."

He had a lot in common with Falcon. So far he liked what he'd heard from the Russian, enough to have confidence that he might be the right man to find Josh Levy.

Behind the counter the Spanish cook and a couple of Latino waitresses talked to each other in Spanish. A couple of customers sat on stools bent over their food. One of them was a middle-aged man, worn down by winter and life, who looked like he'd seen a ghost but the vision no longer scared him. The man seated next to him chewed on a Havana cigar that looked like it predated Castro. Otherwise, the diner was empty.

"Your cousin Nero says you're from Bangkok," said Falcon.

"I'm from New York."

"I owe Nero Garelli a favor. That's why I'm here. I want to be clear about that."

"Keep Nero's favor for another time. I'm paying to hire you."

The ex-cop looked at Calvino like a fisherman with a three-pound salmon, trying to decide whether to keep it or throw it back.

"You used to be from New York," he said. Falcon's narrowing of the eyes was an old habit from the back-and-forth done inside interrogation rooms with men with cordite on their hands and lies on their tongues.

"No one born in New York is ever someone who used to be from New York. I hear that someone born in Moscow feels the same way."

The ex-cop turned private investigator stared at him hard, like he had some wisecrack on the tip of his tongue. He swallowed it.

"This friend, Josh Levy, is he from New York?"

"We grew up together."

"Nero said that Levy spent time with you in Bangkok."

Calvino nodded.

"Did Levy have any problems while he was in Bangkok? Make any enemies? Piss someone off enough to grab him in New York?"

"He was in town for business. His boss asked him to pick up some old Thai coins and bring them back to New York. A gift for the boss's grandson."

Falcon's eyes widened. "Yeah?"

"Gold bullet coins with a history."

"Like a woman, coins always come with a history."

"But not all coins come with a Russian history. They were a gift to Nicholas II. And they came with a letter from King Chulalongkorn to Nicholas."

In the early 1900s, monarchs exchanged letters, presents, visits, and representatives, but the age of absolute power was drawing to an end. These men confidently rode history like a proud mount and had every intention of riding, like their ancestors, into the future.

Falcon put down his pen and sipped his coffee. He was interested, as he had been on the phone when arranging the appointment. His family was from Saint Petersburg; he had a great uncle who worked at the Hermitage.

"You think his disappearance is connected with the coins?"

"It's not what I think. It's what Josh said the men holding him want."

"And exactly how did your friend come to have the coins and the letter?"

"When Josh came to Bangkok, he got involved."

"You make it sound like this was a mistake on his part."

Calvino nodded, sipped his coffee, and waited as Falcon turned the page in his notebook.

Falcon picked up his pen. "Who has the coins now?"

Part 2

A Couple of Months Earlier in Bangkok

ONE

"There's always a downside," said Calvino.

A SOUR SMELL that might have been soup or sewer gas seeped from the kitchen—the kind of smell that occupied the border between hunger and death. Josh Levy sat in a booth facing the front door of the Lonesome Hawk Bar in Washington Square. He glanced back.

"What are they cooking?" he asked.

"The special," said Calvino. "Different every day. Only the smell is the same."

It had been more than twenty years since Calvino had last seen him. No man can withstand the weight of twenty years stepping on his waistline, on his shoulder line, and in Josh's case, hairline. Balding, with no discernible chin; thick black eyebrows, gray flecked; and his sideburns looked like a snow blower had broadsided him.

Josh was that late-middle-age guy sucking in wind, waiting for the referee to finish the standing eight count. When Josh tilted his head forward to look at his beer, the bottom half of his face collapsed like an accordion, aging him twenty years. He had worn a beret to cover up his baldness. This wasn't Paris, and in Bangkok the first thing a serving *ying* does is lift the beret and have a look underneath—the old habit of checking the nest for fresh eggs. This nest was bare. In the Lonesome Hawk one of the *yings* who had grandchildren herself giggled like a schoolgirl as she ran her hands over Josh's head for good luck.

"What's she doing, Vinny?"

"Getting some good luck. Don't worry about it."

Hua laan was one of the first phrases Calvino had learnt in Thai. It means bald. Thais use it like a punch line in an old joke. Everyone always laughs, even though they've heard the joke a hundred times. In some African countries baldness is a sign of wisdom and garners respect. But Josh wasn't in Africa. Here, deforestation of the head was always going to be a running joke.

"What brings you to Bangkok, Josh?"

Josh put his beret back on at a crooked angle.

"I'm getting married."

"Congratulations," said Calvino. "You want another beer?"

Josh nodded, finishing the last of the first bottle. "Yeah, I'll have another."

"You're getting married here?"

"In the Hamptons."

"You still haven't answered my question. What brings you to Thailand?"

"I want you to be my best man, Vinny."

Calvino hadn't been back to New York since the late '80s. The Chinese triad contract on him worked like a *fatwa* that could never be lifted once issued; it lingered like a dull headache that never quite went away.

"I'd like to, but there's some unfinished business I'd rather leave unfinished in New York."

"The triad?" asked Josh as the new beer arrived.

"These guys have memories like an elephant."

"What if I told you that I checked around and the Chinese are no longer interested in squaring things from the past? Even by Chinese standards, what happened was a very long time ago."

"The Chinese think in terms of centuries. Twenty years is nothing."

"Of the three Chinese involved back then, one died of cancer—throat cancer. Smoked himself to death, or talked too much, depending on who you asked. Another one is in prison for life on a double murder rap. No chance of parole. And the third one is a respectable member of the Chinese community who is on a state commission and gets invitations to Washington to brief politicians on Chinese trade issues. He's not in the business of turning the clock back to settle something that happened long ago. At this time of his life he'd rather not think about it. I had it all checked out."

"You just picked up the phone and called around?" said Calvino.

"I hired a Chinese private investigator, a professional, and he wasn't cheap. But he came back with a clean bill of health. Nothing and no one is stopping you from going back to New York. So what do you say, Vinny? Will you stand up for me at my wedding? I'd appreciate it."

From the back, someone slipped a Bob Dylan on the ancient stereo deck. The lyrics of "Jokerman" screamed across the bar.

Calvino remembered the music, the skin he'd shed and left behind, the old friend sitting across from him.

Josh nodded to the rhythm of the music. "The '80s music and films are in for a major revival."

"I've been waiting for the *Karate Kid* sequel. The kid's thirty years older. They still call him 'Kid' and he's grieving that his 401(k) plan is down for the count," said Calvino.

The roar of the mechanical rear hatch of a green garbage truck gorging on trash filtered into the bar. Calvino smiled at the groaning of garbage being crushed under a hot sun. The crushing noise shuddered before stopping.

"The '80s were the best," said Josh.

Calvino had been on the run. "The best" wasn't the way he'd have described the '80s. If it had been a filing cabinet filled with hopes, dreams, and fears, Calvino would have tried to make it to disappear. But that wasn't going to happen. He sat across from a man who was intent on opening all of the drawers and going through every folder.

The meaning of the '80s had been crystal clear—Calvino had strayed too far and had disappeared. Almost. And now, just when he'd thought he'd put New York behind him, an old friend had slipped into a booth with him at the Lonesome Hawk and told him the distant past wasn't dead; it was in for a revival. And Calvino was being rehabilitated. It seemed he could be that rare person: a time traveler with a chance to go back to the past.

Reagan had been president. It had been sunshine all over America except for that small black cloud that hung over Calvino's head. The storm front that had blew him out of New York and into Thailand. Now Josh had arrived with a new weather report—a deep motionless depression hovered over America.

Josh was saying that the special dark cloud over Calvino had cleared. If he went back to New York now, when he looked up, he'd stand under the same dark sky as everyone else. Calvino had lived outside the great transition of American life experience that started with Reagan and bookended with Obama. There was a large library in between them and Calvino had some catching up to do.

"You came to Bangkok to ask me to be your best man?"

Calvino was touched by the thought. Out of the blue one of his oldest friends appears, looking like hell but still recognizable, and it was as if nothing had changed except the pull of gravity reshaping his friend's body and face.

"What's that?" asked Josh, nodding at a dog waddling down the space between the bar and the booths.

"Her name is Fish."

"A dog named Fish?"

"A dog that used to be a he."

"What's that mean, 'used to be a he?' "

"It's complex, Josh."

Josh rolled his eyes. "Make it simple so I can understand it."

The discussion about New York evaporated as a surgically altered dog—part basset hound, part beagle, with a pinch of bonobo mixed in for spice—waddled out of the kitchen with Baby Cook's enormous pink bra over her head. The year before a Norwegian rigger had convinced Baby Cook that Plah would be much better off as a bitch than as a dog. She couldn't tell whether he was joking. That changed when he offered to pay for a sex change operation. Baby Cook was drunk one night and agreed. The operation seemed to make Plah into a different kind of fish that no one could quite identify. Baby Cook insisted that everyone use the name Plah—she and not he. A bitch rather than a dog.

Plah's loose jaws jiggled as she made her way across the bar. She went straight to the front door and barked twice. As she shook her head, spittle sprayed on the glass door. The bra stayed in place on her head. One of the waitresses opened the door and Plah walked outside as if she owned the place. She soon found what she had been sniffing for at the door—a mongrel stray that hung out at the massage parlor across the road. Plah mounted the mongrel in one of the parking bays in front of the Lonesome Hawk. Plah had been changed, that much was sure, but the equipment and hormones no longer fired the way they should. Plah still liked humping other dogs in the Square.

Calvino walked Josh out onto the balcony of the Lonesome Hawk, where a small crowd had gathered. Plah was working up a lather in the shade of a beat-up pickup with Buriram registration plates.

Calvino and Josh gazed at Plah, her long, pink tongue extended, panting, trying to catch her breath, trying to figure out in that confused dog way why there was something different about the humping. Nothing in Bangkok was ever what it seemed to be.

The dog with the pink bra returned to applause from the drunks lining the balcony in the front of the bar. Plah waddled back to the door of the Lonesome Hawk and barked. The door opened, and she headed straight back toward the kitchen, one cup of the pink bra covering an eye, making her look like a pirate from a botched hijacking.

"Josh."

He tapped Josh on the shoulder.

"That was a female dog?"

"As you said inside, it's a new world."

"I said that?"

"I'd be pleased to be your best man."

"You would?"

Calvino slammed his arm around Josh and led him to the balcony door. "Let's go back inside. Then you can tell me the real reason why you've come to Bangkok."

The Lonesome Hawk and a randy bitch with a pink bra draped over her head, humping like a stud, worked better than truth serum.

"You're right. Let's go inside," said Josh.

Although they had stayed in the shade, Josh was sweating. Calvino understood that a lot of things other than heat made people sweat in Bangkok. And judging from the way Josh had suddenly appeared out of nowhere with a story of marriage and asking him to be his best man, even hiring a private investigator to clear up an old problem, Calvino figured there had to be something else that was causing Levy's sweat glands to open.

One of the *yings* came from around the bar with a Mekong and Coke and set it in front of Calvino. He sipped it. His lips tightened into a grimace of a smile. The bartender had been heavy on the Mekong. Just the way that Calvino liked it—strong drinks, strong women, and long nights to linger over both, keeping in mind either one could pull him below the waterline. But that, he knew, is the nature of pleasure—death is always waiting on the other side.

"I flew to Bangkok from Tajikistan. My law firm has a client who is the brains behind a big oil concession partnership. Exploration business, development, and the usual logistical bullshit. The client wrote the software that makes the whole thing run, but I'm the one who runs the deal. The client calls and asks for a favor. Could I pass through Bangkok before heading back to New York? At first, I thought, shit, I don't want to go to Bangkok. Then I remembered you lived there. I was getting married, and I thought, why not ask Vinny to be my best man? The second reason is money. My firm billed him two million dollars last year. He paid the bill in full. No whining, no 'Where is my discount? Why did this associate bill for that? Why was the photocopy expense in excess of ten grand?'"

"You owe him."

"Of course, the firm owes him."

"Who do you have to kill?"

Josh spewed his beer from his nose like a sophomore at a fraternity party. "You've got quite an imagination, Vinny."

He was right; Calvino couldn't imagine Josh Levy being asked to kill a fly.

"Who is this guy?"

"Andrei Smirnov. Russian. A billionaire. A genius. What else do you need to know?"

"I didn't think the Russians used lawyers."

"Man, the Berlin Wall fell. The Soviet Union imploded. You're living in a time warp."

"Andrei Smirnov asks you to go to Bangkok and you can't say no."

"I'm saying I don't want to disappoint him," said Josh.

Calvino stared at him, thinking those words were something Josh should have carved in stone. His headstone. Most people disappointed others for most of their lives. By the time they died, all of those disappointments gathered up like industrial foam covering their lives with a surface of despair, and everyone huddled around their coffin and pretended that the life had been one of those rare inlet reservoirs filled with a clear, blue pool of pure water. Then there were guys like Josh Levy, who prided themselves on never disappointing anyone. Their mission in life was to please. They came to Thailand and married bar *yings* and made it their goal to please them. Josh, ever since he'd been a kid, had had the tendency to appease, please, comfort. He should have been an aid worker. He'd lived to please his first wife (she'd been killed in a skiing accident in Aspen), his kids (two of them now out of college and working on Wall Street), his family, his law firm, and his friends. Calvino was undecided which of their two lives, stretched out and measured at their funerals, would ultimately be sadder or more pointless.

"What's the favor?"

"He wants some coins for his grandson."

"Has he ever heard of FedEx?"

"We represent them, too," said Josh. "But he wants me to bring them."

"So you're a courier with a law degree."

"Come on, Vinny. It's no big deal. I get down time in Bangkok. We can hang out together. What's not to like?"

Calvino went silent as he sipped his Mekong and Coke. "I'm just trying to understand the situation. What kind of coins are we talking about?"

"Thai coins."

Calvino pursed his lips, tasting the Mekong on his tongue. "I presumed they weren't Russian coins. So let me get this straight. This Andrei flies you in from Tajikistan, and you check into a suite at the Oriental Hotel, which I presume he's paying for, and all you have to do is carry back some coins for his grandson?"

"He's rich and eccentric. A genius."

"You keep saying he's a genius. But it doesn't take a genius to figure out that a client doesn't send a five hundred dollar an hour corporate lawyer to Bangkok so his grandson's coin collection has something new, no matter how fucking rich he is."

The Mekong curled his tongue. He ordered another one, holding up the empty glass. A passing *ying* took it and, holding it aloft in a Statue of Liberty pose, disappeared behind the bar.

"You want the truth, Vinny?"

"Try me."

"I've resigned from the law firm. Andrei's hired me as in-house counsel. He knows that I'm getting married, and he said he wanted to give me a present. Ten days in Bangkok. Why Bangkok? Because I told him about how we were kids together and how I was thinking about asking you to be my best man, and how we'd been out of touch all of these years, so I needed some time to get to know who you were. It couldn't be more straightforward."

"So why didn't you tell me that in the first place?"

Josh shrugged. "I didn't want you to think that... I don't know. I wasn't sure we could pick up where we left off and thought asking you to be my best man might be a crazy thing to ask. I had some doubts."

"There's always a downside," said Calvino.

"The glass is half empty or it's half full. It depends on how you see life."

"You sure you want me as best man?"

Josh leaned across the table and kissed Calvino on the forehead. "I wouldn't have anyone else."

The *ying* appeared with Calvino's Mekong and Coke, at the same time snatching Josh's beret.

"Hey, come back with that!"

She disappeared into the kitchen at the end of the bar. A couple of minutes later, Plah waddled out with Josh's beret tied on her head.

"There's your hat," said Calvino. "Taking it off Plah, you'll get to decide if your hand is half gone or half left."

Josh Levy watched as Plah stopped at their table, defying him to make a move. He frowned at Plah and peeled a hundred baht note from a roll and gave it to the heavyset *ying* who appeared from the kitchen after the dog.

"I want my hat."

Calvino interpreted the request into Thai. Baby Cook stuffed the note in her bra and swiped the beret from Plah's head, giving her a kick that sent her squealing back into the kitchen.

"Those two make quite a combination," said Josh.

"Best friends," said Calvino.

"I see I've got a lot to learn," said Josh, not wanting to disappoint.

"When do you go back to New York?"

"A week from Friday, the eleventh of September."

Even as a kid, Josh had been precise with facts, numbers, and dates.

That was a lot of nights at the Oriental Hotel. Those had to be some coins for the grandson. Josh said his new boss was a billionaire. And for someone like that, the price had the same meaning as the purchase of another Singha beer by one of the pensioners at the bar. Calvino raised his glass, looking hard at Josh Levy. It had been twenty-three years. He'd never expected to see him again. There he was, wearing a beret, looking fifteen years older than he should, and still unaware that a man sent to collect coins in Bangkok should have been asking some much harder questions.

"So you've hit the big time," said Calvino. "What happens when a lawyer goes from representing a client to working for a boss? Is it a little like the difference between dating and marriage?"

Josh's smile looked like it had every intention of going on for miles, folding back in a time warp and coming out somewhere in the '80s.

The silent gaps in their conversation increased as the afternoon wore on. It came as no surprise that Josh would want to talk about people from the old days. Calvino and Levy had grown up in the same neighborhood, gone to school together.

"You ever hear anything from Janet?"

That had been the first time in two decades anyone had mentioned the name of his ex-wife to Calvino. No one had ever asked him about her. Men arrived in Bangkok to forget ex-wives.

"Not a word," said Calvino. Janet and Josh's wife, Helen, had been friends. Janet had gone to Helen's funeral. Calvino hadn't.

"People should stay in touch. Make an effort to keep some connection."

"So they say."

"She's invited to the wedding. I hope that's not going to be a problem."

Calvino shrugged. "Not for me. Why should it be a problem?"

"No reason. But thought I'd ask."

Calvino looked at him but said nothing. Janet was one of those shed layers of skin. Jokerman.

"You never remarried."

Calvino blinked and looked away with a shrug. No, he hadn't. It seemed that marriage was the only space of living that Josh could understand. Calvino thought Josh would drop the subject, but he was wrong.

"Living in Bangkok, you wouldn't." He laughed one of those phony laughs. "Some men hate marriage. I'm not one of them. You remember Helen. I never regretted marrying her. And would still be married to her. When she died, I was clinically depressed for nearly a year."

Helen had hit a tree at sixty miles an hour and cashed out. She'd had everything: husband, a partner in a powerful law firm, brownstone on the Upper West Side, club membership, patron of the arts. And she'd crumpled up into a bloody ball on a Colorado slope and died. It was almost as if she'd wanted to die.

There was that Mekong whispering in his ear, he thought.

"Josh, can we talk about something other than my ex-wife?" asked Calvino, raising his glass just in time for the *ying* to grab it and rush to the back of the bar.

"I buy for you, Vinny," said Baby Cook, slumped against the door to the kitchen with Plah stretched out near her feet.

"What do you want to talk about?"

"Anything," said Calvino. "Anything but the old days."

Josh got that excited look on his face. "The Yankees are going to the World Series this year. I've got a grand on it."

Baseball in general, and the Yankees in particular, were subjects that two New Yorkers could discuss for hours.

"A grand?"

"If they win, I get four grand."

"Those are good odds."

"I can lay off half the bet with you if you want."

"Five hundred. I'm in."

"I knew you'd still follow the Yankees," said Josh, raising his glass for another drink.

Josh had moved on from asking about Calvino's ex-wife. The bartender saw Josh and called out to Baby Cook, who hovered nearby. She looked at Calvino for confirmation.

"Another, Baby Cook, one more for the road. Another beer for Khun Josh, and he wants to buy you a whiskey."

"Your friend has no hair," Baby Cook said in Thai. "He looks like he has a good heart. I don't mind bald."

Josh hadn't understood a word; nor had he any idea that Baby Cook was trying to get Calvino to pimp her to his friend.

McPhail stumbled like a boxer coming out of his corner in the twelfth round as he entered the bar. Plah looked up and saw McPhail before putting her huge head with floppy beagle ears back onto Baby Cook's shoe, the one that Baby Cook used to kick her for reasons neither the dog nor anyone else could figured out. McPhail slipped into the booth next to Calvino and Josh and introduced himself.

"Who are you?"

"An old friend of Vinny's."

"I didn't know he had any who were still alive," said McPhail, shaking a cigarette from his pack and offering it to Josh, who screwed up his face.

McPhail took the cigarette and lit it.

"McPhail is also an old friend," said Calvino.

"Are you in the private investigation business, too?" asked Josh.

McPhail hollered at the bar for a gin and tonic.

"I sometimes help Vinny out. So what brings you to Bangkok?"

"I have a meeting with an associate of my client."

McPhail had managed to get new information about Josh's other business. Interesting, thought Calvino. Josh hadn't mentioned meeting an associate, and he still couldn't bring himself to call Andrei his boss. He held onto the word "client" like an army general clutching an amulet.

"You're another lawyer."

Josh shrugged like someone fingered for a crime with too many eyewitnesses to deny his guilt. "Vinny and I were in law school together." He winked at Calvino.

"Let me know if you need any gems to take back. I'm the guy. Ask Calvino."

They both turned and looked at Calvino. "McPhail is the man."

Baby Cook had drunk the whiskey Josh had bought her and now asked him for another one. Josh didn't seem to know that it was all right to say no. Maybe he thought she was like a client. Soon she came back with another glass and insisted on clinking each man's glass or bottle. Downing the drink in one gulp, she started massaging Josh's neck.

"Before you get your fingers into him, get me a gin and tonic, Baby," said McPhail.

Calvino waited for Baby Cook to sic Plah on McPhail— she did that when a customer stepped over the line and upset her, especially when she had landed such a rich and good-hearted customer. McPhail blew smoke across the table, catching her in the face. She coughed and fanned the air with her hand.

"Smoking is against the law," she said.

"Arrest me. But get me a drink first."

Her long, mournful sigh announced an intention that Plah heard a couple of seconds too late as Baby Cook's foot connected with the bitch's rib cage. The dog screamed like a woman in a bad porno film and fled to the safety of the kitchen.

"Did Calvino tell you that dog used to catch rats in the kitchen?" said McPhail. "Rats as big as cats. Then one day she stopped. She wouldn't run after a rat if one ran over her paw and ate out of her bowl. The sex change operation destroyed her desire to kill rats. The vet said it was one of those one in-a-million cases. Plah's the only *katoey* dog in the Square—maybe the city. We had a guy with a grant who came all the way from Australia to study Plah and write some bullshit article about the sociological implications of her operation. He got one thing right—it changed her life. But that kind of operation always does. Anyway, it's made Plah a celebrity. And turned Baby Cook into a stage mother."

Josh's eyes, bloodshot from travel, blinked in astonishment as McPhail puffed on his cigarette, blew out smoke, and downed his first gin and tonic of the day in one long swallow.

"Don't forget, if you want gems, let Vinny know. I can find a star sapphire that'll knock you out it's so beautiful."

"If I want to get knocked out, I'll call you," said Josh.

McPhail paid his bill, slapped Baby Cook on the ass, slid out of his booth and left. Josh glanced down at the dog. Her large, gloomy eyes were alert and focused like they were trained on the Norwegian who'd paid for her sex change operation. When Josh looked up, he found Calvino smiling.

"Is that true what he said about the dog?"

"Mostly," said Calvino. He was thinking it was about as true as Josh's story about coming to Bangkok because after all these years he'd decided out of the blue that no one but him could be Josh's best man. But Calvino was in an expansive mood, and when he saw the tortured look on Josh's face, as if the knife that had fixed up Plah were being sharpened for him, Calvino decided to do something he'd sworn off a long time ago. He gave Josh the benefit of the doubt.

TWO

Bangkok, Chao Phraya River—Friday, September 4

"Last Money. Good name for a boat from Pattaya,"
said Calvino.

THE DISTANCE BETWEEN the Lonesome Hawk Bar
and the Oriental Hotel was no more than eight kilometers,
but the real distance was closer to a couple of thousand light
years. Serious money bunked at the Oriental; those down
on their luck rested on their elbows over their drinks at
the Lonesome Hawk Bar. Josh sat at a table with a fancy
umbrella overlooking the Chao Phraya River. When
Calvino arrived, the headwaiter escorted him to the table,
pulled back the chair, removed the white napkin, shook it
out, and spread it on Calvino's lap. This series of actions was
executed in a single continuous motion.

Sitting on the balcony of a luxury hotel, Josh was
transformed from his hollowed out, jet-lagged appearance
of the day before. He wore a blue Oxford shirt, collar open,
tan trousers, and dock shoes with no socks. He looked like
he'd materialized from the Hamptons, climbing out of a
time machine.

"Baby Cook and Plah send their best," said Calvino,
leaning forward and opening the cloth over the bread basket.
He removed a bagel and used a knife to cut it open.

"When I woke up this morning, I was certain none of
that had happened."

"Next time you're at a dinner party, you can talk about the trouble you had in Bangkok with a dog that had been changed from male to female."

"I don't think they'd understand," said Josh.

"Then let's leave it as a moment you can only share with your best man."

"I like that."

Relaxed, confident, and on a turf of his own choosing, Josh was his old self. Waiters hovered nearby, awaiting his command. With every second sip of water, the pitcher appeared to refill the glass.

"So where's your coin man?" asked Calvino. "I thought he'd already be here."

"He's running late."

"Traffic jam is an old Bangkok excuse for taking your sweet fucking time."

"When he phoned, he didn't say anything about traffic."

"That's something," said Calvino, watching a coal barge being pulled by a tugboat down the river. Long-tail boats, ferries, barges, and pleasure boats passed. Calvino removed his sunglasses and bounced the wing end against his chin. "Are you going to tell me about this woman you're marrying?"

The questioned brightened Josh up. "She's thirty-seven. Divorced seven years ago. She got the house in the Hamptons. Made a couple of good investments."

"She's not marrying you for your money?" said Calvino.

"She's the one who encouraged me to take this new job."

"An influential woman."

"Tess is smart as a whip. Harvard."

"Tess."

"Didn't I mention that before?"

Josh had left a fair amount of information out.

"Is she a lawyer?"

Where else would Josh have met her? The guy had no life other than sitting in rooms with lawyers and clients.

"Short résumé—Tess Reynolds; Harvard MBA; worked for Goldman Sachs; retired at thirty-five."

"She made a couple of good investments," repeated Calvino. "Tess should be the one advising Andrei on these coins for his grandson."

Josh laughed. "You can't leave that alone. It's no big deal, Vinny. If you had ever stayed in a major practice, you'd know that these are the small things a partner does for a big client."

"Josh, Andrei is your boss. Why do you keep calling him your client?"

Josh's face collapsed for a second into that old man's deflation.

"You're right."

"No, you're right. Most of my clients never had enough money to pay me, and not one of them ever asked me to fly halfway around the world for his grandkid. Most of my clients died without leaving heirs. . ."

Calvino stopped in mid-sentence as if distracted.

Josh turned around in his seat and they watched as a yacht named *Last Money*, flying a Thai flag, slipped alongside the dock. The yacht looked like it had been sculpted out of a mountain of white marble, with a speedboat and jet skis added on the top deck. On the main deck several *farangs* in white and blue uniforms secured the ropes. One of the men stood on a gangplank, talking to security guards. The dual engines had been cut. A tall, blond man dressed in a white silk shirt and trousers, wearing sunglasses, waved at the balcony. Around his neck was a gold chain as thick as a wrestler's thumb. The sunlight struck the gold, and a trick of light reflected the gold like a rainbow across his face as if it were a smile.

"That's Maxim," said Calvino.

"He's too far away. You can't see his face from here."

"*Last Money*. I can read that from here. From what I hear on the street, Maxim's the owner. Some say the yacht should be called *Fast Money* or *Easy Money*. *Dirty Money* also comes to mind."

"What's that mean?"

"He's Russian mafia. Lives in Pattaya. But I'm certain he's an all-around wonderful guy, once you get to know him."

Maxim walked straight past Calvino as if he didn't exist and hugged Josh, kissing him on one cheek and then the other.

"The last time I saw you, in Tajikistan, you were making my head hurt with all of this law talk. Now you work for us, we can forget that bullshit."

"*Last Money*. Good name for a boat from Pattaya," said Calvino.

Maxim tilted his head, eying Calvino like a man with a spear gun eyeing a shark.

"And you would be?"

The sleeve on the shirt lifted far enough to reveal an inlaid set of diamonds in a Rolex. A ruby the size of a baby's fist was on his right hand, and an emerald like a pigeon egg on the left hand. Close up the gold chain looked thick enough to hook to a tugboat and tow Mr. Maxim back to Pattaya.

"Vincent Calvino," Josh said. "This is Andrei's associate, Mr. Maxim. Vincent is a childhood friend. Vincent will be my best man. November's around the corner."

The serious expression on Maxim's face dissolved into a full belly laugh.

"Yes, now I remember. You said your friend was joining you."

He smacked his head with the heel of his hand. Moored at the dock behind him, Maxim's yacht looked like a frigate, with its rotating sonar tower, captain's bridge, and empty landing spot. He must have forgotten his helicopter in Pattaya, thought Calvino.

"I forgot," Maxim continued. "I forget so many things these days. Which is good for my enemies."

He gestured at a waiter and ordered a magnum of champagne and a bowl of fresh strawberries and clotted cream.

"It's friends who forget you," he added. "Enemies, they never forget."

As the Russian reached into his pocket, for a moment Calvino thought that the coins Josh had been waiting for would emerge. Instead, the Russian produced a jewelry box with a red satin finish and handed it to Josh.

"Go on, open it."

Josh pulled up the lid to find a pair of diamond earrings. He looked up, surprised, turning the box to show Calvino.

"Josh doesn't wear earrings."

"They are for his wife!" thundered Maxim. He almost choked with laughter. He drank water and gasped. "You are such a funny man. They are a wedding gift. But if you want to wear them, we can keep a little secret, can't we, Mr. Calvino?"

Maxim wasn't exactly the delivery boy that Calvino had expected. And judging from the expression on Josh's face, he was noticing that the box had not yielded a single coin. The only gold was hanging in a thick rope around the Russian's throat.

"You don't like the earrings?" asked Maxim in a hurt tone. "You look disappointed, my friend."

"I thought you had the coins for Andrei in the box."

Maxim's hands shot up as if in surrender. "Andrei and his precious gold bullet coins. What? You think that Maxim forgot? No, of course, how can I forget? I get text messages. Emails. Phone calls. I have images of nine bullets engraved inside my head. And that is no place for bullets, you would agree, no?"

"No. I mean, yes, I agree. I thought the purpose of lunch today was that you would bring them along."

"I will have them on Sunday."

"You said today," Josh said.

Maxim shook his head. "Andrei may have told you today."

The boss had said Friday. Josh wondered why this misinformation had been passed to him. He saw no reason to press the point.

"Sunday for sure?" asked Josh.

The big Russian sighed as if such questions were beneath him. "Josh, I want peace in my life. Sunday you will have them. Andrei will be off your back. Off my back. Onto someone else's back."

Maxim raised an iPhone to his ear and spoke in Russian, paused, spoke again, and laid the phone on the table. The strawberries arrived. A waiter carried a silver bucket with ice and a bottle of champagne. Maxim clapped with approval. He removed his sunglasses, peeled a five hundred baht note from a thick wad, and handed it to the headwaiter. Diamond earrings for a lawyer; five hundred baht bank notes to the serving staff. Maxim delighted in flashing around expensive gifts and money. The waiter gave him a deep *wai*, pocketed the note, and opened the champagne.

The Russian made a production out of chomping his lips as he tasted the first drops from the bottle. "Yes, very good."

The headwaiter filled the other two glasses before topping up Maxim's glass.

"I propose a toast," he said, holding the champagne glass by the stem. "To your wedding, to Andrei's gold bullets, and to the deal."

He clicked Josh's glass, turned, and clicked Calvino's glass. He winked at Josh before he slipped the sunglasses back on.

Calvino was the only one at the table who hadn't received cash or goods. The Russian studied him as he sipped the champagne.

"You look familiar. Have we met before?"

"Not that I recall."

The Russian lowered his glass, studying Calvino. A waiter immediately refilled his glass with champagne, the bubbles fizzing to the top but not spilling over the edge. A perfectly executed refill.

A crew member from the yacht brought Maxim a leather briefcase. As he handed it to Maxim, they spoke in Russian. The hired hand nodded as Maxim grunted something to him. The Russian sailor turned on his heels and walked back to the *Last Money*. Unsnapping the briefcase, Maxim pulled out a folder. Inside was a contract.

"This is finished," said Maxim, waving the papers. "Tell me it is so. I need to sign this. We are two, three weeks over schedule. Change this, revise that. It gives me a big headache. Andrei told me to give it to you to look over and say it's okay, so I can sign it. And he can sign. Signing takes only a minute. Look it over. Then I can tell Andrei you approve."

"I'll look at it this afternoon."

Josh made no effort to pick up the document. He didn't bother to glance at it. He knew the contents inside out already.

Maxim removed his sunglasses and rolled his eyes. He carefully folded the sunglasses and put them on the table.

Shaking his head and sighing, he said, "Every time I give you these papers, you say the same thing. An hour. Then a day. A week becomes weeks. We can't do business like this. It's just a paper. Lift it. It weighs nothing. How can something that weighs nothing sink tons and tons of equipment and ships? I have no answer. You are the lawyer. Can you explain this to me?"

The power over others that had danced like music across his eyes had faded. In its place was a cold anger. The hotheaded type of anger flies out like a solar burst, but the cold kind of anger, like a frozen mountain, sits still, looming, impassable.

"What Josh is saying," Calvino said, "is that you can sign whatever you want. It's no skin off his nose. But if you want him to approve something, then he has to sign off. Signing off without reading the contract isn't skin off his nose, it's off his ass if there is something he should have told you about."

"Now lawyers have lawyers. It is never-ending," growled the Russian.

"We're like Russian dolls, Mr. Maxim."

"Okay, okay, read it. But in Russia we say no agreement can protect you against a .50 caliber round."

He folded his arms and nodded at the agreement. He shotgunned the champagne only to have it refilled immediately. He threw the glass into the river and stood up.

"I will meet you here at 8:00 p.m. on Sunday. You tell Andrei it is approved, and I'll have his coins."

"They're not connected," said Josh.

"In Russia everything is connected. But you need to know where to look."

They watched him pick up his briefcase and stroll along the pavement to the dock. He climbed the gangplank and boarded the *Last Money*, disappearing into the main cabin without so much as looking back. He'd finished his business, broken the connection. The sudden departure rattled Josh, who sat in front of his strawberries, his hands shaking.

"Now it's Sunday," said Josh.

Calvino spooned the clotted cream over his strawberries.

"You're unhappy, and Mr. Buddha Hill is unhappy," said Calvino.

"Why do you call him that?"

"It's his local nickname."

"He was right. You have met."

"Briefly. That's why he doesn't recall."

Calvino had had a case that involved a member of the Pattaya Yacht Club. A member's wife had lost a necklace. The club hadn't wanted to involve the police and had hired Calvino to investigate whether the woman had lost it or there had been a theft. It turned out that she had pawned it in Korat, but that was another story. Maxim had been on the committee that approved Calvino's final bill. When he drove to Pattaya to pick up the check, he'd had lunch at the club and Maxim had been at the next table. They'd nodded to one another. But Maxim had been on the phone and not long afterwards had disappeared from the room.

Josh dialed Maxim's cell phone. "When you deliver the gold bullet coins Sunday, I will have it done," he said.

Calvino was proud of Josh. He'd showed some spine. Though Calvino would have been prouder had Josh had had the balls to say it in front of Maxim. Barking over a phone was just that: barking. Josh had no clue how someone like Maxim gamed the system with the best of them, and it was a hard-as-nails tough system to game unless a man was connected on the inside, but foreigners rarely breached those inner walls. If a man wanted to impress the Thais, all he had to do was park his private yacht along the pier near the Oriental Hotel. That arrival scaled up several degrees of magnitude the usual stepping out of a chauffeur-driven Benz. Maxim arrived with a crew of eight.

Josh wasn't just any delivery boy dropping off some merchandise for some grandkid in Manhattan. This was an unexpected development—a gangster on a yacht, wanting approval for a deal in one of the countries with "stan" in the name and negotiating with what leverage he seemed to have: some Thai bullet coins. Mr. Buddha Hill had taken his yacht out of Pattaya for a trivial errand. Taking *Last Money* for a Pattaya–Bangkok return trip would cost Maxim several grand. People working in the high-end hotel business noticed that kind of entry. That was the whole purpose of doing it: to get noticed by people who understood what that kind of money meant.

It all came back to Josh's ex-client, his new boss, someone to whom even Mr. Buddha Hill had to defer. An important man with his own, bigger yacht moored in Malta. A man who had his private reasons for choosing Maxim and Josh as his custodians.

It had been during the investigation into the Pattaya Yacht Club wayward wife case that Calvino had come across Maxim's nickname, Mr. Buddha Hill. A section of the Pattaya hill with that name was filled with Russians. They had taken it over by buying businesses, condos, restaurants, and minor wives. Maxim controlled the turf, which stretched from the beach up to the top of the hill. It had become a playground for thousands of Russians who flew directly into the local airport on charter flights and headed straight to the sandy beach at the bottom of the hill, stepped out of their clothes and into tiny swimsuits, and flopped their three hundred pound bodies in neat rows in the sand. An aerial shot of the beach could have passed for a tragic natural disaster with hundreds of stranded whales washed up on the shore by a red tide. But the tide was no longer red; it was capitalistic red, white, and blue, and Maxim had come to Pattaya at the right time.

"The Yacht Club wife you were talking about, didn't happen to be Maxim's wife?" asked Josh.

Calvino smiled. Maxim's wife, in the same circumstances, would now have been swimming with the fishes.

"A retired American airline pilot's wife."

Calvino explained that the Yacht Club member hadn't married a Harvard MBA, but a Rice Planting 201, Buriram edition, with a gambling habit and enough problems in her family to keep a TV soap running indefinitely. But the details of an old airline pilot's domestic problems didn't interest Josh. He shrugged it off in that New York way where the focus was so tightly controlled that anything on the margin was chopped off like fat on a hunk of steak.

"Maxim's got a small piece of a big deal," said Josh. "Andrei needs him, but he's not indispensable. Without Andrei he is out of business. That's what upsets him."

"In his mind this is his deal," said Calvino. "What I'm saying is, his deal is the big deal, and he's showing up in the *Last Money* to make certain you don't forget that."

"I've run into this before. I know how to handle him."

"Never be sure about handling someone like Maxim. His life is built on not getting handled. He likes to keep his finger on the remote control to get what he wants or needs. Just so you know, Mr. Buddha Hill has been mentioned in connection with a couple of murder cases in the past."

"You're joking, right?"

"I hear things, Josh. I know people who hear things. Thailand is a place where the voices whisper where the bodies are buried. But nothing sticks on someone like Maxim. Take the right people out on a big yacht, show them a good time, your problems go away. Evidence doesn't depend on how you look at it but on who is looking at it and what he owes you. Guys like Maxim may personally hate boats. But he's got the right idea. When you've gone to the trouble to start a private navy, no one is gonna fuck with you over the murder of a couple of nobodies."

Josh picked at his food. A faint industrial smell blew over the balcony from the river as if fish oil had been heated in a vat of ball bearings. Secured to the pier, the *Last Money*, a monument of sleek, glistening white molded polymer, as dramatic as an ancient Indian temple sculpture, sensual and visceral, waited in the distance. The means to wealth and privilege rocked gently as a large barge pushed a wave to shore.

"Maxim's a big fish in Thailand," said Calvino. "It's about time you told me about Tajikistan. It keeps coming up. Andrei was there. You were there. Your new best friend Maxim has rolled into it as well. What were you doing there?"

"It's complex."

"Give me the simple version. Tajikistan for dummies."

Calvino stretched back in his chair, looking at Maxim's yacht. A couple of young Thai *yings* in bikinis emerged on the upper deck, walking around, laughing, carrying those pink and green drinks in a tall glass with a tiny bamboo umbrella hanging on the rim. They looked happy standing next to the speedboat suspended above them. Why shouldn't they be? Standing on a rich man's yacht, wishing everyone in their village and bar could see them now: tall— well, as tall as one hundred and fifty-five centimeters can be stretched—and on top of the world, wobbling on the deck in high heels. Their presence suggested the *Last Money* didn't represent Maxim's last money; he had plenty left over and he intended to enjoy it.

"Andrei is the main stockholder in a consulting firm. The business makes tons of money from financial, logistical, and probability studies. They come to Andrei, who does the formulas that show how and where they can save money, reallocate resources, and maximize profits. The deal in Tajikistan involves French, English, and Russian companies. They each have a piece of the action. They've won a fifteen-year oil concession. We're talking huge amounts of cash flow. Tajikistan's got a government that is happy so long as some of that cash flows to them."

"How do Andrei and Mr. Buddha Hill fit in?"

"They do business together."

"And you're in the middle. But your boss is in New York..."

Josh nodded.

"And Maxim and the *Last Money* are for the moment in Bangkok. That makes you the in-between guy, trying to keep all the plates spinning on the ends of sticks. But I'm missing the relationship between the two Russians."

"They knew each other from Moscow. Andrei is older. Maxim's uncle was also a famous mathematician, and the uncle won one of those Nobel Prizes for math years ago. Andrei was a great admirer and friend of the uncle. He's been Maxim's mentor, teaching him..."

"The ropes," said Calvino, finishing Josh's sentence. "But from where I sit, unless you're not telling me something about Andrei, Mr. Buddha Hill doesn't need him for a mentor. So what is the relationship between them?"

"Don't know, beyond what I already told you," said Josh.

"Sounds like the military. Don't ask, don't tell. Come on, Josh. So Maxim's uncle could sit around and talk numbers with Andrei all day. That doesn't tell me much."

Josh turned around and looked at Maxim's yacht.

"Nice boat," said Calvino.

"Maxim made money in the transportation business in Africa and Central Asia," said Josh. "That's all I know. He operates a fleet of planes and ships. In Tajikistan one of his companies has the transportation contract to supply the concession with equipment, supplies, people. That's it. All above board, documented, and legal."

"That would likely be a first for a guy like Maxim."

"What's that mean?"

"Maxim's got a short reputation for doing anything legal. That must hurt him. These documents. You keep crossing things out, putting things in, as if that matters. The whole process makes him lose face with his comrades."

Josh sat back and speared one of the strawberries with his fork. He smiled to himself before sticking it in his mouth.

"Last time I saw Maxim, he said, 'You Americans have three gates: Watergate, Colgate, and Billgate.' "

"Russians don't joke about gates. They drive tanks through them."

"On that happy note, I am going to my room to read through the contract."

Josh gestured to the waiter for the bill.

"Easy on the red ink, Josh."

Calvino stood and looked at Josh, who signed his name and room number on the bill.

"Red ink is what the client pays for," said Josh.

"Remember he's your boss. Bosses hate red ink. It leaves an internal trail. That's the one that always nails them."

Josh added a tip and handed the signed bill to the waiter. With the glare of the sun off the river in his eyes, Josh glanced up at Calvino and grinned.

"Vinny, I know these guys. This is the usual bullshit. I can handle it. Stop worrying."

Calvino stretched out his hand. "You got it."

Calvino looked at his watch. His secretary, Ratana, was expecting him for John-John's after-school birthday party, but there was no chance Calvino could hitch a ride on Maxim's yacht to Klong Toey port.

Rather than head back through the hotel with Josh, Calvino walked over to the dock and stood beside the impressive yacht, all one hundred and ten feet of fiberglass, two eighteen-hundred-and-fifty horsepower diesel engines, and the latest high technology. One of the deckhands must have alerted Maxim, who pulled back the sliding door from the main cabin and walked out onto the deck. He stood with his hands on his hips and stared at Calvino.

"You're right. We have met. I remember now," said Calvino. "The Pattaya Yacht Club. Jefferson's wife said she'd lost her diamond ring. She'd pawned it. When she got caught with her scam, do you know what she said?"

The Russian stood still, staring at him.

"She said, 'I'd rather be a winner in hell than a loser in paradise.' Not the kind of thing you'd ever expect a Thai to say, the fear of ghosts and devils being what it is. It turned out she learned it from a Russian boyfriend at the yacht club. We never found out who that was, although I had a theory."

"Theories, like bowls of noodles on the street, are cheap, Mr. Calvino."

"It depends on how they're packaged."

"What do you want?"

"I'm having some trouble understanding why everyone's pulling out their hair over gold bullet coins for a kid in New York."

The Russian laughed. "Did Levy send you to tell me this?"

"He told me your gate joke."

The smile appeared. "What else did he tell you?"

"Your uncle was good at math."

"More than good, Mr. Calvino."

"Okay, he won a Nobel Prize."

"He was awarded the Fields Medal. An award that is above a Nobel Prize."

"Does Andrei have one?"

Maxim laughed. "A Fields Medal? Only in his dreams."

Maxim explained that the Fields Medal wasn't something anyone could buy. Only a few brilliant mathematicians ever earned one. Calvino started to understand what Andrei was about—he was about the mathematics of respect. He might have made a fortune in his business, but a freight train loaded with money couldn't buy a Fields Medal. Something that paid a ten grand prize packed as much deference as a black hole and sucked the respect out of every other genius in the room.

Calvino thought to himself that the scaffolding of dreams rarely holds, and when it finally collapses, there's nothing to break the force of the fall.

THREE

Inside lay a one-baht gold bullet, curled up like a tiny embryo.

THE GUTTURAL GROWL of a *tuk-tuk*, sounding like a VW engine with a bad case of pneumonia, passed on Sukhumvit Road. Manee, Colonel Pratt's wife, waited behind the wheel of her Benz, turn signal flashing, until the Saturday shopping traffic cleared and she drove into the *soi* and parked in front of Calvino's office building. The windscreen had stickers announcing the police department connection, club affiliation, and Siam Society. In the not-too-distant past, those stickers would have stopped traffic and allowed her to pass. The *tuk-tuk* driver was likely some poor Isan boy who hadn't been paying attention, she thought. But the bus, motorcycle, and van drivers had also not let her turn in; they couldn't all be poor Isan peasants. She thought about the implications of waiting. Her husband never seemed to have this problem. Drivers automatically gave way to him when he was behind the wheel.

Earlier, she'd had an appointment with her fortune teller and then lunched with the wife of her husband's boss at the Royal Thai Police Department. Manee got out of her car carrying a bouquet of roses and a gift-wrapped book. She locked the Benz and climbed the stairs to Calvino's office.

She would have chosen another day, but it wasn't possible. This was a special day. It was John-John's fifth birthday, and he had begun to read. She felt a responsibility to see that the *luk-krueng* boy, half *farang*, half Thai, was exposed to the right literature about Thai culture. Otherwise he would not understand what was expected of him, or what he could expect of others. Much like those boys who hadn't stopped to let her turn across their lane into Calvino's *soi*.

She had bought a copy of *When Our Grandparents Were Children*. Her children had loved reading it. When she was a child, she had also read it many times. It was a Thai classic. She particularly liked the way her generation's grandparents had grown up in the 1930s and '40s. The women scrubbed themselves until their skin positively glowed an unmistakable golden color. And they learned how to cut fruit into beautiful shapes, and make gold crisps rolled into a cylinder shape. *Khanom thongmuan* could be slipped over a child's fingers and popped into the mouth, one at a time. What a wonderful game that had been, one of her favorite childhood treats. In her handbag she had brought a bag of *khanom thongmuan* to get John-John into the spirit of the book.

The birthday party was under way as Manee walked into the office. John-John and five of his friends wore hats and chased after a boy who had an iPod spitting gunfire flashes from its screen. Ratana *waied* Manee, who stepped out of her shoes and handed over the roses.

"They are beautiful," said Ratana.

Manee knelt down and called John-John over. She handed him the book wrapped in gold paper.

"Happy birthday, John-John," she said.

He tore the wrapping off, dropped it on the floor, turned the book over, looked at it, shrugged, and handed it to his mother.

Looking up with the profound, intense expression of a five-year-old, he said, "In Rangoon Zoo they have thousands of striped snakes, and the soldiers throw bad people in the snake pit, only they aren't really bad, just unhappy, because the lights don't stay on for more than two hours a day."

It was the kind of nonsense peppered with sublime truths that five-year-olds speak. Calvino and Ratana had grown accustomed to witnessing John-John piece together the world from inside a five-year-old brain as he tried to make sense of what he saw and heard.

"He'll love it," said Ratana. "Just as I did when I was young."

"I'm afraid there are no snakes in it. Or anything about Burma."

"He's been on this poison snake craze for almost a week. The book will bring him back to Thailand. That is a very good thing. Thank you."

This saved Manee from any loss of face. She opened her handbag and took out the bag. "*Khanom thongmuan*," said Manee.

"I used to wear them on my fingers," said Ratana.

"Yes, we all did. But that was a very long time ago."

Colonel Pratt emerged from Calvino's office, grinning. "I thought I heard you," he said.

Manee looked surprised to see her husband. He hadn't said anything about coming to John-John's birthday party, but he was the sort of sweet, kind, gentle man who wouldn't make a fuss but would just turn up. She swelled with pride.

Calvino appeared a moment later behind Colonel Pratt.

"Vincent had an urgent matter to discuss. He told me it was John-John's birthday."

"I told you last week," said Manee.

"It must have slipped my mind. Still, I am here."

Ratana went behind her desk, opened the drawer, and pulled out a small box.

"Your husband brought this for John-John." She handed it to Manee.

Inside lay a one-baht gold bullet, curled up like a tiny embryo.

"Vincent had a question about gold bullets. I thought now here's a chance to increase John-John's knowledge about Thai culture. Coins tell a remarkable story. Shakespeare used coins often. And in the world of coinage there is no more beautiful object than a Thai gold bullet."

"*Thongmuan*," said Manee, smiling. "Gold that you can eat is the best kind of gold."

Calvino and Colonel Pratt watched as the two women admired the gold bullet coin. Like the book, the coin had held John-John's interest for a nanosecond. Books and coins lack the graphic interface that a modern five-year-old boy appreciates. His favorite present had been the iPod from Ratana. It had been Calvino's idea.

Calvino pulled Colonel Pratt back into his office.

"One more thing, Colonel."

With Calvino there was always one more thing.

Colonel Pratt sat in the chair in front of Calvino's desk. On his computer screen, which he'd turned around for Colonel Pratt to read, a catalogue of the coins appeared. The Colonel had chased down a friend who knew a coin dealer who had told him about the auction. When he'd come to Calvino's office, the Colonel had told him a big coin auction had been scheduled for Wednesday at the Nara Hotel on Silom Road. Catalogue Number 1298 was for a complete set of nine gold bullet coins, Rama V, with a letter to Czar Nicholas II from King Chulalongkorn dated 1907.

"There's the Russian connection I was looking for," Calvino said.

Colonel Pratt raised an eyebrow. The reserve price was twenty million baht.

"That's a great deal of money."

"Not in the world of yachts and oil fields in Tajikistan."

Calvino was a betting man, and he bet the auction would be the place to get information about why and how these coins had brought Josh Levy to Bangkok.

"Your friend is bidding on these coins?"

Calvino's forehead wrinkled and one eyebrow shot up. "I don't think he even knows they are for sale."

"You should tell him about the auction."

"I'm thinking about it. Maybe he already knows," said Calvino.

"If he knew, he'd have told you."

Calvino had already decided that Josh had no position in the coin deal. So far it looked to be a strictly Russian-to-Russian side deal. Josh was tapped to carry the coins back to New York. If some kind of side deal existed between Andrei and Maxim, they hadn't told Josh. He hadn't asked. He didn't seem to care. Josh was a paper and red ink lawyer, and the activity outside the paper was flying around like moths in a windstorm, with the occasional one catching its wings on fire. It wasn't a healthy attitude for someone coming to do business in Bangkok. The devil was always in residence, waiting for a new soul. While men like Josh said that the devil was in the details, in Bangkok the devil was everywhere.

FOUR

Bangkok, Silom Road—Sunday, September 6

Wirot grinned. "Everything is under control."

THE COIN AUCTION was to start at ten in the morning. It was in an old hotel with threadbare carpets, faded wallpaper, and sturdy benches and chairs scattered around the second floor lobby. At a table, dealers sat with jeweler's loupes in their eyes, looking like ancient cyborgs, turning over coins, and examining the fine details. Money and coins were changing hands as people scratched their itch for action before the auction started. Discreet deals hatched between dealers who knew each other for coins that weren't in the auction catalogue.

Calvino and Colonel Pratt walked through the lobby. A Thai-Chinese man in black cotton trousers held up by black suspenders worn over an orange shirt walked over and introduced himself.

"Excuse me, are you Colonel Pratt? I am Wirot," he said, *waiing* the Colonel. "My good friend Ajarn Pinit said I should look for you."

Ajarn Pinit taught history at Chiang Mai University. He had also written a book about Thai coins. Colonel Pratt had traced the professor down through a colleague who had graduated from Chiang Mai University. "Wirot is the expert," Pinit had said.

He hadn't warned him that Wirot was also an eccentric. He had bits of fruit, cake, and ice cream on the front of his shirt. On the far side of the lobby were tables filled with food.

"Are you hungry?" Wirot asked, gesturing at the tables.

Colonel Pratt told him that they'd already eaten. He introduced Calvino.

Wirot focused on Calvino for the first time. "A collector?"

"I'm interested in one collection," said Calvino.

He'd avoided answering Wirot's question, but Wirot didn't seem to mind. Wirot was far more interested in Colonel Pratt.

The three men moved through the largely elderly crowd. Thai men and women in their seventies and eighties were not so much sitting in the chairs as they looked like they had chair implants as they rested on their canes. The elders waited for the start of the auction—some excitement in their lives, a chance to buy a coin as old as they were.

"Ajarn said you were asking about the nine gold bullets that were a gift to Czar Nicholas II from His Majesty."

Colonel Pratt smiled. "I am surprised they are being auctioned."

Wirot grinned. "Everything is under control."

Wirot led them from the lobby to an official registration and operational area. Behind tables were rows of women with computers, files, and boxes. Behind them were larger boxes with the coins carefully sealed inside individual plastic bags. At one end were statues of Buddha and kings, military medals, and large medallions.

"If you want to bid, then you need one of these cards, and to get one, you go over to that man and pay him a fifty thousand baht deposit. You can use a credit card. Personally I never give them cash, always a card. It's safer."

"I'm not buying," said Colonel Pratt. "And neither is my friend. We've come to observe."

Wirot smiled. "I see. You want to see how it works."

"Any idea who'd want to buy the gold bullet set from Rama V?" asked Calvino.

"All dealers would love to buy this set," said Wirot.

"Where's this set been all this time?" asked Colonel Pratt.

"Ajarn Pinit mentioned this historical interest." He looked Calvino over, thumbs hooked in his suspenders. "Have you heard of Daniel Richelieu?"

Calvino drew a blank; he had no idea who Wirot was talking about. Thais often assumed every foreigner knew every other foreigner.

"Where's he from?"

"France. But he's long dead. He was a great coin collector and most trusted foreigner. He was a Lord Admiral of the Thai fleet."

"That would have been some time ago," said Calvino.

"In 1902 he led us in a battle against the French. We only had teakwood cannons. And that wasn't good enough. We lost. We had to pay the French compensation and they demanded gold. What could we do? We printed paper money but had no gold to support it. Not until five years later did we have the gold to back our money."

"How did Daniel Richelieu get the coins out of Russia?" asked Calvino.

Wirot shrugged. "He must have had a way. It was during the revolution."

Colonel Pratt opened the catalogue and turned to the page with the coins.

"It doesn't say who is selling them," said the Colonel.

"The owner didn't want his name mentioned. It's common in an auction. You don't want your friends to think you're running out of money."

Colonel Pratt and Calvino exchanged a look.

"Can they be taken out of Thailand?" asked the Colonel.

"As far as I know, that's not a problem. But you're a policeman. I am certain it hasn't come to that," said Wirot. A radiant smile crossed his face as if some shred of knowledge had registered.

Inside the L-shaped reception area, Calvino counted twenty-five staff working the tables. It looked like a bookie operation or a boiler room where everyone talked on the phone at the same time. Video cameras covered every corner. The cashiers sat behind the tables, relaxed, and drank coffee as they helped people through the registration. Calvino and the Colonel followed Wirot inside the main ballroom, which had a high ceiling and a huge video screen in the center.

The crowd looked like a cross-section of people from a combined temple fair and Chinese wedding. Calvino took in the sea of faces—talking, laughing, gossiping, eating, and smiling. He was looking for someone. Most people had been pooled at one end of the room. He waited as someone turned around, moved on, and continued scanning the room. He wasn't the only person rubbernecking, looking for familiar faces. They were surrounded by men on high platforms who wore earphones and stood behind TV cameras pointed like machine guns at those below. He let Colonel Pratt and Wirot work their way toward the front.

The auctioneer stood behind a podium, reading through papers silently. The hum of conversation rose as people came in and out, carrying coffee and sandwiches.

A bleached out image of Item 1, a limited edition of a Buddha statue, flashed on the screen. A strict protocol dictated the order of the items auctioned. The Buddha statues were the first items on the block.

Calvino worked his way down the rows until he came alongside Wirot. The old man had been stopping every second step to say hello to another dealer, introducing Colonel Pratt. When he was no longer actively looking, Calvino spotted Maxim in the back with two other foreigners.

Maxim sat in the middle chair. He wasn't the same man Calvino had seen the previous day standing on the deck of the *Last Money* and the balcony of the Oriental. This morning's version of Maxim looked slightly chewed up—grayish, gaunt, with bloodshot eyes—the way a man looks after a pool is drained and they find his body at the bottom. That was Maxim's face. Tired, moody, and self-absorbed. He sat with arms folded, listening to one of his men whispering in his ear, occasionally nodding, occasionally talking into his cell phone. He could have passed for any other *farang* businessman in the room. That pretty well summed up Maxim. Someone who was looking to play in the big time but meanwhile was stuck at the bottom of this large, empty pool, waiting for the head lifeguard to call the audience to attention.

Wirot had led Colonel Pratt up toward the front, where there were empty seats.

Calvino tapped the Colonel on the shoulder. "I'll be back. Keep a chair for me." He nodded at the foreigners in the corner.

"Tell them not to bother," said Colonel Pratt.

"I'll mention it," said Calvino.

Calvino walked to the back of the room, circled behind the camera platform, and came up from behind Maxim.

"If I owned a yacht like the *Last Money*, I couldn't see myself dragging my ass out of bed on a Sunday morning. For what? To buy some coins?"

The Russian slowly looked up, closing his cell phone. "Is Josh with you?"

Calvino shot him a crooked grin. "Should he be?"

"What do you want?"

Maxim shifted his weight, the way a man does when he's under stress or is getting hot under the cloth. In Maxim's case it was both.

"Thought I'd pass along a message."

"Send me an email," said Maxim.

Calvino glanced at the two men with Maxim. Each held a large briefcase, the kind litigators use for documents.

"I'd forget about Lot 19," Calvino said. "I should have sent you an email."

"Maybe I'll see you later tonight, Mr. Calvino."

Above the background chatter it was hard to gauge the tone. The menace in the expression didn't require any further explanation, though.

"I don't remember you telling Josh about this auction," said Calvino.

With his peace offering declined, Maxim turned away. "I'd like to discuss this with you some other time. I am quite busy now. So if you don't mind, I will make time for you later."

That's how the Russian wanted to play it. Tough and hard, playing up the role of godfather in front of his men.

"See you later, Maxim."

But what was going on inside Maxim's head? Judging from the look on his face, Calvino thought not much. Maxim was like the empty plastic box the military bought to detect bombs. On the outside it looked like the real thing. Calvino wondered whether he would have the chance to open Maxim's head and look around inside the vast open space that was Russia.

"Don't have an accident on the way to the hotel tonight, Mr. Calvino."

That didn't sound like an empty box talking.

The two men stared at each other. One of the bodyguards with a briefcase handed Maxim a cell phone, and Calvino drifted away from the threat as he walked to the front of the room.

The auction started at precisely ten.

The first couple of lots sold quickly. Others had no bidders and were quickly replaced by new lots. The first of the coins appeared on the large screen. An enormous image of Rama V appeared on the white screen. One of the Thais held up a white card showing "172" in red numbers. Other white-and-red numbered cards shot up as the TV crews filmed them. All the red numbers to 500 were reserved for Thais; for 501 and up the number appeared on a yellow card. Maxim fingered a yellow card like a man at bingo night. Expectation and boredom fought for control in his mind.

The auctioneer stood behind the podium dressed in a pink shirt, yellow tie, and banker's gold-rimmed glasses, looking like a game show host. Banging his hammer to announce that the bidding had ended, he pressed his lips to a microphone and barked out the number of the winner—one of Wirot's friends. The room was filled with Wirot's friends. That meant good luck, according to Wirot.

At 10:33 a.m. the auctioneer cleared his throat, lips close to the microphone, and paused, allowing a touch of drama to rise before he announced Lot 19. The gold bullets flashed onto the large screen. Bigger than life, the nine gold bullet coins didn't look like coins; they looked like tiny statues from Easter Island. There was something remote, abandoned, unknowable about these exotic, elegant, folded twists of gold. Stonehenge had its field of stone tablets. Thailand had gold bullets.

The auctioneer told the audience that the minimum bid would be twenty million baht. A couple of people gasped, and a murmur escaped from the audience. Then it started. One member of the audience applauded, another person joined, and the applause went viral. Everyone in the room clapped, stood on their feet, and applauded. The auctioneer rocked on his heels, smiling, as if accepting the applause. Calvino glanced over his shoulder to the back of the ballroom. Maxim wasn't applauding. Nor was he standing. Maxim slumped forward in his chair, holding in his right hand a yellow card with the number 529. Ready to raise his arm. His men sat tensely beside him, clutching briefcases.

Colonel Pratt leaned over and whispered to Calvino. "Wirot's ready for his moment."

Wirot raised his card with the number 33. Red on white, a Thai card. His face tense, he focused on catching the eye of the auctioneer, who had kept the audience waiting. Wirot held up the card, but the auctioneer wasn't ready to give up such a special moment. He made a speech about the history of the coins, the letter written to Czar Nicholas II by Rama V. He described Rama V's journey to Moscow in 1897. He lectured the audience about the relationship between the Thai and Russian monarchs. The Thai audience, attentive and respectful, listened to the speech. Sweat rolled down Wirot's face. He wiped his neck with a handkerchief. The delay made him nervous, and he shifted his feet.

"Wirot looks ready," said Calvino.

"This is for our country." Colonel Pratt smiled and focused his attention back on the auctioneer. The speech had fired up the Colonel as well as the rest of the audience.

The Colonel had discovered the network of people and their plans the previous evening. Ajarn Pinit was one of those people. A Chinese-Thai family from Chiang Mai had put up the funds. That hadn't been easy to arrange, but once the money was in place, Wirot was selected as the front man. He knew his business; dealers trusted him. He was reliable.

Calvino glanced back at Maxim, wondering how the Russian would react once he discovered the fix was in. The mistake for Maxim would be to focus on Wirot. But he would likely find that Wirot was the tip of an iceberg, and the solid mass lurking below had real power and wealth, more than enough to scuttle Maxim and his yacht. The Rama V set of gold bullets was headed, according to the plan, to the National Coin Museum. Everything had been arranged.

The auction started with the auctioneer acknowledging Wirot's opening bid of twenty million baht.

"Do I hear twenty-one million baht?"

One of the spotters pointed at Maxim's card and the number 529 flashed on the screen. People in the audience saw the foreigner's number, and none of the home team liked seeing competition emerge from the back of the room. Maxim's bid caused them to stir.

The auctioneer's voice boomed through the speakers around the room. "Do I hear twenty-two million baht?"

Wirot held up his card, and the number 33 appeared on the screen. There was a round of applause. In the back Maxim already held up his card before the auctioneer had increased the bid.

The auctioneer's sigh filtered through the ballroom. "Do I hear twenty-three million baht?"

Maxim's number again flashed on the screen. The auctioneer quickly ran up the bidding to thirty-three million baht. The US dollar conversion showed one million dollars, to the awe of the audience. It was then the auctioneer's hammer dropped. Wirot's number 33 was on the screen. Thirty-three million baht flashed on the screen. Half of the audience was making a mental note to buy a lottery ticket ending with the number 33.

Maxim was on his feet. "I bid forty million baht," he shouted.

At first the auctioneer ignored the Russian, pretending not to hear him above the roar of applause from the audience.

"I said, why did you stop the bidding? I was not finished."

"Your bid was too late," said the auctioneer. "Lot number 20 is a set of three gold bullets from the reign of Rama V." He continued his speech, ignoring the Russian.

"Look at your tapes. You will see I was holding up my card when you asked for thirty-four million baht. Why do you ignore me?"

Three security men closed into the area. Maxim looked around the ballroom. He had three men. There were hundreds of people inside. None of them were going to back him. He had to make a decision.

"If you wish to make a complaint, number 529, please do so."

"No complaint. It is a small misunderstanding," he said.

The auctioneer smiled. He'd restored balance and order. The audience applauded again. A few minutes later Calvino saw Maxim and one of his men walking out of the ballroom. One of them stayed behind with the number 529 and the catalogue open on his lap.

By noon Wirot looked exhausted but elated. The auctioneer announced a ten-minute break. Wirot gobbled down three sandwiches. A stream of people leaned over him as he munched. He'd mastered holding a sandwich and *waiing*. They patted him on the back. A couple of dozen dealers lined up to congratulate him. It may have been the first time in his life that Wirot had been treated like a hero. The winning bid had made him an instant celebrity in the room. He called Ajarn Pinit and gave him the good news.

Colonel Pratt sat inside Wirot's inner circle, happy and content. The win had been a victory for Thailand. Everyone agreed the auctioneer hadn't made a mistake. The crazy foreigner in the back of the room had been too slow. It had been his own fault, and besides, why would a foreigner want to snatch away a piece of the national heritage from the Thais? After the dealers, a crowd of people formed a line, holding out their catalogues and asking Wirot to sign his name. It was good luck, they said.

"That Russian shouldn't have caused a problem," said Colonel Pratt. "No one cheated him."

Calvino had a feeling that Maxim had a decidedly different view.

The coin auction world was like the racetrack. Punters sweated over the racing form, checking off win, place, and show possibilities. But in this room most people felt as if their horse had won. The plan to keep the coins in Thailand had succeeded. Winning had been a patriotic act and, like a drug, flooded the emotions with a collective high. Wirot puffed out his chest, pulling out his black suspenders, his face as big as a face could grow, bigger than the moon, the sun, and the stars. It was his moment.

"Did your friend Josh tell you about this?" asked Colonel Pratt as they left the ballroom.

Calvino shrugged. "I don't think he has any idea. Josh doesn't know squat about coins. He can tell a quarter from a dime, but after that what would he know?"

"That set of coins carries a historical memory of a time and place. That is magic. You would have to be Thai to understand."

"A million bucks for a set of coins? Magic? They ought to come with a flying carpet for that price," said Calvino. "It has to be a screw-up somewhere. Josh was told they were coins for a kid in New York. Why would his boss spend that kind of money on a kid's coin collection?"

Outside the hotel Colonel Pratt walked alongside Calvino until they reached the street. They stopped for the light.

"Shakespeare said gold is a shelter for friends and binds them like brothers. You saw it happen before your eyes."

"It's done," said Calvino, as the light changed. "Maybe all of that good feeling will catch on. Who knows?"

The Sunday traffic was thin.

"No one knows. But it might be a start in the right direction."

It had been Calvino who had suggested that a foreigner had shown interest in some gold bullet coins. He had had no idea they were some rare national treasure, one that had fallen between the cracks. The foreigners had been excluded from the group of Thais who had made plans for the coins. It looked like Josh and his friends had gone into a situation with imperfect information.

Calvino wasn't so sure that Josh Levy was going to be happy that his best man got involved in something he should've stayed clear of. Privileged information had been leaked and Calvino had done the leaking. Maxim had been handed the chance to lay off the failure on to Calvino and his interfering friends. It wasn't much, but Maxim didn't need much, just a seed of doubt to shift the blame for the problem.

FIVE

Bangkok, Silom Road—Monday, September 7

"Use it to buy a parachute," said Calvino.

SITTING ON THE sixty-fifth story, the linen covered table was the highest in Bangkok. Anyone wanting dinner above that altitude would have had to rent a helicopter. Looking down, the lights painted the Bangkok sky with gold, red, and chrome, pooling in eddies near the river, launching out in long lines along the Rama IX Bridge, and shimmering against the blackness, leaving a trail of tiny red taillights, motionless in the heavy traffic. Maxim had insisted on the rooftop restaurant. It was near the Oriental Hotel, where Silom Road and Charoen Krung Road meet in a lovers' embrace.

Having arrived together, Calvino and Josh waited on the ground floor for the lift.

"I'd go easy on him," said Calvino. "Maxim's ego is bigger than sixty-five stories."

"He's okay."

"He was ready to bid forty million baht," said Calvino. "Doesn't sound like coins you'd give to a kid."

The doors opened and Calvino walked in first. Josh grinned and followed.

"Yeah? How much is that in dollars?"

"A million and a quarter."

"I'm certain there's an explanation. People get carried away at auctions."

"Josh, these weren't any coins. You're not getting it. Why was Maxim after that set?"

"He's a businessman. Maybe he collects coins. And Andrei asked him as a favor to buy some for his grandson." The digital numbers started as the lift shot upward.

There was no point hitting the wall again. In Josh's mind there wasn't anything unusual in the Russian bidding over a million dollars for coins. He worked with these men, and it seemed nothing surprised him.

In the dim elevator lighting Calvino caught a glimpse of that kid from years before. Josh had a kind of radar that could pick up the faint distress signals of a sinking ship. It was a good mentality for a lawyer. Josh prided himself on knowing when to jump, bend, or retreat. The story about Maxim at the auction hadn't caused him to flinch.

"You're getting married," said Calvino. "You've changed jobs. You're dealing with Russians who are up to something that anyone would think should be investigated. But Josh Levy rises high above Bangkok grinning as if he doesn't have a care in the world."

"Just a lucky guy."

They stepped out of the lift. Ahead of them was a restaurant that appeared to float in the sky.

Luck comes in many shapes, but like chance, it is random. Everyone believes their own luck is something special, just as everyone thinks they're unique. That's when the alarm bells ought to bang loud and clear. Only Josh didn't hear them.

"Lucky, how so?"

A waitress asked them if they had reservations. Josh handed her a name card and she found his booking.

"Tess, to start with. And by jumping when I did into this new job."

They followed her to the table. The city shimmered in a dusting of lights that stretched to the horizon. Josh slowly rotated his head, letting the view sink in.

"The city's huge," he said. "You don't look so good."

Calvino hated heights. "At this height, it's not a city; it's an abstract painting."

"You're afraid of heights. I'd forgotten about that." Calvino's weakness seemed to amuse Josh, who made a point of sucking in the air. "Fear's a terrible thing."

Calvino looked away from the edge. "I remember you had no fear of getting high."

"Touchy. But don't worry; you're with me, Vinny. No one is going to throw you over the side."

He'd remembered Calvino's fear of heights when he'd chosen the restaurant. The event was to test whether that old fear was under control. They sat at a table with only a small rail separating them from the 650-foot drop.

"You okay?"

Calvino nodded, ordering a double whiskey.

"Feeling lucky?"

That was one of Josh's stock phrases.

Josh Levy had gathered baskets of luck over the years. He had to have been pulling in a million two, a million five a year from his law firm. The great slump that had run like wildfire through the big law firms had burnt the forest around him but left Josh standing—no burn marks, not even a whiff of fire. He'd gotten out because he could. He'd been safe but felt unsafe. It was irrational, but most fear was exactly that. His record had been sterling. Josh had done big international deals and had a reputation for getting the precise details right before signing off on the deal. When a client had ignored his advice—not something that often happened—he'd counter-offered, saying he'd transfer the work to another lawyer who might be easier, more flexible. Clients with that much money at stake had never called his bluff. Careful, methodical, dogged, and disciplined, he possessed a sixth sense of what could go wrong, a sense forged over twenty-five years in the trenches, where he'd witnessed major battles, blunders, retreats, treaties made and broken, and defeats as well as victories.

Still, he had jumped. And Calvino wondered whether his friend knew where he'd landed.

Josh thought that, having made his own luck, deal by deal, until he became an indispensable part of the deal, that kind of luck was transportable.

"Any chance you might go back to the law firm?"

Josh shook his head. "That's over, Vinny."

"Just you and Andrei. And Maxim. Did you make any changes in the contract Maxim gave you?"

Josh shook his head as the menus arrived.

"That's good. I don't think that sailor can take two sinkings in one day."

"There was a tax issue," said Josh.

"Isn't there always?"

"I cleared it with Ben Harris. If Ben says no problem, it's okay by me. So to answer your question, it's cleared. I am still using the old law firm. Now I'm a client. I can pressure Ben in ways I could only dream of before."

"I bet he likes that."

"I make him sweat a little."

"Like Maxim?"

"Don't make things too easy."

"Or they treat you like a whore."

"Exactly."

"Maxim looked pissed off at the auction."

"You afraid he'll throw you off the roof?"

Calvino tried to read the menu in the semi-darkness.

"Maxim gets other people to do his heavy lifting. He doesn't want to mess up his Armani shirt."

The same waitress returned to the deck with Maxim, leading him through the tables ringed along the iron railing. Maxim smoked a Cuban cigar and yapped on his cell phone. Right behind Maxim Calvino recognized the two Russians from the auction. Maxim and his men sat down at the table.

"Too bad about the auction. But anyone with *Last Money* can't be a loser," said Calvino as he glanced over at the two Russians, who stared back unblinking like a couple of gargoyles mounted on twin Humvee chassis.

"You always like to say the funny thing, Mr. Calvino. In Moscow we call such performers circus people. You see, I happen to like the circus. When I was a child, my father took me to the circus many times. So I have no prejudice against circus people. But I like them best at the circus."

The waitress arrived with more menus and handed them out. The action broke the tension. The Russians scanned the restaurant and the scenery like computer software hunting for a virus. They stuck out among the tables of tourists who looked like they'd parachuted into a tight spot and were trying not to appear scared. Calvino noticed that the muscle that traveled with Maxim had refused the menus. They had the look of men who ate everything ripped from the carcass of a downed beast except the antlers, which they carved into dice.

The three diners each had a drink.

"I recommend the steak," said Maxim. "It's imported from Australia."

Josh ordered the steak medium rare with saffron soup to start, and Maxim followed, ordering a dozen fresh oysters and no soup. Calvino turned the page in the menu, looked up, smiled at the waitress who stood an elbow away, and ordered a single malt whiskey. He asked her to make it a double just like the first one. She repeated the order and gave Calvino a big smile. He avoided looking over the edge of the rooftop. One of the Russians was leaning over the railing. How could he do that? Calvino wondered.

The waitress returned with a single malt whiskey, set it down, and disappeared, hips moving against the distant lights below. Calvino thought he caught Josh watching her ass swaying against the night, but that wasn't the case. Starstruck by the view of the city, Josh had drifted away inside his own thoughts. At least for a moment he was off somewhere far removed from Bangkok.

Maxim reached inside his jacket pocket and pulled out a thick white envelope. He reached across the table with it.

"Your two thousand, Mr. Calvino."

Calvino nearly choked on the whiskey. "Two grand for what?"

"For coming back to warn me the fix was in. At first, I think, 'He's fucking with me.' But you were right. Take it."

Calvino took it. Two grand had a certain heft. He peeked inside and put it in his inside jacket pocket. Picking up his glass, he raised it to Maxim.

"To Tajikistan, gold bullets, and circus people."

"Why not go double or nothing with the two grand?" Maxim asked.

"What do I have to do? Play Russian roulette with you?"

"Circus people," he said under his breath, sighing.

He fished inside one pocket, then another, until he emerged with a leather bag. He unzipped it. The lighting wasn't that good. Maxim ordered a lamp from the waiter. The waiter came back with a flashlight. Maxim took it and shone the light on the contents of the bag—gold bullets.

"If you had stayed at the auction, you would have seen one of my men buy these. Andrei is happy with the results. He says that his grandson will be happy. It doesn't matter that they are different from Lot 19. Andrei understands. National pride is also strong in Russia. We understand this. We have no problem. I have done my part. Now I'd like my agreement back from you, Josh."

Josh tried not to look bored as Maxim showed him each of the nine gold bullets. In that light they looked like

110

progressively larger molars extracted from age six up to advanced old age. Maxim fondled them as if the gold could be absorbed into his blood.

"As it happens, I have good news about your agreement."

"It's approved," said Maxim, slightly bored.

"How do you know?"

"I talked with Andrei."

"I just talked with Andrei, and he didn't mention your conversation."

Maxim raised a hand. "Mr. Calvino, I'd like a private conversation with my lawyer."

Technically Josh wasn't representing Maxim, but given the circumstances it was a fine detail.

Calvino finished the whiskey, took the white envelope from his jacket pocket, and rose from his chair. He dropped the envelope on his plate. He'd been kicked out of better places but never a higher place. That, he had to admit, was a first.

"Use it to buy a parachute," said Calvino.

"I'll give you a call tomorrow, Vinny," said Josh.

"Come around to the office. We'll go for lunch. Some place under four stories."

There had been nine gold bullets inside the bag. Maxim now laid them out in the palm of his hand and held the flashlight on them. He smiled, saying over and over how beautiful they were and how proud he was to be passing them along to Andrei's grandson. As far as Maxim was concerned, Calvino no longer existed. The same couldn't be said of his men. Calvino felt the eyes of Maxim's men on his back as he walked back to the main terrace. When he turned to look back, he saw Maxim laughing as he reached across the table to give Josh a bear hug.

Descending in the lift, Calvino realized he had no idea what words could have motivated the bear of a man to spring across the table and embrace Josh Levy. He had to admit there were gaps in what he knew about his old friend, who turned out to be something of a mystery man with enough magic to turn a clown like Maxim into an entertaining circus performer.

As the elevator door opened and Calvino walked out, he wondered how it is that people remember characters more than they remember stories. It's the characters and how they react, feel, survive, struggle, doubt, hope, fail, persevere, love, and die that we hunger for. These are the elements that stick with us over time. Maxim's story ran like a trim line around him and shaped his character, but for Calvino the Russian essentially remained, like Josh, a phantom shuffling through his thoughts and dreams. The two men were like shadows Calvino reached out for but couldn't quite touch.

SIX

Bangkok, Lad Phrao Road—Wednesday, September 9

It was impossible for the Colonel to say no to such a request.

RATANA LOOKED UP from her computer as Calvino opened a white envelope and dumped out two thousand US dollars on her desk. She looked as he examined the money. The wrinkled bills smelled of age.

"Who left them?" asked Calvino.

"He didn't give me a name."

"Was he Thai or a *farang*?"

"A *farang*. He said you forgot the envelope last night."

"I didn't forget," said Calvino.

Ratana shrugged. "It's a lot of money to forget."

Bending down, he wrinkled his nose over one of the bills. It smelled similar but different. A trace smell of drugs that Maxim's men must have worked half a day to get just right. Maxim could have easily said he'd won the bet; he had indeed delivered nine gold bullets, and a lawyer's argument among lawyers was bound to prevail. But Maxim was a businessman and had seen an opportunity that was worth two thousand dollars. By afternoon someone from the police would come around and ask to examine the notes for traces of drugs. It would be too late, as the notes would no longer be in Calvino's office.

He had been careful not to touch the notes. He didn't want his fingerprints on them. He didn't want Ratana's either.

"Don't touch them. Use tissue and put them back in the envelope."

"What are you going to do with the money?"

When she looked up, Calvino had already walked into his office and downloaded his email. Ratana stood in the doorway.

"I said, what do you want me to do with the money?"

"Phone the Mercy Center and tell Father Joe's secretary that we've got a donation for him. Ask him to send a messenger this morning."

He had a second thought. "Tell him to send a messenger over immediately."

"Who should I say is the donor?"

"A Russian named Maxim. Ask Father Joe to make out a receipt in Maxim's name."

"What's the address?"

"A boat named *Last Money*, near the Oriental Hotel pier. And ask Father Joe to say a mass for him. He's a man who has some sins to atone for."

"What sins? In case I'm asked."

Calvino looked up from his keyboard. "Tell Father Joe the usual ones. He'll know he comes inside the ninety-five percent rule."

Ratana cracked a smile. Calvino had once explained this element of trade-craft—an ion scan of American currency will show a trace of cocaine contamination on ninety-five percent of all hundred-dollar bills. The cross-contamination happens because of the rollers inside automatic banking machines, which spread traces of cocaine on currency like mayonnaise on toast. Such evidence was no longer admissible in American courts. But in Thailand Calvino could look forward to being processed not by the gentle hands of a chef but by a meat grinder of a system that had a different view of what was probative.

"John-John came back from school and said he felt sorry for Jesus."

Calvino smiled, waiting for the latest piece of wisdom to have uncoiled from John-John's undeveloped brain.

"Why sorry?"

"He said Jesus was born on December 25 and died in April. He said that made him less than a year old when he died. He'd done the math. Jesus lived four months in his mind. He asked me why he'd died so young."

"What did you tell him?"

"It's a mystery."

"Father Joe can set him straight."

Ratana nodded, smiling. "It's better to keep focused on the donation."

"One more thing. Use gloves when you touch the money."

Kid gloves were required to touch anything connected with Maxim.

It was mid-morning when Colonel Pratt got the anxious call from Chiang Mai. A professor was on the other end. The Colonel sat in his office and put down the newspaper as the professor came on the line. Overnight, Wirot had disappeared, along with the Rama V set of nine gold bullets. Wirot's family was frantic. The upcountry godfather who had paid for the gold bullets was frantic. Government officials planning a campaign featuring the gold bullet coins were in a panic. The Colonel thought all of this was too much worry just because Wirot had been out of contact. It was likely nothing.

"Do you have some reason to believe Wirot has disappeared?" Colonel Pratt asked.

"His wife is upset."

"If he didn't come home, his wife would be upset. That's normal."

The direct, straightforward approach set Ajarn Pinit back. The Colonel had so rationally explained the situation that Pinit felt slightly foolish. But the professor continued the conversation in a roundabout, academic way. He wondered, given the circumstances, as the Colonel was acquainted with Wirot, whether he might make a few discreet inquiries, starting with Wirot's wife, who seemed to be very upset that her husband hadn't called.

"You were with him at the auction. It would be a comfort to Khun Wirot's wife if you could call on her and the family."

It was impossible for the Colonel to say no to such a request.

Instead of going to lunch, Colonel Pratt, who was in uniform, walked to the parking lot and climbed into his police car. He headed down Ratchadapisek Road, flashing the red light on top. Even with the red light it took ages to drive the ten kilometers to Wirot's house. The house was on a *sub-soi* hidden in a maze of other *sois*, which shot off Lad Phrao Road like the broken veins in a drunk's nose. The Colonel overshot the *sub-soi* the first time and had to turn the car around, backing into the driveway of a mansion. He wondered who lived inside.

By the time the Colonel arrived, nearly an hour had passed, and the stress of driving had knotted the muscles in his shoulders. He sat in the car on the side of the road beside the family compound, massaging one shoulder, then the other. Finally he got out, put on his policeman's cap, and went to ring the bell.

A skinny Burmese maid in Chinese pajamas opened the gate. Two large golden labs bounded through and sniffed the Colonel's trousers, tails wagging. He slipped inside the compound and the maid closed the gate. Inside were four

116

houses with gardens. A driveway ran down the center with two houses on either side. Judging from the new cars in the parking area, the family was one car short of opening a BMW distributorship. The lawns in front were green and rimmed with mango and banana trees. A large gray cat looked down from the branch of a gnarled Bo tree, front legs stretched out and ears erect, watching the Colonel pass beneath.

Standing in the driveway, wringing her hands and consoled by two younger women, a heavyset woman with eyeliner, lip-gloss and rouge, her cheeks streaked from crying waited to greet him.

She gave the Colonel a deep *wai* and brushed away a tear.

"My husband..." she said, her lower lip trembling. "He's missing. Please help me find him."

Wirot's wife wore a black dress that tented over her plump hips. Her surprised eyes made the Colonel wonder whether her expression was the collateral damage of Botox or whether she was in shock over the disappearance of her husband. She could have passed for forty-something; she could have been sixty. She requested that he call her Wan, and with a hint of a smile she *waied* him again.

Missing, is he? thought Colonel Pratt. There was no immediate need for him to commit himself to a position on Wirot's status.

"Ajarn Pinit said you were his good friend and that you would find my husband."

As she held the *wai*, the Colonel studied the skin on the top of her hands —loose, bumpy, with blue veins and liver spots. They were the hands of a woman running the last couple of laps of her fifties. Not all parts of the body aged at the same rate, a friend had once told him. The fear was that the parts that gave the most satisfaction would age the fastest.

117

It was impossible to tell Wan that he wasn't really her husband's friend. From a Thai point of view, they were friends and that was it. The amount of time they'd known each other mattered for nothing. He was resigned to his status as Wirot's friend as he followed Wan and her two attendants into the largest house in the compound. It was a solid upper-middle-class house with a traditional sloping Thai-styled roof and shutters on the windows, which opened onto the lawn. In the sitting room they joined more family and friends. As the Colonel glanced around the room, he felt all eyes were focused on him.

"Ajarn Pinit said you were in charge," said Wan.

The others nodded.

"Ajarn phoned my mother and said not to worry," said one of the younger women, who obviously was Wirot's daughter. "He told us that you were quite concerned and would be personally investigating the missing person case."

He had landed in the middle of a family who had been the object of a misinformation campaign. Nothing unusual, he thought; people love to gossip and jump to conclusions. Colonel Pratt sighed, wishing that somehow he might be spared and the family would jump over him and come down on another authority figure. It must be my karma, he thought.

Colonel Pratt was introduced to everyone in the room. He was told of each person's relationship to Wirot. He was briefed on the history of the family in Lad Phrao. More *wais* and pleasantries. Based on the single phone conversation with Ajarn Pinit, they were convinced that the Colonel was in command of the investigation and that every resource in the department would be used to find Wirot. Wan asked the Colonel what information his investigation had already unearthed.

He decided to try and handle the family in the modern way. He'd clear away the web of misunderstanding. He started by explaining that he'd only met Wirot for the first time at the auction. That the Colonel and Wirot hadn't known each before didn't register. He said that he'd only received the call from Pinit a couple of hours ago. There hadn't been any investigation. So far as he knew, there was nothing to investigate. He had come to the family compound as a courtesy to Ajarn Pinit, who had helped him with some information about the Rama V coin collection. The information about the gold bullets was to help a foreigner, a friend, who had asked about them. One thing had led to another, and he'd found himself at the auction. There had been a misunderstanding about his involvement.

The modern approach failed. He looked at the faces in the room. They told him that his explanation fell short of dislodging their belief that the Colonel and Wirot were good friends. Colonel Pratt sighed, he'd done all he could to rescue the truth but the truth was dead on arrival.

"My father said you were a great comfort at the auction," said Wirot's daughter.

"You talked with him?"

"After he bought the coins. He was so happy. So proud."

Wirot phoned his daughter after the auction and said that Colonel Pratt was at his side, giving him support and encouragement during the most crucial auction of his life. And Wirot, the family agreed, loved coin auctions, and for him to say this was the most important coin auction ever was a first.

Colonel Pratt took out a notebook and pen. He had no real choice. After noting the date, time, and location at the top of the page, he looked up and addressed his first question to Wan.

"When was the last time you saw your husband?"

She pursed her lips, looking at the ceiling and then at the floor. "Two weeks ago."

Colonel Pratt put down his pen. "I don't understand. I saw him yesterday."

"But you are his friend. I am his wife, and we aren't speaking to each other."

"Let me understand this. You and your husband were having marital problems?"

He smiled. Wirot hadn't disappeared; he had simply stayed out of contact with his wife, with whom he had a conflict. Perfectly understandable behavior, thought Colonel Pratt, who felt that at last he was getting somewhere. He didn't want to admit that it was a case or this was an investigation. Not yet.

He pursued the matter, asking the wife what this problem was all about; he had a feeling that it was nothing more than a domestic quarrel. The wife had got hold of information about the auction. The news had caught fire and spread through the compound, with everyone wondering exactly where Wirot had come up with a million dollars to buy coins. So it was about the money. Not the man, but the man and the money. Where had he got his hands on a million dollars, they wanted to know.

"He had dinner planned with Seven," said Wan.

Colonel Pratt looked up from his notebook. "What is Seven's relationship with Wirot?"

"I am his daughter," said Seven, who had been talking to him earlier. She had gone over and stood in the corner, arms crossed and chewing gum, wearing a white cotton shirt and a tight and too short black dress. The button on her blouse announced her university. Seven had been one of the women giving support to Wan as she'd stood crying in the driveway. "And he asked me to meet him last night at seven o'clock. 'Seven at seven,' he liked to say. It was to be a celebration. He wanted to show me the Rama V coins. But he never arrived. My father has never done that before."

"Where was this?"

120

"Siam Paragon. The food court. Father loves pizza with pineapple and anchovies."

Colonel Pratt remembered the bits of food that had clung to Wirot's clothing. He had no doubt that his daughter had correctly gauged her father's affection.

"It's not far from that woman's condo," said Wan.

Colonel Pratt looked at the anger boiling in Wan's face.

"What woman might that be?"

"Father's minor wife. Her name is Anne," said Seven.

"She doesn't even use a Thai name. How can he bear it? A man who loves history and tradition, sleeping with a Thai named Anne. It's too much, Colonel."

The larger question was, how did the minor wife bear Wirot? Given Wirot's physical condition and carelessness with where his food landed, the Colonel assumed that Anne had found other qualities to her liking.

"Is it possible that Khun Wirot has been delayed at Anne's condo?"

Wan's eyes narrowed like a cat watching a mouse cross its path. "I will not hear that woman's name inside my house."

"Mother, you just used her name yourself."

"That's different."

Colonel Pratt held up a hand as the conversation veered off the main road.

"When did Khun Wirot last see this woman?"

Wan appeared to receive vindication from the fact that the Colonel had found a way to refer to Anne without using her name. She liked the Colonel. If only Wirot could have been more like this policeman.

"I talked with Anne," said Seven. "She told me that Father left early last night and didn't come back."

"How can you talk about that woman in my house?"

"Mom, I asked her about Father. I didn't invite her to be my Facebook friend."

"You will find him?" Wan tilted her head, smiling at the Colonel.

Colonel Pratt looked at his watch. It was nearly two and he hadn't eaten. His stomach had started to rumble like a two-stroke motorcycle. All eyes focused on him, waiting for his answer. He studied his notebook, reading his notes. It seemed that Wirot had left his minor wife's condo in the early evening. It was now not quite midday. From early evening to midday was hardly a period of time that qualified to label Wirot as a missing person. People often wandered off for days, distracted by this or that—a pretty girl, an old friend they'd not seen for some time, an invitation to a cockfight or a kickboxing match. To launch a missing person case in every such circumstance would take every waking minute of every policeman in the country.

"I will make some inquiries," said Colonel Pratt.

That brightened up the faces in the room as if someone had plugged them into an electrical socket. "Inquiries" sounded solemn, official, something that a loved one could clutch onto because it suggested action and prompted hope. All Colonel Pratt wanted to do was to eat a late lunch.

"Now, if you will excuse me, I need to get back to my office."

He went to put on his shoes. Seven escorted him from the house as the others *waied* him. Dabbing her eyes with a tissue, Wan stayed on the sofa with a relative on either side.

"It's not like him," said Seven.

"What do you mean?" asked Colonel Pratt, as one of the compound maids unlocked the main gate.

"To not come back. I don't mean to Mother. I mean to Anne's condo. He had no other place to go."

"There are lots of places," said Colonel Pratt, not wishing to be precise.

122

"If you knew my father, you'd understand he hates going out."

"I must go if I'm going to make any headway," he said.

"He paid over thirty million baht for those gold coins," said Seven. "Mother's right. Where did Father get that kind of money? It has to be family money. All the family thinks that he had no right to use that much of the family money for his coins."

"Do you agree?" asked Colonel Pratt.

"It doesn't matter what I think," she said.

Everyone in the room worried about the money. The minor wife would have been, too, had she been present. By any standard, that was a lot of money for a coin collection. But it wasn't the Colonel's place to discuss with the family the nature of the financial arrangements that had made the funds available to Wirot.

The family suffered from the delusion that Wirot had squirreled away the money from them to indulge his hobby. Ajarn Pinit apparently neglected to confide in Wan that the funding of the coins came from a powerful individual in Chiang Mai. Colonel Pratt wondered why he wouldn't have told her. The salient fact was not so much that Wirot was missing but that millions of baht worth of gold coins had vanished with him.

Seven walked him to his car, giving him Anne's address, a condo building off Soi 22, Sukhumvit Road—near the Lonesome Hawk and Washington Square. Anne was three years older than Seven, and they sometimes had gone shopping together, but the Colonel had to promise never to mention the shopping to her mother. Or that Anne was one of her Facebook friends.

It was a family with a warehouse full of secrets.

As with all families, those who knew didn't talk, and those who didn't know had firm opinions on everything under the sun. He started his car and, as he adjusted his rear-view mirror, suddenly thought of a passage from Shakespeare: "All that glitters is not gold; / Often have you heard that told: / Many a man his life hath sold / But my outside to behold: / Gilded tombs do worms enfold."

He smiled and set off. Somewhere in the city Wirot was holding the gold coins, smiling at his good fortune and at the history he held in his hands. He'd been a hero, and like many heroes he wanted to experience that state just a while longer before going back to the everyday life where heroes are soon forgotten.

SEVEN

*Bangkok, Washington Square—Friday,
September 11, 12:34 p.m.*

*"No truer word ever came out of your mouth, Calvino,"
said Old Bill.*

JOSH LEVY'S LAST day in Bangkok included a lunchtime stop at the Lonesome Hawk. Sitting across from Vincent Calvino, he was told, "You're officially short."

"Old military slang for someone close to finishing a tour of duty," said Old Bill from the bar. "Hell, I thought everyone knew that. Where have you been?"

Josh smiled and raised his beer to Old Bill. "Tajikistan."

"Where the hell is that?" asked Old Bill.

McPhail shook his head, blowing a cloud of smoke across the booth table. "Another oil tanker stand. Desert. Oil. Camels. And too many fucking guns."

"You've been there," said Josh.

McPhail shook his head, cracking his knuckles. "I follow it on the Internet."

"In between porn sites," said Old Bill.

"Fuck you," said McPhail. He'd worn his T-shirt with the ink-black skulls. Before Old Bill could answer the insult, Colonel Pratt walked in, passed along the counter, stepped over Plah—stretched out, sleeping, in the middle of the floor—and squeezed into the booth next to McPhail. He removed his policeman's cap and put it on the table.

"I hope that I am not interrupting."

When he was dressed like that, no one was going to tell him his presence was an interruption.

Josh offered his hand and Colonel Pratt introduced himself.

"Vincent said he had a friend in from New York. He said you and your associates had an interest in Thai coins."

"The part about being from New York is right. But I'm not an expert on coins or a collector. My client wanted some Thai coins for his grandson. The boy has a birthday coming up, and he likes foreign coins."

"And did you get the Thai coins?" asked the Colonel.

"As a matter of fact, I did. Last night. Vinny was there."

Colonel Pratt knew that Vinny had been there because afterward Calvino had phoned the Colonel and told him about Maxim delivering coins to Josh at the rooftop restaurant. They agreed that the Colonel would come around and meet Josh and have a look at the coins.

"Could I ask what coins?"

"Show him the coins," said Calvino.

Josh shifted his weight, dug into his pocket, and pulled out a leather pouch. He unzipped it.

"Gold bullet coins. A set of nine."

Colonel Pratt raised an eyebrow, looking inside the pouch. "Do you mind taking them out?" asked Colonel Pratt.

"Where you going?" Calvino asked as McPhail paid his bill.

"I've got a massage appointment with Snake Woman," said McPhail.

The Colonel got up to make room for McPhail, who walked past Old Bill. Josh carefully laid the bullet coins out in a row.

"Where you going?" asked Old Bill. "I'm not finished with you."

"After my massage I'm meeting a man who bought one of my rubies. One as big as your thumb." He looked over his shoulder at Josh. "Some people I know buy quality gems to take back home. Some buy coins. I never figured out why people collect coins."

"Because it gives them pleasure," said Old Bill.

"When it comes to pleasure, I prefer Snake Woman."

McPhail disappeared out of the bar and into the hot afternoon sun.

"Did Maxim say where he got these coins?" asked Colonel Pratt a moment after McPhail wandered out. The Colonel had turned over each of the coins.

"At an auction last Sunday."

"They look expensive," said Colonel Pratt.

"They weren't cheap. Seventeen thousand dollars."

"Did Vincent tell you that one lot of gold bullets, a set of nine, sold for about a million dollars?"

"He told me that Maxim had been stupid enough to bid for that historical set. I asked him why he'd done that. You know what he said? 'I got carried away. I thought Andrei might like them because of the Russian connection.' But he lost. 'You won by losing,' I said to him."

The gold bullets were individually sealed in plastic. The Colonel studied each coin before putting it on the table and taking up the next one. Neither Calvino nor Josh spoke as they waited for the Colonel to finish his examination.

Baby Cook came screaming out of the kitchen, chasing Plah with a frying pan. When she saw the Colonel in his policeman's uniform, she froze, frying pan held above her head, turned, and ran back into the kitchen, squealing as if she'd seen a ghost. Colonel Pratt hadn't noticed her. What he had noticed, though, was that the set of nine included three half-baht bullets, two quarter-baht bullets, two one-baht bullets, and two one-sixteenth-baht bullets. There were no four-, two-, one-eighth-, one-thirty-second-, or one-sixty-fourth-baht bullets among them. It wasn't a true set. The set Wirot had bought at auction had been complete with one of each: four, two, one, one half, one quarter, one eighth, one sixteenth, one thirty-second, and one sixty-fourth gold bullets. The coins Josh was showing him looked like the genuine article. But they certainly weren't the special Rama V Russian collection that Wirot had bought. Following his inspection, Colonel Pratt put the coins back in the leather bag and slid it across the table. Josh picked up the leather bag and returned it to his pocket.

"I believe your client's grandson will enjoy these coins."

"In the days of the Internet, it's good to know some children still appreciate collecting," said Josh.

"You said that you weren't a collector, Mr. Levy," said Colonel Pratt, his cop instinct finding the inconsistency.

Josh shook his head. "Baseball cards when I was ten. But never coins. That doesn't mean I can't appreciate the sentiment behind collecting coins. It's not one that I personally share."

"I never developed the interest either," said Colonel Pratt. "What about you, Vinny? What do you collect?"

Calvino had quietly sat back to watch the Colonel interrogate Josh. He grinned at the Colonel and raised his glass.

"Me? What do I collect? Problems."

"No truer word ever came out of your mouth, Calvino," said Old Bill.

"Who asked you, you old fart?" said Calvino.

"We all collect those, Vincent," said Colonel Pratt, sliding out of the booth.

"But you've not eaten," said Baby Cook, who'd wedged her large body in the doorway to the kitchen. Baby Cook practiced the Thai twenty-four-hour food mantra—part concern and part worry about whether someone has eaten. Having enough to eat was still a national preoccupation.

"I ate earlier," he said. "I have an appointment and am running late," he said, sounding like the rabbit in "Alice in Wonderland."

Not long after Colonel Pratt's police car pulled out of the parking bay in front of the Lonesome Hawk, Plah exploded out of the kitchen with Baby Cook's handbag.

As the dog ran past, Calvino leaned out of the booth to watch. "Ever since that sex operation, Plah's been attracted to feminine things—bras, bags, shoes. Soon she'll have her own wardrobe."

Josh finished his beer. "Did you see the way that cop looked at the coins? Like he was looking for something. Like he was looking at potential evidence."

Calvino resented Josh calling Colonel Pratt "that cop." But with Josh having only one day left in country, there was little point in getting into an argument. Calvino let the remark pass. The thing with Josh Levy, Calvino had begun to notice, was the number of things that he had no right to let pass. That worried him. Nothing passed Vincent Calvino without the kind of inspection Colonel Pratt had given the coins. It was his trademark. One more day, he thought, and life would return to normal.

"The auction got him interested in bullets."

"Cops don't need an auction to get them interested in bullets," said Josh.

"The Thai who bought the special set of coins on Sunday has disappeared. He took the coins with him."

Josh sipped his drink, his eyes glancing around the room.

"Josh, I said the buyer has gone missing. The cops have Maxim on videotape making his big-mouthed protest after he lost that set. Colonel Pratt is interested in whether Maxim had something to do with Wirot vanishing."

"The cops should ask Maxim."

The police had already talked to Maxim. Or tried to talk to him. He'd asked for a Russian interpreter. After the interrogation the police had written down Maxim's alibis—all of his time was accounted for, like an associate in a law firm. There had been no more than a six-minute gap as Maxim recalled places and witnesses who vouched for his presence. If Maxim had been involved, the witnesses were lying or others acting under Maxim's instructions had snatched Wirot. The problem was the police had no evidence. Suspicion was good enough to round up a local, but with a foreigner the cops needed actual evidence. Or the embassy would cry out. The press would cry out. And all that crying would focus attention where no one wished to have people from the outside looking in.

EIGHT

Bangkok, Soi 22, Sukhumvit Road—Friday,
September 11, 1:10 p.m.

"You can buy me a nine-baht gold chain if you like," she hinted.

WIROT'S MINOR WIFE sat on the sofa across from the Colonel, her folded hands resting easily on her lap. The fingernails, freshly done, weren't quite dry. Anne blew on them as the Colonel sipped from a glass of water. He took out his notebook and waited until she looked up. He looked at her and around the room. It was a waste of time, a waste of money. With no place else to go for leads, the Colonel seemed to be sitting at a dead end—a place that might be the essence of hell.

Whatever anyone might say about Wirot, the Colonel couldn't imagine anyone accusing him of being a big spender. The room occupied by Wirot's minor wife rented for six thousand baht a month. The eight floor building housed mainly other minor wives and bar *yings* waiting for a minor wife slot to open so they could quit the bar and paint their fingernails at one in the afternoon without any worries of where the money would come from for the rent, electricity, mother, father, brother, and secret boyfriend. It was a long food chain, and what was left was never enough for all the mouths waiting to take a bite.

Some people love company, love to talk. Anne fell into that category. Colonel Pratt hadn't been in the room more than a few minutes when she started to open up. With

131

talkers, once they started, it was like the mainsail on a ship catching the wind.

In mid-August Wirot had moved in with her. Suddenly. No warning. He had showed up one afternoon with a suitcase, opened it, taken out his clothes, and hung them in the closet. At first she thought it was a joke. The best part of being a minor wife was that the husband was rarely around. It disturbed her to think that he would actually be living in the room, next to her, eating, sleeping, and bathing, hanging out in the same space twenty-four hours a day. Wirot had had a fight with his wife over the money he was spending on coins, and she had thrown him out of the house. His daughter, Seven, offered a slightly expanded edition of the story—Wirot had stormed out of the house after Wan had thrown his favorite coin book at his head. He'd ducked, and the book had crashed through a window. She'd blamed him for the broken window. That had been the last straw.

Once he'd moved into Anne's apartment, Wirot had spent hours poring over the glossy catalogues filled with pictures of old coins. He had stacks of these catalogues. Anne walked over and pointed at a pile of them.

"Catalogues," she said. "All with coins in them."

She made her boredom quite clear, and no doubt Wirot would have noticed her lack of interest. But apparently it hadn't bothered him. The point was that Anne hadn't thrown any book or other object at him. Quiet discontent was something Wirot easily dealt with. The physical aspect of violence made his knees wobbly.

Anne told the Colonel how Wirot stretched out on the bed, a plate balanced on his stomach, dropping crumbs everywhere, chewing and looking through his thick reading glasses at the catalogues. Sometimes he'd make a phone call; other times phone calls would come in. The subject of the telephone conversations was always the same. Old coins. He'd bragged that he was going to buy an expensive set of gold bullet coins. She'd yawned and hadn't bothered looking up from the domestic drama on TV involving servants, minor wives, and the high society family who lived in a big mansion.

"You can buy me a nine-baht gold chain if you like," she had hinted.

He wasn't biting that hook. "Not a good investment," he said.

Colonel Pratt worked the conversation around to the events of the previous Sunday and Monday evenings. Wirot had gone straight back to the room after the auction and carefully placed each of the nine gold bullets on her pillow. "You are looking at a treasure," he had said.

All Anne could see were coins. She'd had enough of Wirot's old coins to last a lifetime. All she wanted was a nine-baht gold chain.

"Do you have any idea how much I paid for these coins?"

She had shrugged.

"Thirty-three million baht."

She had thought that Wirot was joking or insane. She had ignored him until later, when he'd answered his cell phone. His voice had switched to its formal tone, and a large smile flickered across his face.

After the call ended, he had said, "Do you know who that was?"

"Your wife?"

He shook his head. "I am not talking to her. Please don't mention her in my presence. I was talking to the secretary to the Russian ambassador. He is personally sending an embassy car to this apartment. The car will take me to his private residence for dinner this evening. His secretary said the ambassador wished to personally congratulate me on the winning bid for the Rama V collection. It was a considerable victory, she said. Someone from an important

Moscow newspaper will be there to take my picture with him and the gold bullets."

Wirot had spoken Thai over the phone. Judging from the thin, small voice coming from Wirot's phone, it was clear that he was speaking with a Thai woman.

As soon as the call had ended, Wirot had jumped out of bed, scooped up the coins, and put them in a case—carefully, mind you, handling the coins as if they were eggs. When the phone had rung again at 6:30 p.m., Wirot was already dressed in his best red suspenders, purple shirt, lucky yellow tie, and green sports jacket with the soya sauce stain on the right elbow and black trousers with shiny knees. They were the same pair of trousers he'd worn to the *wat* to make merit. Crawling on the cement floors had taken a toll on the knees. He had stood in front of the mirror adjusting his beret so it was at exactly the right angle to meet a Russian ambassador. Then he had turned to the door, carrying his briefcase, and, as if he had forgotten something, looked back and asked Anne, "How do I look?" It would have been a lie to say that he looked like a million dollars. Besides, Anne wouldn't have calculated his looks in dollars; she was still thinking about the gold baht necklace, wondering whether he'd ever buy it for her.

Anne had gone to the window overlooking the street and waited until Wirot had appeared on the pavement. He had emerged from the building, briefcase clutched in his right hand, and walked over to the sleek, silver-gray Benz. The back door had opened and he had climbed in. The door had closed, and the car had pulled away from the curb, heading toward Sukhumvit Road. No, she hadn't seen the license plate. She hadn't seen if there was anyone else other than the driver in the car.

She had expected him to return late. She knew the Russians loved drinking. Perhaps he had got drunk, confused, and lost. By early Monday morning Anne had started to worry about him. She waited until ten in the morning before she phoned Seven, asking if she'd heard anything from her father. That call caused Seven to chew her fingernails. Worry, like a forest fire, soon spreads across the acreage called a family.

Colonel Pratt's call to the Russian Embassy confirmed that the ambassador was in Beijing, but someone else at the embassy would be happy to grant the Colonel an audience. He declined, hung up the phone, and started the engine of his Benz. Had Wirot, badgered on one side by his major wife and the other by his minor wife, done a runner? Was he the kind of man who could set up such an escape?

The Colonel thought about what Vincent Calvino had said at the Lonesome Hawk: "I collect problems." The Colonel agreed that the collection was part of his own destiny. It was human nature how this shared way of collecting forged a bond between them. Each had the other to listen to their latest problem and sift through evidence looking for answers.

What a man has to do, he thought, is weigh the evidence. Judge it. Then flip a coin. Any coin. Only don't make it a bullet coin.

A gold bullet was a different kind of coin. Gold bullets were like individuals—each one unique and all of them the same. They didn't look like money. They were small handmade objects that were folded like a sculpture, leaving no head or tail. They looked not so much like bullets as bullet slugs pulled out of a body. The Colonel would have chosen to test his luck with a modern coin.

In the Colonel's mind the outcome for Wirot was the same as if the coin had come up heads on every toss. He had been grabbed.

Colonel Pratt had only met him once, and under extraordinary circumstances. But having talked with the family and now the minor wife, the Colonel found a picture emerging of a man who wasn't a likely candidate to drop his existing life and take off to start a new one. His love of Thai coins anchored him to Thailand. At the auction the Colonel had seen how all the dealers were like members of a club. It was as much about friendship as collecting. A man like that had one burning passion, and prying him from that object of desire was like removing the dead hand of a minor wife from a nine-baht gold chain.

Inside the room of Wirot's minor wife, Colonel Pratt came to the conclusion that something bad had happened to Wirot. How many shady types in Bangkok would take a shot at stealing a million dollars worth of coins? Once the calculations were done, the list of possible suspects would take a lifetime to go through.

NINE

Bangkok, Soi Cowboy—Friday night, September 11

"That's a brief summary of life in ying land," Calvino said.

IT WAS PAST midnight when Calvino steered Josh into one final bar on Soi Cowboy for a nightcap. As they stood inside the door, an Englishman with close-cropped gray hair, carrying an extra thirty pounds around his waist like a lifejacket, came from the back to shake Calvino's hand.

"Haven't seen you since the cops stopped the girls here from showing," Colin Jasper said, standing to the side, a little drunk, his eyes a debris of red veins.

"That's been a long time."

"They're showing again. Cleopatra is again number one."

Calvino glanced back at Josh, who stood off to the side, a little drunk. Calvino caught the blank expression on his face.

"He's talking about the bar, not the Egyptian queen."

"Reincarnated before your eyes every night, right on stage," said Colin. "So what are you and your friend drinking?"

"Gin and tonic for me," said Josh.

"The usual," said Calvino.

"Give me a hint."

"Make it two gin and tonics. I want to go upstairs with Josh."

"You two want to be alone?" Colin rolled his eyes.

"We've got some business to discuss," said Calvino.

"You want me to send a couple of girls up?" asked Colin.

"I'll let you know," said Calvino.

Josh was no longer listening to Calvino's conversation with the bar owner. His attention had locked onto one of Colin's stars, number 19, who made eyes and blew kisses at Josh from behind a veil. She executed that impossible double-jointed gesture with her hands and fingers, all fingers fanned back, flexible as if the bones had been removed and plastic stitched in. He stepped up to the stage. Number 19 squatted down, reached out with one hand, and brushed it slowly against his face. It was almost tender the way she touched him, as if she were comforting him in some strange way. She whispered something. He nodded. Josh leaned forward and kissed her on the forehead. She stood back up on her high heels and rejoined a couple of dozen *yings* in Egyptian slave girl harem pants—the *mamasan* had insisted on flimsy material that produced blue sparks of static electricity against the black light.

She turned her back on him and resumed her search through the audience for that crucial eye contact. Not the leer of a hooker but the pleading, seductive eyes of that instant girlfriend whom every man had longed for but never found. Josh stood with his mouth open, watching the bare-breasted *yings* in translucent silk pantaloon trousers dance a harem routine. Something they'd learned from a porno movie.

"Those girls look fourteen, fifteen," said Josh, standing in the bar's interior darkness, pierced by neon flashes from the stage.

"Twenty-three, twenty-four years old," said Calvino. "She was born about the time I last saw you in New York."

Josh sighed. "We were still just kids then. What did we know about anything?"

It was a sobering thought, which caused both men to stare down at their hands. Number 19 had been getting herself born about the time they'd last said goodbye. Calvino had been afraid and on the run when he'd left New York. In what seemed like no time, he'd found himself in a Soi Cowboy bar talking about an object of desire born out of that moment.

"Number 19 has your number," said Calvino, recovering first. "You want her to come upstairs?"

The thought horrified Josh. "God, no! Why would I want her to come upstairs? I'm getting married in a couple of months."

"A kiss on the cheek? Absorb some of that electric flash?"

Josh shook his head like his hair was on fire.

"You might not get another chance."

"That's fine with me," said Josh. If he was feeling a hint of desire, it wasn't reflected in his voice.

"I thought you two might know each other. The way she touched you."

"A whore's touch."

Calvino thought Josh hadn't been in Bangkok long enough to grow the cynical shell that most of the old crabs in the *soi* crawled into before walking into a bar.

"It looked like she was doing more than just her job."

"That makes her a professional."

Calvino arched an eyebrow. "Maybe, maybe not."

Calvino thought it was pointless to explain they were talking about different kinds of touches, a stroke of the hair, the sniffing ritual on the neck, a kiss on the cheek—bits of intimacy that rise to the level of affection. Old hands could read those gestures in the dark and at a distance.

Colin walked over to talk to another group of customers, leaving Calvino to lead the way through the bar. They climbed the stairs, which opened onto a platform, turned right, walked down a short corridor, and found another flight of stairs that led them to a small, well-lit room with framed paintings of pharaohs, pyramids, and camels in the desert walking against the moonlight.

A couple of tables and chairs were placed in the center of the room. Along one wall were a couple of booths. Sitting down, they were alone in the room. The pulse of deep bass tones of music from downstairs, like thunder, vibrated their table, which had uneven legs. Calvino got up and sat at the other table.

"This one works," said Calvino, waving Josh over.

A couple of minutes later a waitress came with their gin and tonics.

Calvino couldn't extinguish the image of Josh kissing the *ying* who'd leaned down from the stage.

"Number 19 downstairs liked you, Josh."

"Back on that again?"

"The number stuck in my mind. I asked myself where I'd come across that number before. Then I remembered."

"Aren't you going to tell me?"

"At the coin auction. The Rama V collection was Lot 19. The one that went for a million dollars and caused Maxim to roar like a Russian bear passing a kidney stone when he lost."

Josh sipped the gin and tonic and stared at an oil painting of a long train of camels frozen forever on the desert floor. He checked his watch. Calvino noticed that Josh's hands were shaking.

"I should head back to the hotel. I've got a morning flight, and I still haven't packed. And I need a good night's sleep. I have a long day ahead of me. I need to be ready to go to the office once I'm back."

"You okay?" asked Calvino.

Josh nodded and swallowed another mouthful of gin and tonic.

"You're not having a panic attack?"

"It's late. I've got a lot on my mind. I'm okay."

Go with the hurt. Tough it out. A noble enough principle, but Calvino figured that in Josh's line of work, it had robbed him of his life, one billable hour at a time. It was worth another attempt to get through to him, thought Calvino.

"You don't need to be anywhere, Josh. You're here, in the big now. Why pass up a perfectly good chance to talk? Connect. You want me to be your best man? Fine. I've agreed. But I'd like to connect with you in the present time and not fall back on the bullshit that it's because we were best friends when we were ten. We can't pretend the knowledge of a ten-year-old is enough. How about an update?"

Josh closed his eyes, puffed air into his cheeks and slowly exhaled.

"You're right. You sure you want to hear all of this?"

"Try me," said Calvino.

Josh talked non-stop for a half an hour. He explained what his two children were doing, their problems, and issues they'd had over their mother's death, and suggested they had had some issues over the woman he was marrying. But he said the issues about Tess had been worked through. The economic collapse in Wall Street had been a major blow to his law firm, and severance packages had gone to half a dozen partners. Others would follow them. Everyone was worried, covering their ass or looking over their shoulder—two distinctly different ways of keeping in control and in the job. It was like death row, everyone thinking the executive committee would be calling them in next for the exit interview. Since he'd left the firm and joined Andrei's business empire, those security issues no longer kept him awake at night.

After the second round of gin and tonics, Calvino talked about his early years in building a private investigation business, his secretary, various women, and how a windfall a few years earlier had changed his life, allowing him to kick back, relax, and turn away most clients. He'd have closed down the business but didn't know what else to do with the little bit of expertise he'd accumulated over the years. And, besides, he liked solving problems. Others collected them, brought them into his office, like seashells, asking him to identify them, sort them out, and come up with a solution or two to allow them to dissolve into thin air.

By the third round of gin and tonics, Calvino was explaining that not all of the bars in Soi Cowboy had upstairs private rooms. The few bars that did often reserved them for favored customers, the big spenders who bought a bottle, set up, paid several bar fines, and over-tipped the *yings* and *dek serves*. The motto of most bars remained constant over the years—you scratch my back, and I'll get her to scratch yours. Of course there was more than back-scratching going on. Then seven, eight years ago the Japanese salary men with an itch to scratch started throwing big money for the exclusive right to use the rooms. Overnight the rooms were converted into first-class cabins for punters fresh from Tokyo. The center of gravity in the *soi* was constantly changing, depending on currency shifts, the popularity of individual *yings*, the latest blog detailing the amenities of the private rooms, and the cost of a bar fine or a short-time hotel.

"That's a brief summary of life in *ying* land," Calvino said.

"There's no morality. That's what I don't like," said Josh.

"I wouldn't agree."

Calvino told him about how Colin's father had been a prisoner of war, captured by the Japanese in Singapore and mistreated. The bar owner, in memory of his father, had refused their money when they asked to hire the room. He'd preferred to keep the room empty over allowing them to fool around with his *yings* upstairs. But on the main floor his principles yielded to the economies of running a bar.

Josh had let his guard down. Several rounds of gin and tonic had helped to glue the male bonding firmly into place. By opening up and talking about their lives, they'd reached the point where Josh was no longer talking about getting back to his hotel room. Now he was insisting on ordering another round. He tipped the waitress a hundred baht and received a *wai* and smile.

"Nice," he said. "I like it, the *wai*."

After the waitress went downstairs, Calvino said, "The one who just left doesn't go out with everyone who asks. She has to like the customer. The dancers like number 19 downstairs would go out with the elephant man if he had enough money in his trunk."

"It's always about the money," said Josh.

"My friend the Colonel called me late this afternoon."

"You should have invited him along tonight. I was starting to like him."

"It's official that Wirot and Lot 19, the million-dollar Rama V coins, have disappeared. The police suspect someone bumped him."

"Why do they think that? This Wirot might have decided a million was enough to make a break for it."

"Break for what?"

"You know, a new life. An easy life, no more problems. New identity. New place. New everything. In this part of the world, a million would do it."

"And how much would you need to cash out of New York?"

Josh smiled. "I've thought about that. Thirty, forty million would do it."

"Wirot had a good life here. Guys like him almost never run. He had a fight with his wife, so what does he do? He runs to spend a couple of weeks with his mistress. Another week or so and he'd have returned home and everything would've been all right. A Thai doesn't run away with the national treasure and leave his entire family hanging."

"Where is he?"

"Colonel Pratt is going on the theory that bad guys duped him and coaxed him into the back of a car. What's odd is the bad guys haven't contacted his family with a demand for money."

"That's your colonel's opinion. What's yours?"

"Wirot isn't coming back. Nothing personal. It's all about the money."

"It's one of those stories that will get me invited to dinner parties for years."

"You're not understanding one thing. You are part of the story. This isn't something that just happened to some foreigner you never met."

"I've never heard of Wirot. How can I be part of his story?"

"Today, Colonel Pratt had a second interview with Maxim. After a three-hour conversation with your Russian friend, you know what the Colonel found out? Maxim had Josh Levy and Vincent Calvino as his alibis. We sat together sixty-five stories high at a rooftop restaurant that night. I watched as Maxim and two of his men drained a liter of vodka. Wirot was picked up by a Benz at his minor wife's building around 6:30 p.m. He couldn't be at the restaurant and soi 22 at the same time. Maxim told Colonel Pratt he had given you another set of bullet coins. He said I saw him give you the coins. After the Colonel examined the gold bullets at the Lonesome Hawk, he knew they weren't the missing set that Wirot had bought. All the cops have is Maxim boiling up in road rage like a public outburst after losing the bid. That's not enough to hold him. They need something else. Maxim has a crew working for him. He probably covered his ass by sending a couple of his men to grab Wirot instead of doing it himself. You think that's possible?"

"The police are fishing. That's universal. New York, Bangkok."

"Some fish are harder to catch than others," said Calvino. "Especially the big fish that know how to stay clear of the net."

"You don't like Maxim. I understand that. But I wouldn't let it color your judgment. Just because you don't like a man doesn't make him a thief."

"We're talking possible murder and theft."

"This guy has been out of contact with his family for less than a week, and you're saying he was killed? That Maxim somehow had something to do with it?"

"That's what I'm saying."

"Where's the evidence?"

"Are you defending Maxim on this?"

Josh sighed, tried to laugh it off. "I'm a lawyer, Vinny. You were once a lawyer. We don't go on emotion. We look for facts. For evidence that proves guilt."

"The reality is, if you don't find someone who disappears or hear from whoever is holding him within seventy-two hours, you'll never find him alive," said Calvino.

"You're saying . . . ?"

"Wirot's likely dead."

Calvino had been circling the Wirot and Maxim connection, looking for the right place to land, a place where he could clear the air. Alone, inside a private room in Colin's bar, Calvino sensed that Josh had cooled down; the gin was no longer driving the smile. He needed to keep Josh onside. To keep him ticking along as a friend, someone who had to understand that whether he liked it or not, Maxim was a suspect. Maxim had done his homework, overdone it, in fact, providing himself with the sort of extensive coverage that only someone seeking to create an airtight alibi would have bothered with. People were creatures of habit. There are blank spaces in everyone's day where the habit and routine halt and they are alone. No one could have a witness at such times. Maxim had too many witnesses—and still had enough men for a heist. Someone had set up Wirot with the phony story about the embassy inviting him to dinner. Vanity had been the sticky glue to catch a fly.

"If this weren't serious, I'd let it pass. But I need your help."

"What kind of help?"

"You've done deals for the Russians. Have you ever come across anything suspicious about Maxim?"

Josh looked pale. His face collapsed into that old man's sober reflection.

"The Russians reek of suspicion. I try to never get too close to the personal side of their lives."

"Sometimes that's unavoidable. It might be part of the job. Like coming to Bangkok to pick up coins for the boss's grandkid. Sounds like a personal favor."

Watching a lawyer trapped by his own argument is like watching a rabbit freshly snared, desperate, shaking, its eyes wild and doomed.

"What's that have to do with Maxim getting mixed up in Wirot's disappearance?"

"It's not right, Josh. I can see it in your face. There's something you're not telling me. Be straight for a moment. You're not stupid. You understand something is going on. And you've let yourself get involved in it. But you don't know what to do."

Josh tapped his forefinger on the rim of his glass.

"I can see now that was a mistake. I shouldn't have let him bully me into taking them back. But what can I do

146

now? I've given Andrei my word. He's paid for this trip. And Maxim did go to a lot of trouble to get them. I'm getting married soon. I don't really need this kind of shit in my life."

Calvino leaned back in his chair. He stared at his friend. Did he know this man?

"I'm asking you to trust me, Josh. Give me something about Maxim that I can work with."

Josh had been thinking much the same thing. Did he really know Vincent Calvino, and how far could he trust him? Colin came up the stairs holding a bottle of gin. He walked over to the table and put it in front of Calvino.

"How are you two lovebirds getting along?" he asked.

"You trying to get us drunk?" asked Calvino.

"I can't imagine why you'd want to stay sober alone up here."

Colin raised his hand in a two-finger salute and disappeared back down the stairs.

If Josh was hoping the interruption had caused Calvino to forget about Maxim, he was soon disabused.

"Maxim. Give me something, Josh."

Josh took a deep breath with both hands pressed firm on the table. He nodded and looked up at Calvino. His tongue touched his upper lip, and he nodded again.

"Okay, about a year ago I heard rumors about Maxim. He controls a fleet of aircraft. Old planes he picked up for a song when the Soviet Union fell apart. All kinds of hardware sold for next to nothing. People were making fortunes buying off old state enterprise assets. Maxim saw an opportunity. He's a businessman. And he started a transportation company."

Calvino was thinking, not only had the Russian started his own private navy with the gunboat-sized yacht, but he had acquired the core aircraft for a small air force.

"Any idea what he transports?"

"In the last deal, one of his companies had the contract to fly equipment and supplies into Tajikistan for the oil concession."

"Is that the contract he gave you to review?" asked Calvino.

Josh nodded and brushed his fingers through his hair.

"The inward manifest says inside is equipment for oil rigs. But what's in the crates?"

"Am I going to stand on the runway, looking inside the hold to see whether the manifest matches what's inside?

Josh leaned over and punched him on the shoulder.

"I'm sorry about this Wirot guy. I really am," said Josh. He poured gin from the bottle into his glass and drank. When he came up for air, he said, "Maxim's got his rough edges. But he wanted only one thing: the contract approved. You saw how happy he was. The coins were a nuisance assignment, something he was obligated to do out of friendship with Andrei. Sometimes a cigar is just a cigar, and a rose is just a rose."

"He didn't much like losing at that auction," said Calvino.

"How many people were at the auction?"

"Five or six hundred."

"One of them might have hated losing even more."

"What if this doesn't stop in Bangkok and follows you back to New York? This isn't finished."

Calvino picked up the gin bottle, held it up to the light, and then poured the rest of the gin into his glass.

"What are you saying?"

"The coins Maxim gave you. Dump them. Go back and tell Andrei that you don't have them. Tell him Maxim screwed up, and it was too dangerous. Tell him anything. He won't like it, but fuck him, Josh."

"It's officially way past my bedtime, Vinny."

"Listen to what I'm saying, Josh. Right now you don't need a best man. You need a best friend. And I'm sitting across the table from you, telling you to get as far away from these coins and Maxim and that Russian prick you're working for as you can."

Josh rose from the table. He stumbled as he tried to clear his chair.

"A man's got to know what's possible. Once he figures that out, he's got no choice but to do what needs to be done," he said.

"Josh, read my lips. Get rid of the coins."

TEN

Bangkok, Calvino's apartment, Sukhumvit Road—Saturday morning, September 12

Six days had passed and Wirot still hadn't surfaced.

JOSH PHONED FROM the airport at 7:30 a.m. to wake Calvino up.

"Bastard, if I have to suffer, so do you," he said.

His flight was scheduled to depart from Suvarnabhumi Airport at nine in the morning.

"Number 19 will be asking for you," Calvino said, sitting up in bed, his free hand under the sheets, stroking a long, slender leg.

"Bullshit," he said.

"Hello, handsome man," said number 19, as she flipped back her long, black hair and put the phone to her ear. "I like you too much."

Calvino pressed his head in close to hers, and she held the phone back far enough for him to hear the distant voice on the other end.

"Is that really you?"

Calvino smiled. She had him. All she needed to do was pull on the line, sink the hook in a little deeper, and maybe reel him back from the airport.

"My name is Dew. You remember me? Number 19."

"I remember. Of course I remember. What are you doing at Vinny's?"

Calvino swallowed the laugh as it roared up from his throat.

"I asked your friend to give me your number. I want to talk to you."

Josh gave her his cell phone number. Number 19 repeated it twice. She was good with phone numbers. She would have made a good boiler room employee, working the phones, getting old ladies in New Zealand to invest in South African goldmines.

Calvino took back the phone.

"Do you remember George Michael's 'Father Figure'? The one about 'I will be there and the one who loves you until the end of time?' This morning the end of time lasted twenty-eight minutes."

"You're old enough to be her father," said Josh.

"It's an '80s revival, remember?"

Josh sighed into the phone. "And I gave her my phone number. Why would I do that?"

Suddenly it was all about Josh.

"You're going into the problem collection business. Bangkok is the place where you cut your teeth. Have a good flight, pal."

"I don't fucking believe it."

"I'm thinking of bringing Dew to the wedding."

There was a long silence.

"Josh, you still there?"

"Still here."

"You left the coins behind, right?"

"They're calling my flight. Got to run."

The bastard had taken the coins, thought Calvino, watching Number 19 slip into a pair of tight jeans and a Japanese softball shirt with the name "Lions" in bold red letters on the front. In a few minutes she was gone. He walked out onto the balcony.

Josh waited for his plane to take off from Suvarnabhumi Airport—the name translated as "golden land." But it hadn't always been a golden land. Before the airport had been constructed, the area had been called Cobra Swamp. The name difference described two possible ways of looking at Josh's most recent decisions. A cobra swamp could be converted with enough money into golden land. With a couple of wrong moves the gold transformed itself back into a swamp.

Calvino drove to his office, arriving around two.

There was an urgent message from Colonel Pratt.

And someone, at the same time, was banging on the outer door to his office.

Six days had passed and Wirot still hadn't surfaced. He'd made no attempt to contact Anne or Wan. His daughter had heard nothing. No one else in the family had any idea where he might have gone. Wirot's cell phone had been switched off.

When the Russian ambassador had returned from Beijing on Friday morning, he confirmed that neither his secretary nor he had ever come across anyone among his colleagues, contacts, or staff in Thailand with the name Wirot. No one at the embassy had been authorized to phone a Thai named Wirot and invite him to dinner. Logically, how was that possible? The ambassador wasn't even in town. There must have been a mistake, and perhaps the ambassador ought to take up the matter personally with the Foreign Minister.

Apologies were made. Flowers, baskets of fruit, and bottles of vodka were sent to the embassy. No one claimed responsibility until the information was traced back to Colonel Pratt.

"Mistake" was the word on everyone's lips.

The Colonel must have made a mistake. Or Wirot's minor wife had.

Colonel Pratt had his own theory. Wirot had made a mistake, but it wasn't with the Russian ambassador.

Wirot's mistakes had actually been multiple, starting with an innocent belief that his winning bid had made him a celebrity, a big shot to be courted and honored by foreign ambassadors. Poor Wirot had a moment when an entire room of people had applauded him as a hero. He had confused the applause and deep *wais* from every coin dealer in the country as a change in his destiny, a rescaling upward of his life to new heights. Would he have known that he'd be pushed offstage as others came into play? No man who had tasted the glory of a hero was happy to be relegated to the role of intermediary. Others with bigger names and titles would have soon horned in and fought to claim the credit for keeping the Rama V gold bullets in their rightful home in Thailand. Wirot would have found himself shuttled off to the back row, the little old man in the black beret and suspenders, with food hanging like folk art from his shirt.

Someone at the senior level inside the Royal Thai Police Department had started asking questions and wasn't satisfied with the answers as to why no one had interrogated a *farang* named Vincent Calvino. He had been one of the foreigners who had shown an unusual interest in the Rama V collection. Calvino's presence with the Colonel raised awkward questions. What was a foreigner, who claimed to have no interest in collecting coins, doing at the auction? And the mystery was compounded as it emerged that this foreigner had a personal connection with a Thai police colonel. The people in authority asking the questions weren't satisfied with the truth. The problem with truth was it was far too often banal, and looking back on it in time, there were so many other rich possibilities that could make the truth appear a feeble lie.

What had stuck in the minds of senior people in the department was that Calvino must have gone to the auction for a reason, and being part of a conspiracy, a network of ill-intended foreigners, was a motive that was easy to believe. But there was no evidence, Colonel Pratt told himself; no one would move based on such speculation.

Again the Colonel found out that he was wrong.

Calvino hadn't turned on his cell phone. The Colonel had sent him an email. The message was only a one word: "Cooperate."

The visitors banging on Calvino's door turned out to be two police officers. They asked him to go along with them to the Ministry of Finance.

"Not the police station?" He thought he'd heard them wrong.

"No. To the Ministry of Finance."

One of the policemen had the face of a boy. It made him look twelve going on forty, with the smooth, angelic face of a medieval chorister, undestroyed by the more angular lines of age. His cheeks were smooth, as if he hadn't started to shave. His partner, slightly bigger, with large hands, looked like the heavy, the one who got down to business when the boy cop didn't get the answers he wanted.

"You work for the Ministry of Finance?" asked Calvino.

"A crime committed against our country concerns the ministry," said the boy-faced policeman. His English was good. A little on the arrogant side, though.

Colonel Pratt had sent him an email telling him to cooperate. As he looked at the two policemen in his office, he thought the Colonel might have expanded his advice a bit further.

"I know you're doing your job," said Calvino. "When do you want to make an appointment?"

"Now."

The cops were doing their job—though taking him to the Ministry of Finance seemed to be a job that differed from the usual. Calvino told himself that he had nothing to fear. This would be a routine interrogation.

"We could talk in my office," said Calvino.

The baby-faced cop stared at him hard. "We go now."

Calvino got up from his desk and put on his jacket. He reached into his pocket for his cell phone. The gesture made the heavy cop reach for his gun.

"Just taking out my phone," said Calvino. He saw that it hadn't been turned on. He switched it on and phoned Colonel Pratt.

"I'm cooperating," he said. "They're taking me to the Ministry of Finance."

"That's okay. Just tell them exactly what happened, Vincent. Truth is always the best thing. These are special task force police."

"How special?"

"They handle sensitive matters of state."

Calvino found a catch in his throat. "That's special enough."

The two cops were attached to a special unit assigned to investigate crimes that affected the security and welfare of the nation. It was an elite unit operating independently within the department, whose members enjoyed privileges and benefits that made other cops jealous and nervous at the same time. There was no need for Colonel Pratt to spell out that these police had additional powers and in the exercise of those powers were immune. They were the kind of cops who made people disappear.

The police car arrived at the Ministry of Finance, a grand palace of a building with gardens and a lawn. It had once literally been a palace and until the Second World War had housed royalty. Calvino walked with police officers on both sides into one of the main buildings. The cops led him down a long corridor and past a reception desk. During the ride to the ministry and the walk inside, the cops had kept conversation to a minimum: "Get out of the car . . . Turn right . . . Walk straight ahead . . . Don't stop . . . Keep walking."

The three walked through several rooms before entering one devoted to displaying coins. The police officers stopped before a glass-topped display case. Above the case was a photograph of Rama V and Nicholas II, who was dressed in a military uniform. Both men looked dignified as they stared at the camera. The two regally dressed, self-assured men greeted each other as brothers. On the wall next to the display case was a sign that read, "RAMA V 9 gold bullet coins presented to Czar Nicholas II in 1897 during His Majesty's trip to Russia."

Built into the elegant, black lacquered display case was a thick red velvet strip with nine small indentations. Each place was as empty as a bar girl's promise of love. To the side of the case stood a small stand, also empty, for the Rama V letter addressed to Nicholas II. The text had been neatly translated and reproduced in English with the Thai version above the English. It had been beautifully done. The police officers took up positions on opposite sides of the case, like an honor guard, keeping their eyes on Calvino, hoping that the full weight of the heavy loss would sink in.

Calvino didn't need much time; nor did he need an explanation as to their message. Had he been a magician, he would have produced the missing bullets from thin air and restored them to their rightful place. Unfortunately for the police, he had no such skill; nor did he have any immediate answers as to the whereabouts of the coins. They stared at him, waiting. He looked at the exhibit, then at the cops, and shrugged his shoulders. Why they had wasted an afternoon taking him to stare at an empty presentation case hadn't been discussed during the car journey across town. Someone had lost face big time. And these men had been assigned the task of restoring that loss.

"We have brought you to see the preparations that have been made."

Calvino nodded at the empty display case and reread the royal letter. It was like looking at an empty cradle knowing that the baby had left the hospital and hadn't left a forwarding address.

"The last time I saw the coins was Sunday at the auction. Even then it was only pictures on the screen."

The more senior of the two policemen nodded at the other. "Please follow us."

They walked Calvino down another hallway, a door opened, and they entered a small office. They closed the door behind them. Calvino looked around the room. Nothing special. A wooden desk, a couple of chairs, framed photographs of important people on the walls and on a table. The table and walls were running low on space. So many important faces to admire and fear. Fresh orchids had been arranged in a Ming-style vase. Wedged between the framed photographs was a diploma from an American university and some award certificates in gold frames. The university diploma in fine arts and photographs belonged to the Assistant Director for Bullet Coins. Calvino figured that she was the most likely person to have jumped the gun with the display case. The office had the feel of a woman's hand. Clean, orderly—and of course the freshly cut flowers.

"Sit down, Mr. Calvino," said the baby-faced policeman, pointing at a chair.

The cop walked behind the desk and sat down. He stuck a thumb drive into the computer and turned on the monitor. While he busied himself with the computer, his colleague, who stood near the closed door, glared at Calvino.

"We have some questions." The policeman behind the computer looked up.

"Ask them," said Calvino. Give me your best shot, he thought.

The questions came fast, in a torrent, like monsoon rains.

Wasn't it a fact that he had an accomplice bid for the coins? Wasn't it also a fact that he was the leader of a foreign gang? He'd been seen briefing the gang members. They had video footage of him and a Russian national named Maxim having an intense conversation before the auction. The video from the auction appeared on the computer screen. For a moment, both policeman watched the screen and said nothing. Maxim sat on his chair holding his bidding card, looking bored and pissed off.

"You can't deny that is you, Mr. Calvino."

"That's Maxim."

"Then you know this criminal?"

"I've met him."

Calvino appeared in the video frame.

"And that's you talking to him."

Calvino nodded. "Yeah, that's me."

"And you would agree that is Mr. Maxim."

"I already said that's him."

"What instructions is he giving you?"

"He's telling me to get lost."

"I don't think so. You are planning something."

"I asked him what he was doing at the auction."

"He was there because you planned for him to be there. Isn't that right? You planned it at a restaurant."

In the cop's mind any rational man could see two men cementing a criminal partnership, a conspiracy to steal the coins. Hadn't both men met to have dinner at an expensive rooftop restaurant on Silom Road?

"I didn't eat dinner. I had a double single malt whiskey and left. I was asked to leave, come to think of it. I definitely wasn't invited to dinner."

The policeman leaned over the desk, writing Calvino's answer down in a notebook with the insignia of his unit on the front. This wasn't a schoolboy's copybook; this was an official record, and at some stage, Calvino would be asked to sign a statement that included each and every answer. Calvino understood the procedure; he'd been through it before. This time, though, what he signed wouldn't first be passed before Colonel Pratt's eyes. It would go into a file and up the chain of command. Colonel Pratt wouldn't have access to this file.

"Your waitress remembered seeing the Russian hand over a white envelope with money inside," he said, looking like a schoolboy behind the desk.

"How did she know there was money inside?"

"So you admit there was money inside?"

"Did she see me hand the envelope back to him?"

"You gave the money to your secretary with an order to deliver on behalf of the Russian to Father Joe at the Mercy Center."

"Maxim sent it to my office."

"Why would he do that unless he wanted something? Or had planned something? We know a great deal about Mr. Maxim's business in Thailand."

"Then you know I've never dealt with him."

"Until your friend came from New York and the three of you conspired to buy the gold bullet coins. And when you couldn't buy them at auction, you stole them from Khun Wirot."

Calvino leaned back in his chair. It had started when Josh Levy had come to Bangkok after more than twenty years, asking him to be best man at his wedding. Now Josh

159

had left the country. Even before Josh's plane had landed in Japan, the Thai police wanted to charge Calvino with murder and theft. Calvino sighed, shook his head. It was going to be a long afternoon. Showing impatience wouldn't do anything but prolong the interview. A smile flickered at the corner of his mouth and then died like an untended campfire. Elite cops were selected for their passion for the work, their cleverness, loyalty, obedience, and take-no-prisoners attitude. They didn't smile.

The setting for the interrogation hadn't been an accidental choice; the room with all of those influential faces indicated the importance of those behind the interrogation, the significance of the case, and the gravity of the situation that Calvino was involved in, whether he denied it or not.

"Your colonel friend can't help you," said the baby-faced cop. "But you can help us. Was the Colonel involved in this plan?"

All of Calvino's years in Thailand came forward to prevent the words "Fuck you" from slipping out.

"There was no plan. I don't know where Wirot is. Or who has the bullet coins. But I don't have them."

They had tried to break him down by using Colonel Pratt as bait. They knew that Calvino was connected with the Colonel. In normal circumstances that would have given Calvino an edge to stand on and wait until the storm blew over and he could climb back into the window of daily life. Now they used the friendship as the basis of a theory of criminal activity.

The police were sending a message by taking Calvino to the Ministry of Finance, an old palace, an official's room inside the greatest collection of coins in the kingdom. This was an altogether different kind of storm from the ordinary, and the usual protection provided by the Colonel had blown away like a cheap umbrella the moment the power of the ministry had been turned toward him. The investigation would yield whatever they wanted it to, and nothing Calvino could do would stop such men.

The cop with the boyish face and his partner were delivering to the Colonel a coded message that he wouldn't need an Enigma machine to read. Friendship, as important as it was to the Thais, could only be stretched so far. Their duty, other than questioning Calvino, was to work on the bond between the two men, find a weakness, let that bond break, and then go in fast and hard once the foreigner had been isolated. At that stage Calvino would be a foreigner they could control, and once they controlled a man, they owned him.

Calvino knew he could forget about sentimentality and friendship and decency at that point. All of those fine points of life would be thrown on the dust heap. Colonel Pratt, after all, was a practical man, and like all policeman understood his obligation to the force, his rank, his family, and not least of all to his country. And his country was anxious to solve the mystery of the missing coins.

ELEVEN

Bangkok—Monday, September 14

"Josh loves you, sweetheart."

CALVINO HAD BEEN born in New York City on a Monday. The Thais believed that a Monday birth guaranteed popularity, a good nature, but also that beneath the surface lay a talent for deception, and the skill of a tiger stalking prey. He'd not really thought much about the day of his birth until he lived in Bangkok for years. Now Monday had become his lucky day, the day he went shopping, especially for the big item.

It was Monday in Bangkok. Calvino had gone to the Honda dealership managed by a man named Tanaka, whose father was Japanese and whose mother was Thai. Tanaka, a passionate golfer, had dropped into his first conversation with Calvino that he had a Thai mother just like Tiger Woods. Calvino thought such a psychological confusion might just give him some leverage on a deal for a new Honda Accord. Only he hadn't figured out quite how to make that psy-op work in his favor. The latest visit had been his third time to talk about the car, test drive it, and haggle over accessories to be included in the price. After drinking half a dozen small bowls of green tea, they had reached an impasse. Tanaka smacked his lips and sighed deeply. He wanted the sale, but Calvino drove a hard bargain. The bladder-busting tea sessions were a test of each man's resolve. It had become a kind of game.

The cops had trailed him to Tanaka's dealership. Two new plainclothes cops made no effort to conceal that they were following him. The surveillance details were being run in shifts. The latest crew sat in their car outside the dealership, waiting for Calvino to emerge. Now they followed him back to his condo.

A few years before, Calvino had managed to compromise two cops who'd been assigned to babysit him in Pattaya. He'd got them fed and drunk. It had been an embarrassment for the department. The two cops had been quietly reassigned to walk the Burmese–Thai border. The lesson had been learned, and the brass weren't taking any chances this time.

Calvino had expected an escort. He had gone over to their car and asked if they needed anything—cigarettes, whiskey, and food. They were a couple of working stiffs with no particular ax to grind. An hour after returning to the condo, Calvino walked out to the street and gave them a Hawaiian pizza with extra pineapple and cheese. The pizza made both of the cops happy. If you're going to be followed, it's good to make a personal connection with those doing the following. Treat them like people, with dignity, and they can't help but think of you as not just a target but also a person who had reached out.

The pizza wouldn't have worked on the baby-faced cop. Or his heavy sidekick, who would have run his fist through the pizza box, pulling it out dripping with the extra pineapple and cheese before slugging Calvino. The policemen who'd interrogated him had warned him not to leave town. He'd handed his passport to Baby Face, who'd looked at Calvino's picture and then at Calvino.

"It's me on a bad hair day," he had said.

Neither cop had smiled.

Baby Face told Calvino it would be better still if he didn't leave his apartment. This was, Baby Face said, for Calvino's own well-being, a choice of words that the boy-faced policeman, who hadn't smiled, had carefully selected in place of "house arrest." The other cop had said nothing. He never budged from the doorway, never blinked, watching Calvino as if he were calculating the best way to dismantle his body into twelve equal pieces.

"I shop on Mondays," said Calvino.

"Avoid shopping," said Baby Face. "Stay inside."

Calvino smiled and said nothing.

"You are free to go," said Baby Face.

"You have a card?" asked Calvino.

Baby Face produced a card from the front pocket of his uniform and handed it to Calvino. He read the card.

"Major Tinakorn, I want to ask you a question."

Baby Face now had a name. He nodded for Calvino to ask it.

"How long will I be confined to my condo?"

Major Tinakorn thought for a moment. "Until we recover the coins."

Mondays were also the day for a Soi Cowboy run. So far Calvino's confinement hadn't felt much like a house arrest. He'd had tea with Mr. Tanaka at the Honda dealership, delivered pizza to the cops assigned to follow him, and showered and changed his clothes. On the way out again, he stopped at the unmarked police car.

"How was the pizza?"

The cops looked embarrassed. The empty pizza box was on the backseat.

"I wanted to let you know, I'm going to Soi Cowboy. You want to come along?"

"You must stay in your condo," said the cop behind the wheel.

"I'm coming back soon." Calvino walked off in the direction of the MRT station. The cops followed in the car. Calvino looked over his shoulder. One of them got out and walked behind him as he took the escalator to the train platform. Again Calvino looked back, saw the cop, and smiled. The cop couldn't stop himself from smiling back.

So far he didn't feel like he'd been isolated or his movements restricted. The MRT station delivered him to Soi Cowboy better than any conveyor belt could deliver a product to a consumer. He wanted a Monday drink just in case it might be a long time before Wirot and the missing coins surfaced. No man could be certain when he had ordered his last Monday drink. He'd lived long enough in Bangkok to appreciate that almost no *farang* ever lived as if the drink he touched to his lips might be the last, or the *ying* in his bed might be the one who'd wake and find him cold.

In Calvino's experience, Monday people didn't dwell on the endgame. But they didn't pretend that the endgame only happened to someone else.

Calvino stopped at an outside bar in Soi Cowboy, pulled back a stool, sat down, and ordered two drinks. He waved the cop following him over, patting the stool next to him.

"It's okay," said Calvino. "Take a load off your feet."

The cop looked both ways as if he were being tailed, shuffled his feet, and then walked up the two stairs to the outside bar area and sat down at a table behind Calvino.

"If it makes you happy," said Calvino.

When the drinks came, he gestured for the waitress to give one to the cop in the corner. Pizza, then Mekong and coke—soon these cops would be following him even after their superiors assigned them to other jobs.

Calvino didn't sit alone for long.

Number 19, Dew, had heard from the bamboo telegraph that Calvino was on the *soi* and showed up fifteen minutes

165

later. He bought her a lady's drink. She sat down on the stool that the cop had refused. She wore her civilian outfit— jean cutoffs and a t-shirt. The cutoffs were neatly hemmed with a thumbnail-sized paler blue material that ran like a band around her inner thigh. It was the same pair she'd worn when he'd taken her back to the condo on Josh's last night, but her shirt was different. This one read "L.A. Lakers." The most successful *yings* wore expensive shoes. Dew's open-style high heels were made of buffed leather with silver studs on the straps. She had the updated version of the Queen of the Nile look.

She looked good in the sporty gear. Her customers included men who had found a new way to show their team loyalty.

"You pay bar for me," she said, taking his hand, nodding her head.

"I'm trouble," he said.

"Me too," she laughed. "Dew always in trouble."

"I'm double trouble."

She had no idea how trouble could be doubled. But then Major Tinakorn and his bone-crunching colleague hadn't given her the special treatment.

"I think you no like Dew?"

The usual bar *ying* line—half insecure, half bait to get the fisherman's attention. It almost always worked.

"Like but don't like."

"Why you say like that?"

"I thought you and my friend had something going. He seemed to like you."

"Your friend like Dew? I no think so." She screwed up her face and shook her head.

"Josh loves you, sweetheart."

"He tell you that?"

"He didn't have to. I could see the way he looked at you."

"Not love."

"What was it?"

She shrugged. "Mistake."

At least it sounded like "mistake," but after a few drinks a lot of words in a bar sound like "mistake," and most of them are exactly that. Calvino let it ride.

After a couple more lady's drinks, Calvino settled the bill. Turning on his stool, he nodded to the cop, who had finished his third Mekong and coke.

"You phone Dew. Promise?"

Calvino smiled, knowing that hookers' play-for-pay book required them to extract a promise of a next appointment. It was the way the business worked. There were Monday people. And there were people for every night of the week. Booked every night was good luck. Still, he had to give Dew full credit. She'd delivered her line with a hooker's full-toothed, perfect smile, along with the teeth, breasts, nose, and eyes paid for by a hundred men.

Calvino never begrudged a *ying* deploying the weapons in her limited arsenal. They were primitive and transparent but effective on tourists. It was like shooting fish in a barrel. Shooting wasn't even required; hitting them over the head with a stick worked as well. In her world the stakes were high, the nights long, the competition fierce, and the cash machine moaned for a fresh injection every day of every week, month after month. Calvino knew the score. He slipped a five-hundred baht note into Dew's hand. She looked at it, leaned forward on the stool, and kissed him on the lips and then hugged him. Then she ran off, disappearing down the nearly empty *soi* waving the note in her hand as if it were the scalp from a white man who'd strayed onto Indian land. The night hadn't yet started and Dew was already ahead of the game.

Monday shopping had finished. It was time for Calvino and his police escort to return home.

TWELVE

Bangkok—Tuesday morning, September 15

*He parked the car in front of the One Hand Clapping
massage parlor.*

IF MONDAY WAS the best day to shop for a car or a
woman, Tuesday ranked as one of those days when Calvino
was grateful for house confinement. He had no intention
of going out. He'd told Ratana that he'd be working at the
condo. She understood and was happy enough that he'd
been able to stay out of a jail cell.

Calvino read the newspapers. The press had picked up
and run with the news of Wirot's disappearance. They
pumped the story up until it was zeppelin-sized news, filling
everyone's sky with the eccentric coin dealer's image. The
story of his disappearance and the gold bullet coins ran in
the Thai newspapers, TV, and radio, and even made the
English-language dailies. A reward of 250,000 baht had been
offered for information leading to the recovery of Wirot.
"Recovery" was a curious choice of words. In cases when
a ferry capsized, the first phase was search and rescue. The
face of Major Tinakorn, the boy-faced policeman, looked
out from the papers. He was leading the investigation. He
looked even younger in the photograph.

After the weekend had passed with no new leads, Major
Tinakorn's picture no longer appeared on the front page
of the papers, and the rescue phase was abandoned, as was
hope. The men in helicopters with binoculars were shifted

into recovery mode. Officially, no one was coming out to say that the authorities had abandoned hope of finding Wirot alive. But they had ways of saying the same thing indirectly. "Police fear the worst." Calvino had the newspapers spread out on the coffee table in his living room.

Sources close to the police investigation said officers were following leads that pointed to the involvement of foreigners. No foreigners were named. That detail didn't matter. Foreigners left the police a lot of rope, deflecting the possibility that a Thai was responsible for the crime. Calvino sat on the sofa, sipped his coffee, and read the latest update in the *Bangkok Post*.

He hadn't been expecting anyone. When the doorbell rang, he thought it was one of the cops sent to have another little talk. Instead Ratana walked in without a word. And without her usual smile. She seemed undressed in the absence of the smile. Calvino closed the door behind her.

"Something's wrong," he said.

"I don't have much time."

She pulled an envelope from her handbag.

"What is it?"

Obviously it was something that couldn't wait.

"This package came by registered mail. It looked important."

He held the envelope. The return address was the first-class lounge for United Airlines at the airport. The name of the sender: Josh Levy.

"It's from Josh," he said.

"I knew you'd want to have a look."

"You did the right thing."

Setting the package on the counter in the kitchen, he put his coffee mug in the microwave and pressed the button for one minute.

"Aren't you going to open it?" she asked, nodding at the package.

The microwave pinged and he took the mug out.

"Later."

He sipped the coffee. Walking to the fridge, he pulled out the milk and added it to the coffee.

"Sure you don't want a cup?"

John-John was at school. She had the time. There was nothing to do back at the office.

"You don't trust me?" she asked.

He shook his head. "It's not a question of trust. If it's something you need to know about, I'll phone you. Otherwise, assume it's a thank-you note from Josh for the wonderful time I showed him in Bangkok."

"I want to help," she said.

"I'm still thinking silver. Or is a silver Accord too clichéd?"

"Silver isn't the color. But gold is."

She was sharp as ever. Attempts to divert her failed and left him like a baseball player standing over the plate as the umpire called the third strike.

"Gold bullets are my problem. No one I know can build a floor over this trouble. I've got to deal with it in my own way."

"You're trying to protect me. I appreciate it. But you can't. I am only a secretary, but that doesn't mean I can't do something."

He wasn't sure he was getting through.

"Ask John-John what he thinks about the color silver. Let me deal with the question of gold."

"John-John told me this morning on the way to school that foreigners have to wear sunglasses because the sun would make their green and blue eyes go blind. Thai people don't need sunglasses. Brown eyes can stare at the sun for hours without a problem."

"And you told him?"

"His father had blue eyes."

170

"And that satisfied him?"

"He asked if his father died blind."

A look of sadness crossed her face. She looked like she was about to cry. Ratana turned away, hoping Calvino wouldn't see it, or if he did, wouldn't say anything. John-John's father hadn't been blind, not officially blind. But he hadn't seen what was coming. It was another kind of blindness that had caused him to stay in Bangkok when he should have run. Blindness caused by the mistaken idea that it mattered that he had right on his side and believed in a code of honor. Beliefs hadn't shielded him against men who lived outside the code. It was a hard lesson, one that hadn't given him a second chance to get it right. After a moment, Ratana turned around, wiping her eyes.

"I should go," she said.

"If I get any calls, let me know."

She nodded. She was about to say something but left whatever was in her mind unsaid.

Calvino closed the door and returned to the sitting room. He carried the package and placed it beside Major Tinakorn's press photograph. He turned it over, examining the outside of the rectangular box. Someone had gone to a lot of trouble to tape and seal it expertly. He got a paring knife from the kitchen, carefully inserted the blade, and pulled it along the seam. Josh Levy's name had been printed in block capitals on the outside label. It had been years since he'd seen Josh's handwriting. But the lettering on the label didn't look anything like what he remembered. Someone in the VIP lounge might have written it for him. One of those curvy ground crew staff with their big smiles and perfect makeup might have taken it over to the airport post office to get it registered. That would have been going to a lot of effort. Someone would have had to be motivated. Calvino peeled back the thin plastic wrapper that covered the box like a full-body condom. When he looked inside, he saw a leather bag—a plain coffee-brown color with a zipper running down the center. Before Josh had left for New York, Calvino had seen Maxim produce the same bag, unzip it and run a flashlight beam over the nine gold bullet coins inside.

Calvino set the bag down and picked up one of the larger gold bullets. It was in a plastic envelope, the kind that coin dealers use to protect coins. His initial reaction upon seeing the coins was relief and gratitude. The bastard, thought Calvino, smiling as he stared at the gold bullets. Josh had gone back to New York without the coins. The headstrong, willful boy he remembered from the old days had actually listened to his advice and acted upon it. Calvino sat back on the sofa, cradling his cup of coffee and looking at the gold bullets, running in size from horse pills down to a dot smaller than the stem on a child's watch.

He smiled and nodded his head, shouting out, "Yes!" Fucking Josh had walked away from the mess. Calvino reached for his cell phone to call New York and thank him. At the same time he thought about calling Colonel Pratt. But he stopped himself, putting his cell phone back on the coffee table. He leaned back, stretched his arms over his head, and shook his head like a fighter who had taken a hard cross on the chin. If this was something Ratana didn't need to know about, the same thought applied to Colonel Pratt—did he really need to know?

Calvino finished his coffee. He was having second and third thoughts about making the call. As a private investigator, he had to read people's motives. A cop like Major Tinakorn wanted to recover the gold bullets and close the Wirot case. Investigating the box and package would get the Major thinking about connections. Major Tinakorn could use the registered mail receipt and packaging to build a chain of suspects who'd been involved in sending and receiving the coins. Calvino saw the Major working on the theory that the people connected to the package were the same people who had grabbed Wirot and the Nicholas II set of gold bullets. Maxim was connected to both sets. Josh was connected to Calvino, and once the Major had got that far down the floor, he could be expected to dance to the tune of the conspiracy waltz.

The thing about imagining a cop's conspiracy was that it was contagious. Calvino started to wonder about Josh. Why would he send the gold bullets with no note? No nothing but nine gold bullet coins worth a lot of money. What if Major Tinakorn had been right and Josh was covering up for Maxim and Andrei? Every private eye has had an experience or two of people who tried to throw him off by leaving a false trail. Professionals who make a living from crime are smart people. When a false trail works, the diversion allows time for the real trail to grow cold. The cops end up with nothing.

Calvino asked himself who might be laying down a false trail that led to him.

Why, he asked himself, should he take a chance, even though the odds were low odds?

Having made his decision, Calvino rationalized it. He told himself that the coins on the coffee table didn't solve anything. They only increased his chances of being nailed as the scapegoat for Wirot's disappearance, not to mention the loss of the gold bullets, with an important matter of national heritage attached. The newspapers would work themselves up into a nationalistic rage. No one was going to be too concerned about the details when the look of things gave credence to a major crime. This, thought Calvino, was how scapegoats were picked. It wasn't the kind of goat that Calvino would be happy to become.

Opening the outer box wider, he took out the packaging. He asked himself what else would fit inside. He walked around his apartment, considering the possibilities—plates, cups, a collection of opium weights (not a good idea), small temple bells from Rangoon, a Gurkha knife from Nepal. None of the things could remotely pass for something Josh Levy would have sent from the airport. As he leaned against his bookshelf, his shoulder brushed against Mark Twain's *The Adventures of Tom Sawyer*. He pulled the book off the shelf and opened it. "While Tom was eating his supper," he read, "and stealing sugar as opportunity offered, Aunt Polly asked him questions that were full of guile, and very deep—for she wanted to trap him into damaging revelations. Like many other simple-hearted souls, it was her pet vanity to believe she was endowed with a talent for dark and mysterious diplomacy, and she loved to contemplate her most transparent devices as marvels of low cunning."

He closed the book and returned to the sofa, sat down, and picked up a pen. Then he opened the book to the title page and wrote: "To John-John, on his 5th birthday. Have many happy hours reading the adventures about an American boy. With fondness, your Uncle Josh from New York."

Calvino sat back and admired his work. Of all forgeries, sentimentality was the easiest to pull off. Kindness made people innocent to deception. It was a simple difficult to overturn. Calvino read the words, smiling. This was gonna work.

Calvino put the box, repackaged with the book inside, into his large black briefcase and took the elevator to his parking space on the fourth floor. He put the briefcase on the backseat and drove out. He slowed down, letting the surveillance team catch up to him in their white Toyota. Calvino turned and waved at them. They pretended not to see him. He phoned Tanaka.

"I'm driving, so I'll make this short. I want the Bose speakers. Red leather upholstery. Why don't we have tea and discuss the price?"

He parked the car in front of the One Hand Clapping massage parlor. Tuesday afternoon looked to be a slow time. The *yings* squatted on plastic stools out front, fanning themselves in the shade. It had rained hard an hour earlier. The last puddles steamed in the sun. He climbed the stairs, carrying his briefcase. Opening the office door, he glanced over his shoulder. No one was standing at the bottom of the stairs. He closed the door as Ratana looked up from her desk.

"I thought you said . . ."

"Forget about what I said. I just got around to opening that registered box."

"What was in it?"

He made her wait a beat.

"A birthday present for John-John."

"Really?"

Calvino heard a rising in her voice, the way relief turned into joy.

"I told Josh all about John-John. He has kids of his own."

"I don't know what to say."

"Don't say anything. It's a book. Give it to John-John."

"He's only five. Can he read this book?"

"It's *Tom Sawyer.* You can read it to him. It's a book his father would have remembered from when he was a boy."

Every day Ratana woke up and saw John-John's father reflected in the face of their son. That kind of hurt never had a chance to heal. She looked up from the book, her face clouding as she searched Calvino's face.

"There's something else, isn't there?"

"One small thing. If anyone asks, you never took this box out of the office. It came to the office and you opened it"—he looked at his watch—"at around three-thirty. If they ask why you came around to my condo, tell them it was to deliver lunch."

"You're asking me to lie?"

He said nothing, trying not to break eye contact with her. She drummed the cover with Tom Sawyer on the front.

"Blue," she said softly.

"What?"

"I saw a blue Accord. I thought it looked very cool."

"Thanks."

Calvino slipped the book inside the packaging. It fit back into the box as if the box had been made for a book. Talking to her face to face hadn't saved him, despite his efforts to wear his poker face as he told a lie. She'd known straight out that the hand he was holding was different from the one he pretended to hold. Women saw those small twitches and eye movements. But a woman like Ratana had that extra perception; she believed that Calvino had a very good reason to ask her to lie.

Part 3

New York City—November

ONE

New York City, near Chinatown—Monday,
November 2, 11:03 a.m.

"They're letting you sweat," said Falcon.
"I know how these people think."

IT WAS MONDAY morning. That was supposed to be Calvino's lucky day. So far he'd felt no luck breezing into his life. The Yankees were scheduled to start game five of the World Series that evening in Philadelphia. But it didn't look like Calvino was going to catch the game. He figured wherever Josh was he probably wouldn't be watching it either. Falcon had stepped outside the coffee shop to talk on the phone.

Calvino couldn't help thinking that Josh had been talking out of fear long before he'd been grabbed. The confidence Josh had felt in Bangkok had vanished. In its place a kind of bitterness and resignation had broken, the emotions of a man cornered.

"You can't show up after twenty years and expect to pick up where you left off. That doesn't make sense," Josh had said the day after Calvino had arrived in Manhattan. "People on TV aren't the same. You don't know their faces. You have no idea who is famous anymore. Same with the newspapers, the ones still in business. You don't recognize the bylines or the people they're talking about. Kids on the street aren't the same—the way they dress, their music. Their Twitter and Facebook pals are scrambled from Timbuktu to hell and back. Nothing is like the way it was when we were growing up. You knew the kids in your neighborhood. You knew whom to fear. Whom to respect. Whom to avoid. You're back in the old neighborhood not as someone who belongs but as a stranger. Only the buildings are roughly the same, and even most of them are gone or unrecognizable. Subtract from the geographical equation the World Trade towers and a few other buildings and look around. People have moved on. You're Rip Van Winkle."

"I'm back, Josh."

"You're back, but back to a past that's gone."

Josh had scored a few points. Body blows. Calvino was still standing, but he felt the ropes digging into his back. A couple of decades had flown by at the speed of a hooker leaving the room after she counted her money. What happened when Rip Van Winkle woke up? Calvino was, as Josh said, a stranger in his own hometown. That left a hole in the heart.

Everyone from Josh to Nero was telling him the same thing: take time to get adjusted. Get over the past. Better yet, forget about the way things were. The direction of thought was forward. They advised him to pretend that he was a foreigner off the boat, learning a new language and culture. Calvino had seen that happen to others. They were foreigners in their old hometown and foreigners in Thailand. Like one of those guys on the long haul flight that never landed. The old times had died but no one had invited you to a wake or a funeral. What you know is what lies buried in a cemetery or an exhibit inside a museum. But real people don't live in the past or inside museums; they live in the present. And if they passed Rip Van Winkle in the street, ranting about what's happened to the neighborhood, they'd think he's just another street crazy.

Sitting in the coffee shop, Falcon saw how Calvino had drifted off. The conversation had stopped as they waited for the Colonel. Falcon sat erect as an Asian man pushed open the door. He'd been watching that door the whole time he smoked his cigarette. The chilly air from outside blew in with him.

Calvino smiled. "Colonel Pratt, you look cold. You need coffee."

The man who came to the table didn't look like a colonel. He didn't much look like a cop either, thought Falcon. He looked more like a middle-aged librarian or tailor. Or maybe the man could have been cast as an Inuit shaman left on an ice floe. The Colonel climbed out of his heavy black overcoat as if it were a space suit. He removed a scarf and then his hat, his cheeks flushed from going from extreme cold into a heated room. His sweater had a hood that covered his head. The Colonel pushed the hood back and shook off the cold. He stamped his feet and sat down.

"Arctic winds from Canada," said Calvino. "They cut straight through you."

"It's nothing. It's like late summer weather in Moscow," said the Falcon. "This is your partner?"

"Friend," said Calvino. "I am not a member of the Thai police force."

"Never thought for a moment that you were."

Calvino cut through the small talk and introduced the Russian detective to Colonel Pratt. The two men shook hands. Then Falcon turned to Colonel Pratt.

"My Russian name is Sokolov. Most people call me Falcon. That's the meaning in English."

He flicked the ash from his cigarette into a balled-up paper napkin.

"You can call me Pratt, after the institute."

"When I think of Thais, I think of elephants and jungle."

"When I think of Russians, I think of ballerinas and oligarchs."

The Falcon raised an eyebrow, thinking the Colonel was taking the piss out of him. The waitress brought the Colonel a steaming mug of coffee and a menu. The three men stopped butting heads and took the menus.

Falcon hadn't showed any sign of respect since the Colonel had walked into the coffee shop. Calvino thought that the Colonel was handling the situation well. He'd rolled with Falcon's banter, his lack of respect. A lot of Thais would have harbored a grudge. Not showing deference was a hostile act for a Thai; it could cause a loss of face, and that wasn't something anyone wanted to be around to witness. Everyone studied the menu.

"Any news about Josh Levy?" the Colonel asked, looking up. Not rattled, not upset, looking business-like—a cop talking to his partner.

Calvino waited for Falcon's answer.

"They're letting you sweat," said Falcon, tilting his head, a faint wisp of a smile crossing his face. "I know how these people think."

Calvino and the Colonel exchanged a look. They'd lost track of the number of times a *farang* had said the same thing about Thais, and Thais had said it about *farang*. The fact is, Calvino thought, no one knows how others think unless they open their mouths and incriminate themselves. It's language that removes the mystery. Only a word or two is enough to figure out what someone means or wants.

"Vincent gave me some names," said Falcon. "Ben Harris. Andrei. Maxim. Wirot. And he also had the list of people who attended Mr. Levy's bachelor party at Sammy's."

He ran a nicotine-stained finger down his list.

"And Mr. Levy's girlfriend. I have a description of the Thai coins. What I don't have is Mr. Levy's location, but I am working on it. I've put the word out."

According to Falcon, nothing happened in the Russian community that Falcon couldn't locate and figure out who was involved.

"You got the coins?" said Falcon.

Calvino pulled a handful of change from his pocket and laid it on the table. "You tell me," he said.

Colonel Pratt smiled and sipped his coffee. Silly question, the Colonel thought.

"We could give them the coins, and they'd release him."

"Then we wouldn't need you," said Colonel Pratt.

Falcon laughed. "You've got a sense of humor, Colonel."

"He wasn't being funny," said Calvino.

Falcon flicked his ash and shrugged. "What's your point?"

"It doesn't matter if we have them. They think we have the coins. That's the point. We promised them we would deliver the coins. Your job is to set up a meeting."

Falcon eased a chest full of smoke out of his nose, shaking his head.

"This looks like a professional snatch and grab. They're going to stay put until we give them something they can believe is real. You won't bait the trap with a promise. These kinds of men don't believe in promises, or in the world that pumps them out. They are likely hard, practical men. Men who understand that before you can defeat an adversary, you must first respect them as men."

"When do we bring in the NYPD?" asked the Colonel. "Vincent tells me you were on the force."

Falcon shrugged as if that information were irrelevant. "If you think my contacts from the NYPD will help, then I have to say, this won't likely happen."

"We have to bring in the police sooner or later," said the Colonel.

It was inconceivable that Falcon wouldn't have friends he could call on. The way he brushed off involving the NYPD caused the Colonel to doubt whether this was the right man for the job. They needed all available resources. The Russian was acting like an American cowboy.

"We bring in the NYPD when you decide you'd rather have Josh dead than alive."

That answered his question. Falcon might be a cowboy, but he had a clear vision of what was waiting on the other side. It might be New York City, but what it came down to was cowboys facing off, walking down the main street of Dodge City, ready to draw down.

"These coins they want. I've been thinking about them. We could try and give them coins that look the same," said the Falcon.

"It won't work," said the Colonel, shaking his head.

There was no hint of ambiguity in his statement—quite unlike the usual guarded, leave-yourself-an-out Thai approach. America brought out another side of him.

Falcon shrugged and stubbed out his cigarette in the paper napkin.

"You're not leaving me with a lot of options, Colonel."

"These are special coins." The Colonel reached into the pocket of his trousers and put a fistful of nickels, dimes, and quarters on the table. "When you're thinking about coins, this is what is in your mind."

Falcon nodded, looking at the change, then up at the Colonel.

"Thai bullet coins aren't loose change pressed by hundreds of government employees working at a stamping machine. These coins on the table come from a government mint by the millions."

"Can I borrow your pen and notepad?" the Colonel asked.

Falcon pushed them across the table. Colonel Pratt drew an oblong tube and carefully inserted two vertical lines, parallel to each other, an equal distance from the ends. He turned the notebook around.

"Those are called cut lines. Only a handful of highly skilled craftsman ever mastered the art of folding the gold along those lines."

"Folded coins?" asked Falcon.

"By hand. One bullet folded by one man at a time. There's no modern machine or living person who can make a bullet coin. These gold bullet coins have been scanned and photographed. We have to assume whoever is holding Josh has a copy of the scans."

"Like a fingerprint."

"Unique like a fingerprint," said Colonel Pratt, smiling.

"Where are the originals?" asked Falcon.

"We don't know," said Calvino.

"Why do the kidnappers believe you have them?"

"It's a misunderstanding."

Falcon slammed his hand on the table. "Misunderstandings can get a man killed."

Calvino sipped his coffee. "We are aware of that. We hired you so that won't happen. You might start by clearing up this misunderstanding."

"I'm not a diplomat."

"We're asking you to find someone, not negotiate a treaty."

"How much time do I have?"

Falcon had asked the question before. He was hoping each time he asked that the answer would be different. Whether this was a sign of optimism or madness, Calvino wasn't clear.

"Less than three days."

"I can't promise," said Falcon.

The Russian had a grudge against the word "promise," as if it were an ex-wife hammering through a wall to get at a safe where the last of their wealth had been hidden away.

"I hope to have more information later this afternoon," said Calvino.

"Then you call me," Falcon said, sticking his notebook in his pocket. Rising from the table, he buttoned his jacket and disappeared out of the coffee shop.

Calvino and Colonel Pratt watched Falcon, hands dug deep into his pockets, wait until a delivery truck passed before crossing the street. He didn't look back. He walked at a quick pace, head down, as if he was thinking.

"Falcon is the right man for the job," said Colonel Pratt.

"Maybe, maybe not," said Calvino.

"He doesn't make you feel good with a false promise."

The Colonel thought the same thing about Calvino. But it wasn't necessary to tell him. Calvino agreed with the Colonel's point, only he worried that Falcon seemed alienated from the Russian community, that he had gone bitter and cynical like expats in Bangkok. A man who had lost his edge with his own people raised questions. Falcon was like a razor gone to rust; it scraped but didn't cut, and at that point the blade became not just useless but dangerous.

The Colonel changed gears. "It was difficult getting away at the consulate. I was in meetings all morning."

"Any break in finding out what happened to Wirot?"

"None. The government wants the Rama V collection returned."

"I want Josh out alive."

"They want to negotiate payment with the Russians holding Josh."

"What's your role, Colonel?"

That was the question the Colonel had asked himself on the train from Washington earlier that morning. A passenger had asked him why the Chinese had taken all of the jobs from America. He had shrugged and not bothered to explain that he was Thai. It was a miscalculation. The entire plan to buy the coins had been flawed. No one had thought to pick up the coins at the auction before Wirot had left.

"My role is to assist you in finding the Rama V gold bullets and see they are returned."

That's how he had got the authorities to go along with his plan to escort Calvino back to New York, all expenses paid. Only Calvino had had to pay his own way. It had been the only way Calvino would have been allowed to leave the country. They had left it up to him. The Colonel had told him it was a formality and not to think too much about it.

"No reason we can't do both. Find Josh and then take the coins back to Thailand."

"That would be ideal. But this isn't an ideal world, and sometimes we have to choose. I want to know what you will do if a choice has to be made."

"Come to think of it, I'd like to ask you the same question," said Calvino.

The Colonel went quiet, coiled up like a kickboxer who had taken a foot in the eye, a fist in the gut, and was still standing.

They left the coffee shop without either man committing himself. They were rather like a couple dating again after twenty years of marriage. Colonel Pratt had rediscovered an element of Calvino's Thainess, which he'd used instinctively to deflect the Colonel's kick, knowing the Colonel wouldn't ask the same question again. The question both had asked was left hanging like mist in the cold air as they walked in front of the old police headquarters. Bundled up like Inuit looking for movement, white on white, in a snowstorm.

Calvino hadn't given him a direct answer, the Colonel thought, but perhaps by ducking the question, Calvino had answered the question after all. And Calvino was thinking the same thing.

"Where are you going?" asked Colonel Pratt.

"Uptown. Fifty-Sixth and Fifth Avenue. Number 27."

"What's there?"

"The Harvard Club."

They walked a bit farther, hands in their pockets. "You didn't go to Harvard."

"I'm meeting some of Josh's people who did. The woman he's marrying. She graduated from Harvard. So did Ben Harris. And Andrei, a Russian client."

"The one whose grandson wanted the Thai coins."

"Same guy."

"Do they know that you're bring a friend along?"

"I wasn't sure if I should use 'friend.' "

"We agreed not to have this conversation."

Calvino stepped into the street and flagged a taxi. The driver was a Cambodian and spoke to them in Thai all the way uptown, glancing every other second into the rear-view mirror, telling them how happy he was to be speaking Thai. The driver couldn't stop smiling. He rattled on about Asian solidarity, how Asians understood Asians. The fact that one of the men in the taxi was a Thai-speaking *farang* was a detail to be overlooked—like the fact that the Thais and Khmers had nearly come to war over a temple nestled along a disputed border between the two countries. With the three men confined together inside a New York City taxi, those squabbles disappeared. They suddenly had been converted into brothers, speaking Thai, driving uptown with the sun out and the car heater blasting away.

They talked about the old refugee camps along the border. The driver had been inside one of the camps for several years. He stopped short of saying that it was the best time of his life. The rough treatment and abuse inside a refugee camp had faded in his memory, thought Calvino. Go figure. As Colonel Pratt and the driver bantered about old times skinned of the horror and sadness, they made it sound like everyone was a happy camper.

Calvino sat back and thought about the people waiting for them at the Harvard club—Josh's future wife; Ben Harris, the tax partner at Josh's old law firm; and Andrei, his genius boss who appeared to have wanted a million dollar starter set of old Thai coins for his grandson. At Sammy's with his bodyguards, Andrei hadn't looked like a grandfather. Ben Harris and Andrei had been at the same table. Andrei had clutched the rubbery clown's mask in one hand, squeezing it like a puffball after Josh had left.

Calvino wondered what kind of shape Tess Reynolds would be in. He had had no problem discovering a great deal about her mental state up to then, her feelings about Josh, the delay in the wedding—that had been the word, "delay"—as if they were waiting for a traffic light to turn green on Sixth Avenue. Calvino had tapped her inner thoughts, and it had been easy. He'd simply logged on and read the latest hourly updates on her Facebook page. When she'd tired of Facebook, she'd switched to Twitter. Calvino had registered as a follower. She'd left a trail of words, and all a person had to do was follow the crumbs and the bird would be at the end, typing in her iPhone. Thanks to technology, Calvino felt he knew more about Tess Reynolds than just about any woman other than his mother.

Rather than run a glamour photo on her Facebook page, she had chosen a photo where she looked upset. She had the sad, wet look of a woman who'd witnessed a black tide swallow up her wardrobe. He'd wondered why she'd used that shot. His guess was she liked drama; she was a woman who didn't filter her moods but used them to shape others in the ways she wanted.

They got out of the taxi. Colonel Pratt leaned through the window and tipped the Khmer driver. Five bucks. From the grin plastered over the driver's face like wet paint, you'd have thought that he'd won the lottery.

189

TWO

New York City, Harvard Club—Monday,
November 2, 12:35 p.m.

"It's a puzzle with a lot of blue sky pieces that don't fit,"
said Calvino.

THEY STOOD OUTSIDE number 27, looking at the large red awning. Colonel Pratt pulled a camera from his pocket and handed it to Calvino.

"Do you mind?"

The Colonel climbed halfway up the stone stairs, turned, pulled down his hood, and smiled, a frozen early November New York smile. Calvino snapped his picture. The Colonel's wife would show it to her friends—"My husband at the Harvard Club." She'd have a face as big as a messiah coming down the mountain with a wheelbarrow full of stone tablets.

The tourist moment ended. Calvino returned the camera to Colonel Pratt and they entered the club. A Latino with thick black hair, who hadn't smiled since he'd left Guatemala, escorted them to the cloakroom, where they shed their coats. They were given plastic buttons with numbers on them. Calvino looked at the button in the palm of his hand.

"Reminds me of home," he said, staring at the number 19. Another Latino showed them into the bar. Ben Harris waved from a stool.

"Colonel Pratt, Royal Thai Police," said Calvino.

Ben Harris extended his hand. "Good to meet you, Colonel. Can I order you a beer?"

The Colonel smiled. "Something hot would be better."

"Coffee, then," said Harris, smooth as a desert lizard crossing a dune.

They pulled back stools and sat at the bar, with Ben Harris in the middle.

"Guess you aren't used to this cold weather," he continued.

"I'm adjusting," said Colonel Pratt.

"That's the spirit."

"Where are Tess and Andrei?" asked Calvino.

Harris smiled his best reassuring lawyer's grin. "In the dining room having a private powwow. I thought we'd have a drink in the bar first."

Calvino sipped the beer that was set in front of him. On the wall was a Pacific sailfish mounted on a lacquered plaque. Shiny and blue, metallic like a lure, sleek and silvery like one of those stop-action frames in a movie. The sailfish hung in midair in perpetuity. The date of this conquest, the names of the Harvard graduates who had hauled it out of the sea, and the year of their graduation were written behind the fish. Harvard had prepared them to land the big fish.

Inside the horseshoe bar, the waiter poured another Beck's from the tap, leaning the glass in at just the right angle, whistling to himself.

"Let's give them another ten minutes. Then we'll go in," said Ben Harris.

A distinguished looking woman in her sixties came into the bar. She didn't look happy. She was upset and went straight up to the bartender, someone she seemed to know.

"Do you know how long I've been a member of this club?"

"No, madam."

"Thirty-one years and counting. And one of your waiters just told me that it was against city regulations to take the rest of my fish home in a doggy bag. Against the law? How can that be? He said it couldn't go out the door. Well, it came in the door, didn't it? Why can't it go out the door? He had no answer. I asked him could I take home the ice cream. He said, 'No, same as fish.' City regulations forbid it. This is from an immigrant, telling me that my fish and ice cream are forbidden. I've never heard of such a thing. Ice cream is sold on the street all over the city. You need a lawyer at your table to deal with these people. And this nonsense almost made me forget. Have you seen an older man with a cane with a young wife?"

The bartender smiled. That description covered roughly eighty percent of their members.

"No, madam, but I'll keep an eye out."

"Hi, Ben," she said.

Harris waved, just as he had when Calvino and the Colonel had come in the door. She rolled her eyes and left.

Harris shook his head. "That woman is a Frick. She's worth seventy million dollars and she wants to take a doggy bag with fish and ice cream."

Calvino suspected the outburst had been for his benefit as much as for the bartender.

"Another beer, Mr. Harris?" asked the bartender, with a Spanish accent.

"No, Jose. Time for lunch."

"Are the Yankees going to win tomorrow?"

"Bet on it," said Harris. "The series in six games."

Inside the baronial dining hall were tables occupied with patrons, their restrained conversations blending into a murmur. Calvino saw Tess and Andrei seated at one end of a large round table. Tess dabbed her eyes with a handkerchief and nodded as Andrei, leaning in close, spoke. Calvino and the Colonel followed Harris, who in turn had the headwaiter leading the way. The walls were covered with the heads of big game bagged by Teddy Roosevelt while on safari in Africa. Scattered among the dead animals were paintings of dead presidents. Tess and Andrei were seated at a table below a framed painting of John F. Kennedy, suspended between the heads of an antelope and a wild boar felled by Roosevelt's rifle.

Looking up, Tess saw Calvino and nodded. They'd met the second night after he had arrived in New York. Josh had booked dinner at the Harvard Club. A band had played. Tess and Josh had danced, and Calvino had danced with Tess.

"I don't feel I know very much about you, Vincent," she had said that night.

"Strange," he said. "I feel that I know a great deal about you."

They had talked on the phone after Josh had been grabbed, but they hadn't met since that first night. She insisted that Calvino sit next to her, patting the chair beside hers and gesturing to him.

"Vincent, it's so terrible. Do you remember that this was the same table we had dinner at a few nights ago?"

He remembered.

"Today was supposed to be my wedding day," she said, some bitterness in her voice. "I'm sorry, what did you say?"

"This is my friend, Colonel Pratt, Thai Royal Police," said Calvino.

"Thank you for coming, Colonel."

"I still don't understand how the man I'm to marry is being held hostage over some stupid coins."

Her eyes misted, and she touched the corners with the edge of the white handkerchief. None of the men said anything. Andrei patted her hand. Harris dipped his head one way, then the other, like he was stretching a kink out of his neck. The Colonel wore a smile to hide his discomfort. And Calvino looked at the antelope and wondered how many shots Roosevelt had taken to drop him.

"I promised not to cry today. I really did."

She had posted her non-cry pledge on her Facebook page. Though she had resisted posting the reason for bursting into tears. Whatever was said around the table had a fifty-fifty chance of being broadcast to the public. So far she hadn't written the message that her future husband had been kidnapped. Judging from the shape she was in, Calvino wondered how long it would be before Tess's confessional nature broke free of the advice that going public would harm their efforts to get Josh back alive. He assumed the others around the table hadn't gotten where they were without taking into consideration that anything they said in a place like the Harvard Club might be overheard and discussed, from unheated rooms in El Salvador to boardrooms on Wall Street. They were careful.

"Can you tell me why anyone would want to hurt Josh for these coins, Colonel?"

Colonel Pratt nodded. It was his turn to say something to appease her.

"Before I left Thailand my wife was worried about me. She said, '*Sia thong tao hua mai yom sia phua hai krai.*' That means a woman would rather lose a pot of gold than her husband."

"That's exactly how I feel," said Tess. "I want Josh back. I don't care about the gold coins."

"Your fiancé may not have known the importance of these coins. In my country I am not sure the authorities would agree with my wife on what they'd rather lose."

He stopped, choosing his words carefully, all eyes on him as he was expected to give the official position.

"In America if your Declaration of Independence were stolen, your government would do everything to get it back. It would not be a loss that you would bear. The missing coins are that kind of a loss for us. It is difficult to explain."

"But Josh would never do anything like that. Steal some national treasure? That's not him."

The Colonel looked to Calvino for help. Calvino was careful to watch Andrei.

"The Thai police think that Josh might have been set up," said Calvino.

Andrei looked at him without blinking. He's very good, thought Calvino.

"The theory was that Josh was an involuntary mule."

"Josh never had anything to do with drugs," said Tess.

"It's an example of how people make mistakes. Of course Josh wouldn't smuggle drugs. Neither would he knowingly take out coins that are part of the national heritage of Thailand."

"They were for Mr. Andrei's grandson. That's what I don't understand."

"It's a puzzle with a lot of blue sky pieces that don't fit," said Calvino.

She searched his eyes, listening as the waiters hovered, waiting for orders.

"I understand that you've hired a private investigator, Mr. Calvino," said Andrei.

Andrei was turning the conversation away from the puzzle before it could turn into questions about the missing pieces and whether Andrei might know where to look for them. It was a line of inquiry that he understood was unavoidable, but Andrei was prepared, and before that moment arrived, he wanted to assert his position at the table.

"A Russian ex-NYPD named Falcon."

"I am acquainted with the name," said Andrei. "I believe he was fired from the police force some years ago."

"Same guy," said Calvino.

"I've apologized to Ms. Reynolds. I never thought asking Josh to bring a few souvenirs in the form of coins could balloon into an international criminal investigation. It was quite unintentional on my part. And I can assure everyone at this table that I will do everything in my power to see that Josh is released and the coins are returned to the Thai authorities."

"You might start with your friend Maxim," said Calvino, smiling the way a Thai does to throw off the listener, who wondered if he was being serious or joking.

The Russian took it seriously. "Maxim is a business associate who has a minor part, playing a logistical role."

"He's saying Maxim isn't a friend, Mr. Calvino."

"I speak English, Ben."

"Sorry." Harris pulled his head back like a turtle whose nose had touched a flame.

"Any idea why he bid on the historical set at auction? I was there. He bid forty million baht," said Calvino.

"I understand someone else won the bid. It might be best if you asked Maxim yourself."

"I have," said Calvino. "I thought he might have told you that. He said he got carried away. For a guy who named a yacht *Last Money*, that almost seems plausible, but in Maxim's case I don't think so. He wasn't buying the coins for investment or on spec; he had someone lined up. And I can't think of anyone other than you who was looking for nine gold bullets."

"I can't speak for Maxim's other contacts in the coin world," said Andrei.

"I thought you two were friends."

"As Josh and you are friends," said Andrei. "How well do you really know Josh?"

Calvino had begun to understand why Josh called Andrei a genius. Tess tilted her head, staring at him as if to suddenly realize that, in fact, Calvino hardly knew Josh. Taking this in, Colonel Pratt saw a way to turn the conversation back to Andrei's relationship with Maxim.

"Your friend was recently implicated by my government in weapons smuggling," said Colonel Pratt. "Charges are pending against the crew of an aircraft chartered to one of his companies."

"Should Maxim or his crew be found to be involved in such a business, then of course they should feel the full weight of your courts, Colonel. No one disagrees with that position. My dealings with Maxim have been limited. Some people in my country have been known to deal in illegal arms. I condemn such activities. It gives all Russians a bad name. Just as in your country, your women suffer a low international reputation because of the few who prostitute themselves. We all have this burden, an image that others place on us, and we fight to maintain our dignity even though others doubt that we have a right to it."

Calvino saw how Andrei had tagged the Colonel. The Russian, surrounded by dead heads of state and animals, had delivered a good speech. The Harvard Club was a place for such speeches. The waiters brought the soup and salad to the table. Tess didn't touch her food. She looked worn out and had started to fade by the time the main course arrived. Once the plates were cleared and the small talk was finished, Andrei leaned across the table and patted Colonel Pratt's hand.

"I want you to tell your people that I will do whatever I can to help them. I am sitting here today and wish to make it clear that I have nothing to hide. In your investigation, I wish to provide complete and full cooperation."

"I'd like to request an appointment to discuss Mr. Maxim with you," said Colonel Pratt.

"It would be my great pleasure, Colonel."

"Vinny, as Josh's best man, would you take me back to my apartment?" asked Tess Reynolds.

Calvino looked around the table. He locked eyes with Andrei for a moment. The genius had batted away any idea that Maxim was bidding on the historical set of bullets on his account. He'd also preempted the idea that he involved with the cargo plane embargoed in Bangkok. Andrei stuck to his personal formula that denied all proofs of dangerous associations. Like Andrei, none of the other men had finished with lunch. Calvino pushed his chair back, went around and helped Tess out of her chair. Escorting her back to the coat check, he produced the number 19 from his pocket. He tossed it into the air, caught it like a coin, and slapped it on the top of his hand. The number came up. Heads, he thought. He had an idea of his own about investigating Maxim.

THREE

New York City, Upper East Side—Monday, November 2

"A Thai whore named Dew," she said without missing a beat.

ON THE DRIVE from the Harvard Club, Tess invited Calvino into her apartment on the Upper East Side. Her building was in a block stacked with high piles of brownstone. The doorman wore a uniform with gold braids on the shoulders and stripes on the trousers; his hat looked like the ones worn by North Korean generals. He saw Tess and smiled, opening the door. The doorman watched her with the darting eyes of a ceiling gecko following a bluebottle fly. Calvino followed her into the elevator. Tess fumbled for her keys as the door opened on her floor. She stepped out, still fishing inside her handbag for keys. After she found them, it took her a couple of minutes to unlock the three dead bolts. There was almost enough brass on the door to make it worth stealing. Glancing back at Calvino as the last bolt popped, she swung open the door and walked in. It was a large room, professionally decorated so that all of the cushions and carpets and curtains blended in a harmony of white, gray, and polished cherry wood. A bank of tall windows opened onto the trees outside. The leaves had turned yellow and red, part of the cycle of death and renewal played out every autumn on the streets of New York. Or at least those streets where the rich lived and died and the trees remained, shedding leaves the way a widow sheds tears.

He followed her inside.

"Sit down," she said.

"It's quiet here," said Calvino. He sat on the sofa.

"That's why we like it," said Tess, disappearing from the room. "By the way, thanks for giving me a way out of there."

A moment later she appeared with a bottle of wine and two glasses.

"I normally don't drink in the afternoon," she said as she poured the wine. "It will turn out all right, won't it?" she asked, handing him a glass.

He said nothing but only sipped the wine. Putting the glass down, he looked at her eyes—two cat eyes watching him with the concentration of a predator ready for a takedown pounce.

Calvino shrugged. "It depends."

"On what?"

"On everything going right and nothing going wrong."

"Something can always go wrong," she said.

"That's the problem."

She sat back and looked at Calvino. She made it clear that she'd figured out how to switch on a sensual, elegant smile and use her eyes to lock onto the target. That combination worked wonders on most men. He could see she was the kind of woman who got what she wanted. Besides, she was easy on the eyes. And the afternoon light through the window made her light brown hair even lighter. But it was her eyes that stood out. Forest green eyes, the kind that go supernova when they're angry. And turn pastoral—at-sunset soft green—when they want something.

"It looked intense between you and Andrei," he said.

She flexed her bare feet—toenails expertly painted red with sparkles of silver—as she crossed her ankles.

"Meeting that Russian math genius would make anyone intense."

She didn't call him Andrei. Funny that. A few hours earlier at the Harvard Club, she'd been crying on his shoulder, and now, with the man downtown, he became what he did and what his reputation had earned him. It was the uptown way of dividing the world, Calvino thought. She sat forward on the chair, fingering a necklace. It was an upscale gold and diamond throat chain, the kind that made a woman's throat feel special. It had to have cost more than an autoworker's lifetime pension. Calvino stared at it.

"You like the necklace? Josh gave it to me not long after he came back from Bangkok," she said.

"The last time I knew Josh to give a woman a piece of jewelry, it was his high school class ring. It cost twenty-three dollars and fifty-five cents."

She smiled. "That must have been a long time ago."

She worked her finger and thumb, massaging the necklace, as if to make certain it hadn't disappeared—and to make certain Calvino got the point that Josh had an investment in her. He got the point. She slowly shifted her position, folding one leg underneath and dangling the other one like a schoolgirl at a picnic.

"You had something you wanted to discuss in private," said Calvino.

"Josh said that you were a man who liked to get to the point. I like that in a man," she said. "Going round and round just makes me crazy. Do you understand what I'm saying?"

"I understand that Josh is in something way over his head. And I thought you might give me an idea of what he was doing transporting expensive coins from Bangkok to New York for his new boss's grandson."

"You don't believe Josh?"

"Do you believe Andrei?"

She laughed, covering her mouth, and blushed.

"That is exactly the question I sometimes ask myself."

"Has Josh phoned you?"

She shook her head. "Not a word."

From the way she said it, she left the impression she had other things on her mind and she was just waiting for the right opportunity.

"Any idea why he wouldn't phone?" Calvino asked.

"You'd have to ask the men holding him. But I did have one call."

She paused, letting out a long breath.

"About Josh?"

The supernova flashed in those eyes, turning them into an awesome shade of green.

Tess put down her glass and folded her arms. "The call was from Thailand."

Calvino scratched his cheek, wondering who'd phoned. Tess wasn't giving anything away. Time slowed down, as the silence gathered. He could see that she was waiting for him to guess the identity of the caller.

"A Russian named Maxim?" asked Calvino, knotting up the napkin and dropping it on the coffee table.

"A Thai whore named Dew," she said without missing a beat.

"You sure about this?"

"You must keep this in confidence," she said. Her smile disappeared, leaving just the hard green eyes drilling holes in him.

"Tell me about the phone call," he said.

She cocked her head to the side, wondering why he didn't look shocked after being told Josh had been caught red-handed. Had Calvino heard what she'd told Josh? His Thai whore had phoned his fiancée, but Calvino absorbed the information as if it were a recipe for cabbage soup.

"She phoned from a bar where she works."

Calvino smiled.

He wondered whether the tears in the Harvard Club had been caused by the same call. He watched as a new tear slowly zigzagged down her cheek and splashed on her necklace.

"I want to know if Josh was unfaithful to me in Bangkok."

"With Dew?"

"So you do know her?"

"She works in my neighborhood."

"She works in a bar, selling herself."

Tess was circling around the idea.

"How'd she phone you?" asked Calvino. It was a mystery. Except it wasn't.

"The night before the bachelor party, Josh was in the den on the phone. He left his cell phone on the table here." She pointed at the table with the pastries and coffee pot and cups. "I answered it. The operator said it was an important collect call from Thailand. I accepted the charges."

"You were expecting a collect call?"

"I wasn't expecting anything. It was Josh's phone. I thought it might be you."

Calvino's eyes narrowed. She thought he'd phone collect? The man whom Josh had chosen to be his best man? But never interrupt the flow of a woman talking about another woman in her man's life.

"And she spoke in this creepy little girl's voice. I could hardly understand her broken English. She comes on the line and says, 'Josh, I miss you too much. I have bad dream every night. I think you too. Do you miss Dew?' I said, 'Excuse me, who is calling?' She says, 'My name Dew.' She asked me who I was. Imagine that."

He could imagine it all right.

"And you told him that you were his wife."

She nodded. "And she said he never told her he had a wife. That was theoretically true. But as I said, she spoke broken English, and I didn't want to get into a protracted discussion over a technicality."

"What did you do?" asked Calvino.

"I asked how well she knew Josh. And she said, 'He my very good friend. Can I talk with him?' And I asked her, 'What would you like to talk to him about?' She went silent. 'I have big problem. Bad men want to hurt Dew. He knows I speak the truth. I need Josh send me money. Cannot work. I must hide.' I asked her how much money, and she said one hundred thousand baht. At this point I went to the den looking for Josh, but he was still on the phone. I told him it was important. He nodded, holding up two fingers for a couple of more minutes. And I told him that it couldn't wait two minutes. He needed to take the phone call now. He put the other call on hold and picked up the cell phone. He had that 'This better be really important' look as he put the phone to his ear. I sat down in the chair opposite the desk and watched his face."

That was the moment Calvino wished he could have been a fly on the wall. One glimpse at Josh Levy's face as Dew's voice floated through the satellite transponders, bounced through the airwaves, entering his ear and registering in his brain, his brain sending panic signals, twisting his face into a mask of undisguised horror.

"The call lasted less than a minute. But he knew the damage had been done. The first thing I asked him was, 'Where did you meet her? Why did you give her your phone number? Did you sleep with her? Does she have AIDS? She doesn't sound of age on the phone. You could go to prison for sleeping with a child prostitute.'"

That didn't sound like the first thing. It sounded like the drum roll of many first and last things all bundled together.

"And what did he say?"

"Dew was your special friend, not his. That you'd taken him to this bar and she'd been dancing. He'd hardly talked to her."

"I asked Josh how she'd gotten his number."

It turned out that the absence of a convincing answer to that question had cost him the necklace that Tess now wore proudly around her neck.

"Josh is right. Nothing happened," said Calvino.

"You're his best friend. Of course you would cover for him. That's to be expected. But I would like the truth. Did he cheat on me in Bangkok?"

One necklace wasn't enough to quench her thirst for an answer that she could believe in, one that would return her self-respect and pride.

"Nah, not Josh. He's a straight arrow. All he could do was talk about you. I've never seen anyone so head over heels about a woman. At first I thought it was some kind of an act. We're New Yorkers. We don't go around wearing our hearts on our sleeves. But I've been away a long time. People and things change. He was wearing his heart on his sleeve, and he didn't mind that I saw him doing it."

"Is she pretty, this Dew?" She sat Buddha-like with no expression crossing her face.

Women shift their moods, thought Calvino, like a drunk stumbling through Soi Cowboy bars. What did she want to hear? Hardly the truth—skin the shade of nutmeg, hourglass waist, slender thighs, firm breasts that stood to attention as if attending a flag raising, and an infectious smile that could bore through the most jaded heart and nestle inside, hatching dreams of passion.

"Yeah, she's pretty."

"Thanks for not lying about that."

"It's like this, Tess. A man like Josh has control in his little piece of the world. He knows how it all works. In a Bangkok bar, women like Dew are in control of their little piece of the world, but the men don't see it. Giving Dew his phone number surprised even him. It was a spontaneous act. Like throwing a cigarette out of a car window. He wouldn't ordinarily do that either."

"Josh doesn't smoke."

"It's just an example. But say he smoked and threw a cigarette into a forest. It's one of those careless, thoughtless acts. Most of the time nothing happens. Then that one time, it sets a forest on fire. Ten thousand acres burn down. Houses. Schools. Churches. Hospitals. All go up in smoke. Giving his number to Dew was that kind of act. It's up to you whether to let it burn out or spread through the whole forest."

"My therapist said I was in control of the situation. But she didn't put it quite that way. Forest fire. He did start one, didn't he?"

"Let me ask you a question, Tess."

Her eyes said that she was feeling better about herself, more relaxed, as she eased off the emotional accelerator. She was coasting, head back, hands comfortably wrapped around her cup. A picture out of a fancy interior design magazine, a rich woman at home and contented.

"Ask away."

"Do you have any idea if the Rama V bullet coins are in New York?"

She tilted her head and smiled. "Why would they be in New York? Why not Bangkok?"

"You think I have them."

"The men holding Josh think you have one of the two sets. And you're in New York."

"What do you mean, 'one of the two sets'?" She had his full attention.

"The special and not so special one."

"Someone in Thailand was killed over the special set," said Calvino.

She shrugged it off as if the death of someone in a foreign place didn't much matter. Wirot could have been killed on the moon.

"Some of the coins got mixed between the two sets."

"They have one set. Is that what you're saying?"

She nodded. "And they think you'll lead them to the second set."

"How do you know this? You can't, unless you're mixed up with it. Is that it? You and Josh are both in over your heads?"

He finished the last of the wine, rose from the sofa, and walked to the door. They had used him as a decoy to create a false trail to a second set. But a couple of things had gone wrong. Wirot had been murdered. The coins had gotten mixed up. The person who had sent him the second set knew that he had the coins and that he'd been playing a game with the *Tom Sawyer* novel in the box. Calvino had seen Maxim hand Josh the second set. Colonel Pratt had inspected the second set. But who had mailed the box from the airport? He'd wanted to ask Josh, but then he'd have had to admit he'd received them. Others might not be so certain the coins had ever been sent. Gold, he thought, spawns hard to control children named paranoia and greed.

Tess's mood had shifted, as if pulling a heavy load up a steep incline.

"Now I don't know if I'll ever see him again. This thing with Dew is destroying me from the inside. I don't know if I can handle it. I'm fragile."

Nothing about Tess Reynolds looked breakable.

As he stood in the open door, he turned back.

"One more thing."

She nodded.

"Josh's Halloween mask. Did you choose it?"

Again she nodded and smiled, closing the door.

She'd gone for the werewolf look. Maybe her therapist thought it suited Josh Levy, a man with a hooker phoning from Bangkok.

FOUR

New York City, Union Square—Tuesday, November 3

"You've won a golf tournament, Mr. Andrei?"

ANDREI'S OFFICE OVERLOOKED Union Square. His company occupied the entire floor. To gain access to his part of the floor, with its bulldog-faced receptionist of unspecified gender, was like running through airport security. Colonel Pratt was waved through, and a guard led him down a corridor. At the end of the corridor the guard stopped and knocked on the large door before opening it and showing the Colonel inside. At the far end of the room, Andrei stood up and walked around his desk to welcome him.

"Please come in, Colonel."

Colonel Pratt acknowledged Andrei with a nod and crossed the large room while looking out of the corner of his eye at a massive volume of mahogany wood that had been used on the ceiling and walls. Somewhere in Russia, he thought, a forest has gone missing. Andrei's desk was flanked by side tables filled with framed photos. Andrei was in every one of them—sometimes a younger version, dressed in academic gowns and hats. He'd been photographed with corporate big shots and the presidents the big shots bought. There were more photographs of Andrei with politicians, movie stars, and celebrity businessmen.

By comparison, Andrei's office walls made the animal heads and presidential portraits of the Harvard Club look devoid of power and influence. Leather sofas were positioned opposite each other with a table of chrome and glass. Across the room on a shelf were awards, certificates, and bronze statues with his name inscribed for this honor or that donation. It was a display of a man seeking to impress or intimidate his guests.

One of Andrei's aides appeared in a jacket and tie with a tray of porcelain china. He gestured at the aide, who poured Colonel Pratt a cup and then a second cup for Andrei.

"Making a good cup of tea isn't easy," said Andrei. "It takes skill, time, the right tea leaves, and some luck. Not all people can make such a cup of tea, and not all people who receive such a cup appreciate what they have."

"Is that why you asked me here?"

The aide handed the Colonel his cup.

"Go ahead, drink it. Tell me what you think."

The Colonel drank the tea and put the empty cup on the coffee table.

"That was very good."

"I'm disappointed in your friend, Mr. Calvino," Andrei said.

Colonel Pratt said nothing, waiting for Andrei to sip his tea, close his eyes, open them, and finish his thought.

"He's not helping Josh."

"How do you know that?" the Colonel asked.

"They're phoning him. Not me or anyone else. They want something specific from Calvino and he's not delivering it. He's not helping Josh. I asked myself what is going on. I realized Calvino was trying to tell me something. He wants compensation for handing over the ransom. No one has bothered to ask him."

"You're asking me whether Calvino will take your money?"

Colonel Pratt smiled but his eyes narrowed signaling a different message. Calvino would have punched him. But there was no point in the Colonel sharing this thought, as he'd already communicated his message without uttering a single word. That is considered a success.

"I feared that might be the case."

"The same with threats. They don't seem to bother him," said the Colonel, still smiling. He felt Andrei was about to expose his connection with Josh's disappearance.

It was Andrei's turn to smile, but inside he wasn't all that happy of a man. He had one big problem. He had to choose between believing Maxim's story or Calvino's about what had happened to the second set of gold bullets. One of them had it. The way he saw it, Maxim pointed the finger at Calvino (that was to be expected), but Calvino just kept quiet. Didn't say a word, as if pointing a finger at Maxim. He didn't want money. No good threatening him. With Calvino the only options were killing him or walking away. Which man was lying?

He could trust Maxim, or thought he could. Men in modern Russia, as in modern Thailand, are defined by the degree of their polarization and paranoia. It's difficult to determine whose side a man is on, and the paranoia kicks in because whatever side he is on, he could silently shift loyalties as soon as someone else comes along with a better carrot or more lethal stick. Andrei had tried a number of formulas to work out the probabilities but still couldn't make up his mind. He had decided to bring the Thai Colonel to the office, impress him, and see if the Colonel might have information to break the deadlock.

Andrei dropped his smile. "It means I'll lose Josh. It's a pity. He's a very good lawyer. We Russians have a great deal in common with Thais. A hundred years ago plus, our kings met in Moscow. It was a different world then. But we don't forget them or forget to honor them. We teach our children not to forget. It defines who we are."

"No more tea," said the Colonel as the aide reached to make another cup. Colonel Pratt couldn't really say the tea tasted any different from the usual. Certainly one cup had been enough.

He felt comfortable with Andrei in the way that two foreigners do in a big city. The fact was, saying no to the second cup of tea was a good way of saying the personal business was finished. If so, the Colonel would leave. He was in the country on an official mission, and he had his duty as a police officer to consider. The Colonel might not have been a genius, but he wasn't anyone's fool either. Andrei had made the coded offer to pay for the second set. Whatever Calvino wanted. He'd asked Colonel Pratt to his office to make a final decision: Calvino or Maxim.

The Colonel has only drunk one cup of tea, Andrei thought, and now he wants to leave. Why didn't he grill me about the gold bullets, he wondered, staring at the medium-sized Thai with the wide smile. Russians hated cops that always smiled. There was a legend such cops were sadistic. Such cops were full of surprises and the genius was to surprise the cops first.

"In my business we are not cold like the Americans," said Andrei. "We help and rely on our friends. Like the Thais, Russians take time to get to know another person. Who are they? Where do their families go for holidays? What kind of cakes do their children like? We keep in contact with each other not for profit but for the simple reason that we value and respect each other."

"You are doing business in Thailand?"

"Yes. But let's not talk business. Not yet. Let me show you something."

He rose from the sofa and crossed the vast room to a set of cabinets. He opened a drawer to remove a large, polished cherry wood case and returned to the sofa. Setting the case on the table, he opened the brass lock. He slowly lifted the lid and turned the case around.

"Please have a look."

Inside the velvet-lined case were rolls of Thai coins. Gold and silver bullet coins. Colonel Pratt's heart skipped a beat as he counted over fifty coins.

"You are more than an ordinary collector."

"It is a passion, collecting. And I wish to pass my passion for Thai coins along to my grandson. I saw an opportunity to buy bullet coins to start a collection for Nicholas, my grandson."

"Then you did pursue the Rama V gold bullets at the auction. I was there that day."

Andrei held up a hand. "I am aware of that fact. Mr. Maxim, a Russian who lives in Thailand, agreed to buy a collection at that auction. Not the special collection, mind you; that is something that wasn't ever my intention. You trust a man like Maxim and you think that he will honor that trust. Instead he decides to bid on a very valuable set of coins for reasons that I am certain your police will find once they interrogate him. Reasons that I also would like to know. I, too, have been a victim. You must understand that a man like me must be extremely careful in all dealings, in every relationship. I have enemies, as do all men who are in the public eye. Please, Colonel, inspect the coins. Photograph them. Spend as much time as you wish until you are fully satisfied that these coins are not the ones you seek. If you will excuse me, I will leave you in privacy while I go next door to another office."

The Colonel changed his mind and lifted his teacup until he caught the aide's eye. Though the aide seemed torn between acknowledging him and applauding Andrei's little speech, he finally reached for the empty cup. Colonel Pratt opened his briefcase and removed the scanned photographs of each of the nine gold bullet coins. An hour later, he had been through every coin in the box, turning each one over carefully, glancing at the scan and back at the coin. There was no match. When Andrei reappeared as silently as he had left, he eased back on the sofa across from the Colonel.

"Have you finished? Or do you need more time?"

Colonel Pratt shook his head. "No more time is necessary."

His scans of the Rama V set lay on the glass top table. Andrei glanced at them.

"You came prepared."

Colonel Pratt said nothing.

"I can appreciate why your superiors selected you for this mission. You are the most senior official that they can rely upon to get the job done."

Andrei had a way of enlarging another man's face. He was a plastic surgeon with words.

"If Maxim acted on his own," asked the Colonel, "why do Mr. Levy's kidnappers insist that Vincent Calvino has the collection?"

Andrei sighed. "I am starting to wonder if Maxim and Calvino are working together."

"I've known Vincent for more than twenty years," said Colonel Pratt. "I can't believe he'd have business with Maxim."

"Colonel Pratt, in 1988 did anyone believe the Berlin Wall would fall? Or that the Soviet Union would collapse? That wall and union existed for many, many years. They seemed like permanent fixtures. Yet at the end of the day, they both were not as immutable as everyone presumed. Is a man like Calvino any more solid than such a wall? Than an empire?" A long sigh came from his lips. "Maybe your Mr. Calvino has lived in Thailand for too long."

The Colonel resented the observation. Thais reserved exclusively for themselves the right to describe in this way a *farang* in up to his neck in local trouble. So far Calvino was up to his waist in trouble, but it'd hadn't risen above that. Colonel Pratt shrugged, leaving Andrei's question until it fell away into an embarrassed silence. He used that moment to glance at a mini-cemetery of medals and trophies that looked like tombstones. In the clutter, to the far left, Colonel Pratt saw a golf trophy. He adjusted his glasses and read the Thai script on the front of it.

It looked out of place. "You've won a golf tournament, Mr. Andrei?"

The Colonel nodded at the bronzed man in full backswing. He moved forward a couple of steps and read the inscription aloud. Above Andrei's name was the name of a Chonburi golf club—the Jasmine Park Golf Club. It was first choice from the list of the most exclusive golf courses in Thailand. Politicians, generals, big shots were members. And as far as the Colonel remembered, it was one of the few exclusive golf courses that enforced a restriction of players to members and their guests.

Andrei picked up the trophy as if it were an Oscar and handed it to the Colonel.

"I know of the golf course," the Colonel said.

"They say all the important business and political decisions in Thailand are made on that golf course."

Colonel Pratt handed back the trophy.

"I won this because of my handicap. I keep it in my office to remind me that in business, a handicap will bring failure. But in a golf tournament it can work to your advantage."

FIVE

New York City, Nero's apartment—Wednesday,
November 4, 7:03 p.m.

"Falcon's found where they're holding Josh."

FALCON PHONED USING the landline at Calvino's cousin's apartment around seven in the evening. The Colonel had been in the kitchen slicing onions, carrots, and large, plump red tomatoes he'd bought at one of those superstores made to look like an upscale farmers' market. The scent of the freshly steamed kale rising from Nero's vegetable steamer carried throughout the apartment. The Colonel was spooning rice out of a rice cooker when the call came in. He stuck his head out of the kitchen and listened as Calvino gave him the high sign.

"Falcon," he mouthed.

The Colonel stepped out of the kitchen, wiping his hands on a towel.

Calvino had been sitting in front of the TV watching the pre-game commentary to game six of the World Series. The broadcast was live from Yankee Stadium. Pettitte, the Yankee pitcher, was talking about how he felt having had only three days' rest. He said he was going to try to go for as long as he could. That seems like the right attitude, thought Calvino, who kept his eyes on the screen as he put the phone to his ear.

"I've found where they're holding Levy," Falcon said.

Calvino leaned forward on the sofa and pointed the remote at the TV. The screen went blank.

Looking up at Colonel Pratt, he said, "Falcon's found where they're holding Josh."

"Where?" Colonel Pratt asked.

"In a warehouse in Port Elizabeth," said Falcon over the phone. "I've been on stakeout. I've drawn a map of the street, the layout. We go in for him tonight. It's a good time. Everyone is going to be inside watching the World Series."

"When do we go in for him?"

"I'll pick you up in thirty minutes."

Nero had also told Vinny where other hardware was kept in the apartment, if that became necessary. "Just let me know, that's all." Nero had slapped his cousin on the back. Calvino had told him about the 9mm he'd borrowed. Nero said he was surprised his cousin would take a registered gun papered up with a proper permit. It could be traced straight back to him. Instead, if he'd dug a bit deeper, he'd have found the cache of special purpose weapons that no one could trace. Nero never asked why he thought they might need this information. He assumed the Colonel hadn't tagged along with Calvino to sightsee. And when he found out that Calvino had already borrowed one of his guns, Nero had all the information he needed. Nero had no doubt that his cousin would ask if he needed backup.

Calvino hadn't asked him. He'd left it that way. Sometimes a man's got relatives he can appreciate, Calvino had thought.

Calvino descended from the upstairs bedroom closet, a gun in each hand. Both were 9mm Berettas with the serial number filed off. He handed one to Colonel Pratt and checked the clip of his. Colonel Pratt never liked the weight of an automatic. Most cops hated a 9mm. It lacked sufficient stopping power. When shot, a person should immediately go down. With a 9mm, a couple of rounds could hit a man but he could still return fire. That was a bad situation. But if it was a choice between a 9mm and no gun, it was better to accept the limitations of a 9mm. What a man wanted and what he got often diverge, the Colonel thought. In the case of a borrowed gun, it is never wise to criticize the weapon. To do so would bring bad luck. So long as the automatic had a full clip, he'd worry about the stopping power as a minor concern. But it didn't prevent the Colonel from thinking that in a fight in close quarters, while the Beretta was good enough, a shotgun would be better.

SIX

"Let's get him out alive," said Calvino.

TEN MINUTES BEFORE the start of game six in the
World Series, Falcon picked them up in a white SUV with
upstate New York plates and tinted windows. A New York
Yankees decal was stuck to a rear side window.

Falcon removed a cigarette with a damp end from his lips
and dropped it out the window. "We're going to miss the
game," he said.

"We'll listen to it on the radio," said Calvino.

Calvino hadn't taken the Russian ex-cop for a baseball
fan.

Falcon wore a Yankees cap, bill pulled forward, his eyes
like a wolverine peering out as they climbed inside. Lighting
a new cigarette, Falcon nodded, said nothing, signaled,
executed a U-turn in a tight circle in front of their building
the way cops are taught in cadet school, and they were off.

"I'd rather be in the Bronx," he said.

Josh and Calvino had had tickets for the game. Calvino
had tried to persuade Colonel Pratt to go with them. But
the Colonel had thought it too cold, and he'd had a sixth
sense that something was going to break in the case. He'd
been right.

Once they were on the Jersey side of the Holland
Tunnel, there was no traffic. Falcon turned on to a side

218

road, drove two miles, pulled into the gravel parking lot of a bar, and parked beside a Buick, tan and white, with Jersey plates. They got out of the SUV. Falcon locked it and they climbed into the Buick. On the road again Falcon shifted from second into third, gathering speed as they entered the highway. He turned on the radio. It was the top of the second inning and the Phillies were at bat. The score stood at zero after the first inning.

Calvino sat up front with Falcon, and the Colonel was in the back, his jacket zipped up, his hands resting on his lap. Falcon looked in the rear-view mirror at Colonel Pratt.

"Your friend's sleeping," said Falcon.

Calvino looked back. "Meditating."

"Yeah, that's what the Yankees were doing in the first inning."

"It's a Zen thing."

The Russian kept driving and listening to the ball game.

The information about Josh's whereabouts had been sent by email from an anonymous proxy account dead-ended in Bombay. Falcon had tried and failed to trace the identity of the sender. He assumed it wasn't an Indian. But in his line of work, he'd learned the lesson that a man should never make an assumption. He had staked out the warehouse the previous night for long enough to confirm that Levy was inside.

"They're holding him inside a warehouse," Falcon said, cigarette hanging out of the corner of his mouth.

Smoke filled the SUV. Calvino cracked his window. The rush of cold air hit Colonel Pratt in the backseat like a slap in the forehead.

"I counted three men. They're all heeled. It looks like a professional job. They run the operation in shifts."

"Maybe they've moved him," said Colonel Pratt, leaning forward, having come out of his meditative state looking refreshed.

219

"We'll soon find out," said Falcon, shrugging, glancing at the Colonel in the rear-view mirror. "Does that Zen stuff really work?"

"Only if you let it," said Colonel Pratt with a Buddha-like smile.

Falcon's report had been good enough for Calvino and Colonel Pratt. He'd seen Josh as a brief silhouette in a window, with two men on either side of him, talking and gesturing, until one of the men pulled down the blinds. It was long enough to identify the missing Wall Street lawyer. No one said much on the drive to Port Elizabeth. The silence was filled with the baseball game play-by-play. The car interior had the lingering scent of Old Pine and spoiled tomatoes. It wasn't the kind of car that was at a high risk of theft.

The radio announcer's voice picked up. "Hideki Matsui singles for Yankees, pushing their lead to four to one."

"Those Asians can play baseball," said Falcon.

The Colonel sat in the back, thinking that's what Calvino felt like when Thais called him a *farang.*

The Buick passed through a neighborhood of small factories, auto wrecking yards, and storage depots. Finally, along the port, Falcon turned north and the street was dark. Warehouses and dark buildings passed one after another, indistinguishable in the night. Falcon tried to ease the tension by commenting on the score.

"Now we're ahead by three," he said. It was just after nine o'clock.

Neither Calvino nor Colonel Pratt said anything as they looked out the window.

Port Elizabeth smelled like saltwater and oil. It was the Third World, American-style. Not a place included on any tourist map, and the only tourist bus would have been stolen goods wheeled into some auto crushing shop for five hundred dollars cash. Tourists not included.

Falcon parked the Buick by a building where the darkness pooled. He cut the engine but left the radio on as strike three was called. Switching it off, he opened the door of the Buick and got out. Calvino and Colonel Pratt followed. They'd passed the warehouse half a block away. The street was quiet except for horns from the harbor. Calvino stretched his legs. Colonel Pratt stood on the curb, hands in his pockets, the 9mm in his right coat pocket. Falcon walked behind the Buick and opened the trunk. He reached inside and pulled out a pump-action shotgun with the barrel sawed off. He threaded the shotgun down the sleeve of his hunting jacket. Yankees cap, hunting jacket, sawed off shotgun, Russian accent—just your average Yankees fan.

"You look cold, Colonel," said Falcon.

"I'm not worried. I have a feeling I'll warm up soon enough," he said. He softly closed the Buick door. The sound of a door slamming would have echoed down the empty street.

"Let's get him out alive," said Calvino.

They walked down the opposite side of the street, the warehouse ahead of them on the right, and then crossed over and followed Falcon as he turned down an alley. Parked behind a dumpster was a white Caddy fitting the gangbangers' description of the one they'd spotted prowling outside Sammy's. The same tinted windows as they'd seen that night. Calvino leaned over, cupped his hand, and looked inside on the driver's side. The door was locked. Falcon, who had gone a few feet before he realized he'd lost his clients, backtracked.

"This looks like the car they used," said Calvino. His hand felt heat radiating off the hood. "Still feels warm. Half an hour ago or less, someone used it."

Falcon and Calvino exchanged a look, both thinking there might be some reinforcements working inside.

Falcon removed his glove and held his hand on the front grille.

"Someone could have gone out for food," said the Colonel.

The Thai point of view always came down to food, thought Calvino. But in this case the food theory made as much sense as the possibility the Caddy had been used to ferry in new recruits to stand over Josh Levy. Chances were the men who'd grabbed him were the same men who continued to hold him.

Falcon took an oilcloth out of his jacket pocket, unwrapped it, and took out a couple of lock-picking tools. Caddies are built for easy break-ins. The door popped open, and Falcon, the trained cop, took over. He checked the registration and sifted through the glove box, scooping out a handful of cards, pizza fliers, receipts, and old parking tickets. He leaned forward, unzipped his hunting jacket, revealing the butt of his .357 magnum in its shoulder holster, and unbuttoned an interior vest pocket. He stuffed the contents into the pocket and zipped up his jacket. There's a gun with stopping power, the Colonel thought. The Russian knows how to dissuade a determined man.

"We'll go through the stuff later," Falcon said. "If something happens, you let them know where to find the contents."

He climbed out of the Caddy and closed and locked the door. His right arm looked stiff; the straight, hard line of the shotgun gave it a robotic appearance. As one cop watching another, Colonel Pratt liked the professional way Falcon had organized and planned the rescue. He also felt awkward, uncertain. A hard lump had appeared in his throat, and his heart was pounding. Port Elizabeth was about as far away from his turf as he'd ever worked. Informing the consulate before setting out wouldn't have gained anything, Colonel Pratt had concluded. On the ground, walking toward the back of the warehouse, radioing for backup wasn't an option. He was alone with Vincent Calvino. Andrei had made a case that his old friend had been turned. The Colonel couldn't bring himself to believe it. In any case, there was no time for such thinking, or for reading the mind of Falcon, a foreigner who was leading them down a dark, blind alley.

More than halfway down the alley they passed a padlocked door. Falcon walked ahead another twenty feet before he stopped and dropped his cigarette on the wet pavement and ground it with the heel of his boot. Stacking two crates one on top of the other, he climbed up and stretched out to pull the fire escape ladder down to the ground.

"Follow me," he said, climbing up first.

Calvino followed with Colonel Pratt waiting until Falcon disappeared into the building. Below him in the shadows, Calvino could make out Colonel Pratt, one foot on the first step, waiting. He looked up and saw Calvino gesture for him to climb up. The rice had been cooked, the vegetables steamed, the whole trout deboned and grilled. They'd left it all behind in the apartment. He suddenly felt a pang of hunger as he entered the room where Falcon and Calvino knelt.

On the floor in front of them, Falcon held a penlight on a blueprint of the warehouse.

"We're here." He pointed to the map. "We go up one floor, then down this corridor and the second room on the left. That's the one I showed you from the street."

Falcon laid his sawed-off shotgun on the floor next to his right knee, the barrel holding down one end of the map.

"The shotgun is good to clear the room," said Calvino, as he looked at the map. "Only one thing: it can clear it too well. We want Josh out of there alive."

"I'll take that into consideration," said Falcon.

"That is the only consideration to take into account," said Calvino.

Colonel Pratt watched, wondering which man would back down first.

"Once we get inside, we'll know," said the Colonel.

"That's what I figured," said Falcon, glad for the support.

It wasn't as much as Calvino wanted, but it was as much as he was going to get. He took what he could get.

"I'll go in first," said Calvino.

Falcon shrugged, picking up the shotgun as they headed upstairs.

Outside the room where Falcon believed Josh was, light leaked from the bottom of the door. Falcon stood with his back to the wall on one side, Colonel Pratt in the same position on the other side of the door. The corridor smelled of wet concrete and mildew, like something rotting drifting up from below. They could hear the murmur of the play-by-play on the TV. They were watching the game. The announcer on the TV said that Robinson's fly to deep left had been caught by a Phillies outfielder.

Calvino had the 9mm in his hand as he stood with the light touching the top of his shoes. He heard voices inside. They were speaking Russian. He couldn't understand a word. Someone was on the phone. The TV was turned down. Another person shouted in an angry voice. Footsteps echoed on the concrete floor from inside. They came closer, as did the voice, and the door opened. Calvino raised his gun and shot the Russian who had a cell phone to his ear. He fell, the cell phone scattering into the dark corridor. Falcon rolled through the door, his .357 drawn, and dropped another man who had reached for an Uzi beside his chair.

Calvino ducked inside on the right side as the Colonel walked straight into the room, standing tall. It worked. He drew another man who had hidden behind a filing cabinet, who leaned out to take a shot. Falcon shot, as did Calvino. The man dropped face first, his skull hitting the concrete with a dull thud. Falcon stood up, the .357 in his right hand, the sawed off shotgun in his left. Stepping forward, he scanned the room. Colonel Pratt, the 9mm extended, kicked open a door to the toilet in the back of the room. It was empty.

"Josh, are there any others?"

Josh Levy sat holding a piece of hamburger pizza, his mouth open, and tomato sauce dripping from his lip, his hands untied. His shoes and socks were off, his feet tied with a rope to the chair. He could stand up. For an instant he seemed unable to move, in a state of shock. Calvino ran over and shook him.

"Is there anyone else?"

"I knew you'd come, Vinny. I just knew it."

Falcon came over to the table, holstering his .357.

"Are you okay to walk?"

Josh rocked back and forth, anger building with his motion, gathering strength and resolve. He hobbled to the side of one of the dead men, slowly reached to the floor, and picked up a 9mm Smith and Wesson. He held it with both hands but the gun shook as he squeezed off two rounds into the body. Josh dropped to his knees, sobbing, holding the handgun in his hands.

"The son of a bitch cut off my toes," he said.

"Let's go," said Falcon.

Calvino leaned down and took the Smith and Wesson from Josh. He looked down at Josh's feet. One foot was heavily bandaged and bloody.

Later, inside the Buick, Calvino told Josh there was no way they could go back and find the three missing toes that belonged to his right foot. In any event it was too late to have them stitched back on.

Colonel Pratt had got it right. The Russians had been hungry. Someone had taken the Caddy out for pizza. Their hostage with the missing toes had found that the pain had gradually faded until it was overwhelmed by hunger pangs. Three days without food. He'd been hungry enough to understand how cannibalism was the restaurant of last resort. Though he'd been glad that it hadn't come that.

SEVEN

New York City, Lower East Side—Wednesday, November 4

"The Yankees win," said Calvino.

HAVING DITCHED THE Buick in the parking lot in Port Elizabeth, Falcon arrived back at the Lower East Side with the Yankees six outs away from winning the series. He parked the SUV in front of Nero's building. Colonel Pratt and Calvino helped dismantle the weapons, bag them, and throw the bag into the harbor. Calvino helped Josh out of the SUV and Falcon drove away, figuring he'd already done more than he'd signed up for and what they decided on next wasn't anything he wanted to know about. They watched as Falcon's taillights blended into the traffic and disappeared. The main thing was they were back.

Josh rested against Calvino as the three of them hobbled into the elevator and finally through the door of the apartment, where Josh collapsed onto the living room sofa. Josh wasn't ready to head uptown to the Upper East Side and Tess Reynolds.

"You want to phone her?" asked Calvino.

Josh shook his head. "I need to pull myself together first."

"You want something to drink?"

"That would help."

Colonel Pratt came out of the kitchen with plates of rice, kale, fish, steamed carrot and tomato soup with a touch of ginger, and a mug of hot lemon and honey. They both watched as Josh devoured the food. He sat back, looking rocky, before limping to the toilet and vomiting.

"I feel better," he said, voice shaking. He was white as a ghost, sitting with his damaged foot extended.

Calvino threw a blanket over Josh and waited until he'd stopped shivering.

"You got any painkillers?"

In the upstairs bathroom Calvino found a bottle of Aspirin, then a plastic strip of paracetamol. He left the Aspirins and brought down the paracetamol just as Colonel Pratt returned from the kitchen with a glass of whiskey. He handed the tablets to Josh, who tore open the wrapper and took out several. Popping them into his mouth, he drank the whiskey and swallowed.

He groaned and shook his head. "This is all fucked up."

Soon the pills and the whiskey began to ease his pain. It was easy enough to tell. Josh had that urge to talk and the words were about to flood out.

"Can I talk to you alone?" he asked, as the Colonel returned holding a mug of tea.

"Anything you want to say, you can say in front of the Colonel. He put his ass on the line to get you out tonight."

Josh's chin dropped to his chest. His eyes closed. He hadn't thought about it that way.

Colonel Pratt grabbed his topcoat from a hook in the hallway.

"We're out of food. I'll buy some sandwiches at the deli."

"It's not necessary, Colonel."

"Josh has got to be hungry. He couldn't keep down the first food I gave him. I'd like to try again."

It was the Colonel's way of giving Josh the space he wanted. He understood that friends sometimes had things to say that they didn't want strangers to hear. But it was more than that. Colonel Pratt was signing off on a message of trust that whatever Josh Levy had to say about the gold bullets, Calvino would pass along.

After the door closed behind Colonel Pratt, Josh sat forward, head perched on his hands, staring at his mutilated foot.

"You won't be running a marathon anytime soon," said Calvino.

"It wasn't supposed to turn out this way, Vinny. You've got to believe me."

"No one can control the way things turn out."

Josh shook his head. "You killed those men."

"Things didn't turn out the way they thought, either."

Josh had that look that Calvino remembered as a boy. He had something he wanted to get off his chest. He took a deep breath and licked his lips.

"Are the Yankees still ahead?" asked Josh. "I promised to take you to this game."

Calvino turned on the TV in time to see Shane Victorino ground out.

"The Yankees win," said Calvino.

Josh winced. "That's good, Vinny."

"Now are you going to tell me what this is about?"

Josh nodded and drank his whiskey. "You're right. There are some blanks that I need to fill in. It happened like this . . ."

Part 4

A Big League Deal: Grand Slam Home Run

ONE

"I love a man who's sure about himself, Josh."

ON FRIDAY JOSH returned from Bangkok. Saturday afternoon he drove to East Hampton. Tess waited for him at the beach house they had rented for the summer. Though he'd been on the road for more than two weeks, he planned to make it up to her. But he told himself that was the life of a major league player. There were home games and away games. He'd been signed on to play a series of away games. He couldn't wait to tell her about his signing bonus and his contract. He felt good about the arrangements. It was working out just as Andrei had said it would.

When he arrived at the beach house, Tess had a drink waiting for him. She was alone. Ingram, who designed software, his wife, Williams, a member of Josh's old law firm, and his partner had gone into the village for a late lunch. Their absence was a gift to Josh and Tess; they'd left behind some cocaine and were giving them a little space after a couple of weeks apart.

The Bangkok heat trailed behind Josh following him to the Hamptons. What he wanted was a cold beer. What he got once inside was a cold beer and two lines of coke laid out on the coffee table along with a tightly rolled-up hundred-dollar bill.

"You look good," he said.

"You first," she said, handing him the rolled-up bill.

"Ingram says applications he designs have to work like coke. Make people want it day after day because it makes them feel they can't live without it."

That was Ingram creating addiction in the digital world. Enslaving anyone with a keyboard and an Internet connection. He was giving the dealers in Colombia a run for their money. Ingram, like Williams, was on his list for the bachelor party at Sammy's.

Josh ran the bill a hair above the glass table, sucking up the line of coke. When he finished, he wiped his nose with the back of his hand, shivered, and handed the rolled hundred to Tess, who halfway down the line changed nostrils to finish the last half.

She smacked her lips. "Good," she said.

"Good to be back," he said. "Good to be bad."

He sipped beer straight from the bottle, letting her undress him and lead him into the shower.

The coke paved a highway of alertness above his jet-lagged brain.

"You must be tired," she said, as they stood hugging under the showerhead.

"I feeling high on you," he sang, mangling the lyrics to Survivor's song.

He closed his eyes and felt the water running down his neck and back as he stood with his arms wrapped around her waist.

"Vinny agreed to be my best man," he said.

"What was it like after all those years to see him?"

"We picked up right where we'd left off. It was as if we'd seen each other the week before."

She soaped his chest. "Last night you said that you had some important news. That was about Vinny, right?"

He shook his head, laughed, feeling giddy from the coke.

234

"I cut a deal with Andrei in Tajikistan."

"Let's do one more line. Then I want to hear everything," she said.

Tess slipped out of the shower first, dried her hair, fresh and clean, and walked to the living room. She took out her stash and razor blade and cut two more white lines on the glass coffee table. She looked up and saw Josh wearing a towel. He leaned forward, pulled by the neat lines. She slung her arms around his neck and kissed him, handing him the hundred dollar bill.

"You go first," she said.

They had fallen in love inside this beach house—walking along the beach, doing a couple of lines, making love, listening to music, and making meals together. It had cost a fortune to rent for the season. Ingram had talked about buying the house once he cashed out his share options in a startup company, but that wouldn't happen for at least another eighteen months. The possibility of buying the house was in the air and in the minds of everyone who rented it. Ingram had said he wanted the house, but Tess had hinted that Josh was also thinking of buying it. She'd thrown it out one night after everyone was loaded. People around the table smiled and nodded, their faces happy from the blow.

"I had this thought," she had said later, in private. "If we made one of the upstairs rooms into a good office, you wouldn't need to go into the city."

He had already made an inquiry, and the asking price was four million. Josh had the feeling that the owner would take three and half in cash.

"With a house like this," he'd said, "I'd have to bill twelve hours a day, and even then Ingram would buy it first."

"Or you could find a different job," she'd said, as if that could easily be done.

Those had been the magic words. Competition with Ingram over who could pay for the house first was only the start. Tess had thrown the gasoline of a job change onto the flame.

The East Hampton beach house required a lot of up-front cash.

His thoughts fogged from the coke and the jet lag, Josh laid his head back on a cushion and put up his feet.

"I've found a new job," he said, as she curled up against him on the sofa.

"Which law firm?" she asked, kissing his chest. She figured a headhunter had finally come up with a lateral move to another law firm.

"Not a law firm. Inside counsel for an existing client."

"Andrei."

He nodded. "I did the numbers on his latest project. The profit margin works out around sixteen percent. That's a conservative estimate."

"Good for Andrei, but does that help us?"

Josh casually said to Tess, "What is a sixteen percent return on ten mil?"

"Bernie Madoff." The coke had relaxed her. The name made her giggle.

He laughed. "Oil is back. Exploration is in full shit-kicking gear. Extraction is galloping close behind. This is a time to make real money. When you do business in risky places, and the market is rising, you can make this rate of return. Plus Andrei's super-smart, connected, and rich."

She raised her head from his chest. Her mind was racing in the lane right next to his. The coke had kicked their thoughts into overdrive. Her wet hair brushed against his shoulder. It was as if she'd touched him with electricity. If only he could hold that moment.

But the moment passed the instant she replied with a question of doubt.

"Isn't that exactly what Madoff used to say?"

He was slightly wounded. Josh had expected, not a challenge, but a reaction of wonder and glee. His eyes performed a Blue Angels' breaking formation roll as if to say, forget about it.

"Did I hurt your feelings?" she asked.

He smiled. "It's the jet lag. The inner clock on my feelings is out of whack."

"Does that include your feelings about me?"

"No," he said, but he didn't sound convincing, even to himself. He'd expected encouragement, support, some minor cheerleading. Instead he'd gotten questions and Bernie Madoff thrown at him like eggs from an Elizabethan audience in a punishing mood.

She took his answer as a signal to go upstairs and change into a red bikini. "High on You" blasted from the speakers as Josh sat alone on the sofa.

"I can't stop thinking about you girl," Josh sang along with the lyrics.

A couple of minutes later she came down and slid open the glass door.

"I want to walk on the beach."

"Good idea."

"Join me before the night kicks in."

He was hooked, high on her.

"I'm feeling good."

"Me too."

He put on swimming trunks and followed her out of the house and over the dunes to the beach. It was hot outside, though a breeze came off the sea. She grabbed his hand, the waves washing over her feet. She turned and looked back at the beach house in the distance.

"Isn't it beautiful?"

"Ingram is going to be so pissed off," he said.

She leaned forward and kissed him. "What are you saying?"

"I'm going to buy it."

She pulled the towel up and around her breasts. "You'll have to rob a bank."

"Tess, I've gone to work for Andrei. He'll advance the purchase price."

She stopped, withdrew her hand from his, reached down to pick up a small stone, and threw it in the sea. They both watched as the stone made a small ripple and disappeared.

"He'll do that?"

Looking out at the water, he drew in the sea air and smiled.

"He'll do it. I had to make a decision in Tajikistan. I wanted to surprise you."

"Oh my God, you're serious."

"Wait, there's more. Andrei guarantees three million a year. And ten million dollars of shares. At the end of three years, I can sell the shares at market. They could be worth fifty million by then."

Tess's eyes, dilated from the coke, looked like pinpoints in the afternoon sun. She looked at Josh, then at the beach house.

"This is for real?"

"For real," said Josh.

"You're right about Ingram being pissed off. I can't wait to see his face tonight when you tell him."

"I can't tonight."

Her face clouded. "Why not? I want him to meet his new landlord. I want to see his face."

"I can't tonight because of Williams. I haven't given the firm my resignation letter."

"When are you submitting it?"

"Monday."

Monday seemed to her an infinite time away from Saturday afternoon on the beach. She faced the sea, arms folded around her waist, as if trying to decide what she wanted.

"It seems too good to be true," she said.

She searched his eyes waiting for an answer.

"Ten million worth of shares and three million a year. It's true."

"Guaranteed?"

He nodded, breaking into a smile, putting his arm around her waist.

"In writing."

"But you love the law firm. You said so yourself."

"The firm's executive committee is breathing down everyone's neck. I get daily memos about cutbacks, expenses, secretarial help, limos... And I've seen other partners make that silent walk into the chairman's office for that George Clooney moment where they are told this is a chance to start a new life. I don't want that to be me."

The rationalization didn't wash with her. She knew he wouldn't be one of those frog-marched out of the building with their possessions in a cardboard box.

"They'd never lay you off, Josh. You're a star."

"Stars burn out. It happened to our beach house owner."

"Hepford was never in your league. He inherited this house. Otherwise, forget about it. He'd never own a place like this."

"Hepford needs to raise money."

Hepford, their landlord, like other partners in big law firms, had been laid off. He'd joined the ranks of ex-lawyers who sat in their Long Island or Jersey houses with nothing to do, no income, no friends, no prospects of working again, holed up like P.G. Wodehouse without the talent to

239

write down a single coherent sentence about life that didn't reduce them to tears.

"What do you say, Tess?"

Her smile said it.

"You're sure you really want do to this?" she asked.

"I'm sure."

She thought about it as they turned and walked back toward the house.

"I love a man who's sure about himself, Josh."

TWO

"Maxim asked me, 'What do you know about coins?' "

"BEFORE I LEFT Tajikistan," Josh told Calvino, "Andrei told me to be careful with Maxim. I asked him why, and he said he didn't completely trust him. 'No Russian trusts another Russian completely. Sixty percent is okay,' he said.

"How did he come up with sixty percent? It was crazy, like he'd pulled it out of his ass. He wasn't smiling, and I had this weird moment, thinking this is insane or he's testing me. His warning had started to make me paranoid.

"He was sending me to Bangkok because that forty percent possibility required coverage. I'd gotten the tap. I tried to say I had to be back in New York on firm business, but Andrei wasn't finished. He kept on drinking and talking. I told him I didn't want to get in the middle of anything between him and Maxim. He said, 'You're already in the middle of things. That's why I am buying you for three million a year and advancing the cash for your house.'

"Yeah, I wanted that house so bad that I was willing to get in the middle of a herd of elephants. I thought he might be joking, so I asked him, 'In the middle of what?'

"Andrei is a big bear of man, fit like a Navy SEAL. He'd been butting heads with Maxim in Tajikistan over some deal. Several times, when I'd presented paperwork to them, they'd moved into a corner of the room for intense

241

private conversations. Andrei now smiled and reminded me of those private meetings. And it came down to a simple power relationship equation: I was the force that allowed Andrei to act at a distance on Maxim. I allowed him to rotate Maxim as if I were a lever. I wasn't anything more than a mechanical device between a couple of Russians in competition for power and calling it business. Andrei needed me for equilibrium in a basically unstable relationship.

"That's when I got scared. I started to have second thoughts about working for Andrei unless I got some upfront assurances. Before I could say anything, what does Andrei say? He says he wants me to extract a couple of promises from Maxim and oversee a private transaction the two of them were doing on the side.

" 'What kind of promises?' I asked him. 'What kind of transaction? Not drugs, I hope.'

"And Andrei said, 'No I don't ever deal in narcotics. Don't worry, counselor, I am not asking you to break any law. I want Maxim's people in Moscow to keep their hands off my business in Thailand.'

"I asked what kind of business he was talking about.

"He shrugged, gave one of those long, deadly stares, like a man coming back from a shooting range where they use live targets. I told him that I'd come to talk about the transportation contract.

"Andrei smiled. 'You don't understand much, do you?'

" 'My job is to understand the documents,' I said.

"Andrei told me, 'Stalin buried men and then made up all the documents he needed. That's a Russian contract. Paper. Burn it, bury it, shit or spit on it. What matters is the man behind it, his real plans and intentions. The rest is just like a show trial. It's for others, not the players.'

"I hadn't resigned from the firm. I could still back out. I discussed my options with Ben Harris over a phone call. He was at the beach house. I told him to keep it confidential and not even say anything to Tess. I wanted to break the news to her myself. Ben told me to go easy. Think it over. What was the rush? Had I nailed down the details with Andrei? I didn't want to tell him about buying the house. There wasn't a lot of time. Hepford would sell it at three and half million. But Ben was right about one thing—I needed to lock down with Andrei the timing of the delivery of the share transfers, certificates, and the option on the second lot of shares. Ben's a tax guy, and he asked all of the right questions, and I was going, 'Shit, I left some of those details to be worked out.'

"'What have you got for leverage?' Ben asked. I said, 'He needs me.' Even as I said it, I thought to myself, 'What the fuck am I saying?'

"I didn't put on the brakes. I was in glide mode. The forward momentum took me to Bangkok. The first time I met Maxim on his yacht, I saw from his setup how he mixed business with pleasure. He had a small arsenal on that boat, plus champagne, women, a crew that have gone to special forces school in some of those tough-ass countries.

"Maxim asked me, 'What do you know about coins?'

"I thought, here it comes, the Russian twenty questions game. 'Something that interests sweet old ladies and young boys.'

"'Andrei collects coins.'

"I'm watching him with a Thai girl on each arm. Wearing bikinis, massaging his neck and arms. 'There's an exception to every rule,' I told him.

"'There are no rules, only exceptions,' he said, bowing his head as a set of the longest fingers kneaded the flesh on his neck. 'These Thai gold bullet coins, for instance.'

He possessed the same sour, resigned Russian vagueness as Andrei, but his showed, while Andrei kept his hidden under a polished, scholarly veneer.

" 'Insurance is not difficult to buy for the right price,' he said. 'You name the amount and the beneficiaries, and when the shit flies, you have money to take a shower.'

"I underestimated Maxim when I met him in Tajikistan. I pegged him as a wannabe bluffing a weak hand for a better deal with Andrei. I thought I'd seen hustlers like him before. Self-made businessmen with money and power but no firm grasp on reality. Guys used to getting what they want and being in control, surrounded by hangers-on telling them how great they are.

"You tolerate such assholes because the client needs something this guy has to offer. Maxim came into the room looking like another round Russian face with a three-day stubble, sitting around the table, looking tough. Not necessarily stupid but more like a hungry and cunning animal. Maxim and Andrei had their private deal in place before I arrived in Bangkok. It didn't matter that he lost at the auction; he found a way to get the coins. I should have told you before. I should have told you a lot of things before. Mostly I should have listened and left the coins in Thailand and returned to New York without them. Let Andrei make his arrangements directly with Maxim. I kept hearing this little voice in my head. It said, 'Get out of the middle.' But I wasn't listening. I was more worried about closing a deal on the beach house.

"I thought Maxim would flip out when I said I had second thoughts about taking the coins back to New York. He surprised me. He was cool about it and said, 'That's something to think about.' At the airport Maxim was all business, handing over the special set of gold bullets and telling me I had no choice but to take them back. The way he said it made it clear. I had no option. I'd have a big problem. He asked me to give him the other set, the one you saw him deliver at the hotel. I gave it to him. I asked what he was going to do with it. He said he would mail it to you, and when you came for the wedding, you would bring it along. He didn't say anything about switching the coins between the sets. I don't know why he did it. It might have been that forty percent risk of a double cross, or maybe it was an insurance policy against Andrei double-crossing him. Fuck if I know. The fact that what happened in Bangkok put you and me in the shit, Maxim didn't care about. It was just doing business the Russian way. You've got to believe me, Vinny. I thought I had the whole set when I landed in New York.

"I told Tess, 'Baby, look at these gold bullets.' And she said, looking up with a funny look on her face, 'What kind of gun do these go in?'

" 'Baby,' I said, 'these go into a cannon.' "

Josh winced from the pain. To tell the truth, Josh looked like he'd emerged from a tour through hell. The realization of not ever getting back to where he started along with the physical pain of his injuries exploded, turning his face into a frightening mask of resignation and fear. He'd looked better, more human, in his werewolf mask. His captors had cut off several toes. The bandages on Josh's right foot were bloodied.

Josh had been talking non-stop for an hour when the phone rang. Calvino picked it up. He heard Colonel Pratt's voice on the other end, and the horns blaring and people shouting as they celebrated the Yankees' World Series win.

"He's not in great shape," said Calvino.

"How's the foot?"

"He needs to see a doctor."

What Colonel Pratt really wanted to know was whether he could come back and put a few questions of his own to Josh. It was a fair request. They spoke in Thai over the phone. Calvino watched Josh on the sofa, moaning for drugs to kill the pain.

"They held me down and one of them cut off my toes," Josh said, a loud wet sob bleeding through his voice.

"I'm going to take you to the hospital," said Calvino, letting the Colonel on the other end of the phone hear.

"They're going to ask all kinds of questions," Josh said. "I don't want that. The hospital will get the cops involved. Maybe trace things back to New Jersey. Then what happens?"

Calvino didn't answer and went back to speaking Thai to Colonel Pratt.

"I need a little more time. It isn't a good idea to interrupt a man in the middle of a confession."

By the time he put away his cell phone, Calvino knew what the Colonel wanted to ask Josh.

"What happened to Wirot?"

"Who?"

"The Thai with the winning bid at auction."

Josh threw back more tablets, swallowed whiskey, and shuddered. "No fucking idea. You wouldn't happen to have some coke?"

"Fresh out," said Calvino.

Josh's face pale and gaunt looked haunted.

"Did Maxim say anything about Wirot?" Calvino asked him.

Josh was unable to say anything more and broke down, face buried in his hands. Pain and exhaustion crashed down and rolled Josh down the side of an emotional mountain.

"When you got the coins, I wanted you to think, 'Josh is some kind of hero.' I really fucking thought that. Am I total shit? Maxim knew I'd asked you to be my best man. He used that knowledge. In his mind you became part of his way of dealing with Andrei. Send them to Calvino for safekeeping. That way he knew where they'd be, no cops could find them on his yacht or in his house or on his men. But when he needed the coins, he'd find a way to get them from you one way or another. I told him it was a crazy idea. That's why he liked it, he said. It was crazy enough to work. It all came apart in New York after I got back. Andrei went nuts once Maxim told him that I'd switched some of the coins."

"Classic double-cross," said Calvino.

"Nothing classic about it. But I no longer gave a shit about Maxim. I told Andrei what Maxim had done. Of course Maxim denied it. Meanwhile, I've got the coins I brought back and have no clue what to do. I'm in the middle of something. What do I do?"

"Who hired those Russians at the warehouse?"

Josh drank more whiskey. "Andrei thought my kidnapping would get you to turn them over if you had them. I thought he was a joking. He was serious. At first I went along with it. God, I wanted that beach house. I couldn't see beyond it. And I thought that you'd give up the coins. Fuck, man, you didn't. And what could I say—I know that you're holding out? I was the hero who sent them to you, right? Now I want them back because something valuable got mixed up in what I sent?"

"You're saying they worked for Andrei?"

"Exactly. Or so I thought at first. They had to be Andrei's men. It was his idea. But now I don't know. I'm confused. Maxim could have been involved. The two of them could have worked it out together. I don't think I'll ever know, Vinny," Josh said. "All I know is that I'm glad you came when you did. They would have killed me."

"You're not telling me something, Josh. Where are the coins you brought back from Thailand? You handed them over to Andrei, right?"

Josh looked up, wiping his nose with the back of his hand. "You're fucking joking, right? It was the only leverage I had. I'm in the middle of these two guys."

"Where are they?"

Josh's lips tightened, teeth biting the bottom lip.

"You gotta tell me, Josh."

"Or you'll do what? Cut off more toes?" He tried to laugh but only choked on his own bitter joke.

Calvino poured more whiskey into Josh's glass. "You wanted to be a hero like in the old days."

"Not much of a hero, am I?"

Calvino's law—a man who thinks of himself as a hero isn't one.

"Maxim talked about insurance. The coins were your policy," said Calvino.

Josh shrugged and sat back, eyes closed, glass in one hand. "Tess could be part Russian. That first Sunday night after I returned from Bangkok, we talked in the car on the way from East Hampton to Manhattan. I told her I planned to give the coins to Andrei on Monday. Like Maxim, she didn't trust Andrei to come through with the transfer of the money for the beach house. She wanted that house as bad as I did. 'Those documents wouldn't take more than an hour of paperwork,' she said. And she was right. I knew that she was right. So then she said, 'Here's what *we* do. We hold on to the coins. Lock them in the safe. I have one of those built-in safes in the bedroom where I keep papers, some cash, and jewelry. Phone Andrei and tell him that after the paperwork is done, you'll come around with the coins. Make an exchange. Next I would give the firm my letter of resignation.' She'd thought it out. Step by step. You know what my first reaction was?"

Calvino watched the anxiety slowly build as he refilled Josh's glass. The whiskey hadn't slowed him down. His leg propped up on the table looked like the limb of someone who'd come out of a combat zone.

"That she was brilliant," said Josh. "The worst of all worlds was resigning and then finding out that Andrei had decided not to go through with my deal. Where would

I be? Totally fucked. Then I started to think it through. Andrei would see it as blackmail. And he'd have a point. The other thing that bothered me was Tess's secret safe. She'd never mentioned it before. I thought, why hadn't she told me about it? When I asked her, she said, 'Why didn't you tell me about the woman in Bangkok?' I didn't want to go through that again. So I left it.

"She sat on the bed and watched me phone Andrei. He hated the idea. He said it was a provocation. One of those English words that Russians learn before learning to ask where the toilet is. He said what I proposed was hostile. I said, 'Hold on, Andrei, it's only fair.' And he said, 'You work for me. You don't dictate to me terms and talk about what is fair.' We went around and around for ten minutes, and then he says, 'How do I know what you've brought back is the gold bullet set?' I didn't know one coin from another, and he knew it. I thought, 'Yeah, he's got a point.' Then Andrei says, 'Scan each one and give me the scans.' I'd never heard of scanning coins. He explained it. I said okay. I did what he asked.

"Everything seemed set until he phoned and started screaming that I'd fucked up everything. I had no idea what he was talking about. Three of the bullet coins had been switched."

"Maxim," said Calvino.

"Insurance time. Maxim must have switched three of the valuable set with three of the others and mailed them to you. What was I going to say—'Maxim and I are in the insurance business, and those three coins are our ace in the hole?' The point was, Andrei knew that kind of double-cross was something only Maxim would think of pulling off. Me? I settled for blackmailing with nine coins that looked like, well, nine gold coins.

"Andrei hit back. I don't know who he phoned, but it must have been someone working in intelligence. Next thing I know, Thai cops and army have grabbed one of Maxim's planes in Bangkok, arrested the crew, and opened up crates of weapons that God knows what group of criminals or terrorists were buying from him. The Thais came down on Maxim hard, and he felt the heat. Suddenly his money wasn't quite the wall of protection he'd thought it was. He bluffed Andrei into believing that you and I had done the switch. He negotiated a better commission on his transportation contract with Andrei at the same time. That's the way Russians do business. He told Andrei that you'd have the three bullets when you came for the wedding.

"Now Andrei is outraged. I'm not only holding out on delivering the set I promised, I'd fucked with them and involved someone from the outside in a double-cross. Tess and I were caught in the middle of this nightmare. All I wanted to do was go back to my office at the firm and close the door and pretend none of this ever happened. I had no idea what to do or who to turn to. I was lost. Andrei kept saying he was going to have to do something drastic. I was frustrated and joked, 'Let's fake my kidnapping. Make the ransom the coins. He'll hand them over, I'll give you back what I brought, and let's call it square, okay?'

"I put down the phone and told Tess what Andrei had said. And she said, 'I think you should call the police.' And I told her not to be crazy, that the police were the last people I wanted to talk to about any of this. You didn't need to practice criminal law to know that even with a plea bargain, I'd be looking at serious time. 'No,' I said, 'I need to get Andrei off my back. That's the end of it.'

"I can't tell you how many times I wanted to tell you the whole thing. Should've, could've, might've... they all rolled through my head. The world of dones and almost dones. But I wanted to limit my exposure. I thought they'd run the private investigator you hired around in circles. I was glad the guy was Russian. I thought that he'd tell you to hand over what they wanted, that he'd tell you what such men are capable of.

"Tess kept repeating how I had a right to the money for the beach house. I said it didn't matter. Then she said, 'Do you really think that you can go back to the firm after this has happened? Think it through, Josh.' I phoned Andrei back and told him that instead of the share transfers, I'd sign them over to him, and what I wanted was the cash. Funny thing was, he didn't sound surprised. I said I'd get him an offshore account number for the transfer. Once I'd confirmed the transfer online, he'd have the coins. And you know what? I still have no idea why those coins are so fucking important. There's not enough gold to make a gangbanger's gold chain. I don't get it."

That's what had made it work, thought Calvino. Josh Levy would have no clue as to the importance of the coins. Andrei had recruited the perfect courier—a corporate lawyer who had volunteered to cross over to his side for the money. His knowledge of the game in play was limited. All Josh saw was the new life, the shares, the income, the beach house in the Hamptons, and Tess gliding around like an angel darting between her friends on Twitter and Facebook.

"The Thais want the coins."

"What should I do, Vinny?"

"Give the coins to Colonel Pratt."

"Can't." He tore the last paracetamol from the plastic and ate it. "Got anything stronger?"

Calvino ignored the plea. Pain made a man more truthful. That's why it was so highly valued by those searching for information.

"It's the right thing. Colonel Pratt has taken a major hit because of this. I've got my own problems as well. Everyone who's touched the coin set has suffered. It's time to stop and do the right thing."

"I can't give the Colonel the coins. It's not a hand I can play."

"Pull them out of the safe. I'll go with you. Give them to me. Tess and you can clear out of town for a month or two. Don't go to the Hamptons."

Josh's grim smile slashed across his face. "I can't do it."

Calvino held out his cell phone. "Call Tess and tell her we're coming over for the coins."

Josh stared at the phone, folded his hands behind his head, and leaned back.

"There's something else. You won't want to hear it."

Calvino placed the phone on the table. He looked at Josh, wondering what else he'd been holding back.

"Try me," said Calvino.

"Tess was fried after the phone call from Dew. She goes batshit, saying I'd promised her the beach house, and she's thinking everything is perfect. Then Dew phones and all I hear is that I'd been sleeping with a whore in Bangkok. Tess says I'm unpredictable. And she doesn't know if she can trust me. Half of the money from Andrei is hers. That's what she says. I dragged her into this mess. She's in trouble, disappointed, and otherwise fucked up about Dew. In her mind she's entitled. Her word, 'entitled.'"

"You've got the combination to the safe?"

"What do you think?"

"You want me to talk to her?"

Josh tilted his head, swallowed more whiskey. "It won't do any good. She blames you for hooking me up with Dew. She says you're a pimp. No way she wants you to be my best man. She said a woman understands men, and now she understands you."

It didn't take a genius to understand that Josh had thrown Calvino under the infidelity bus at the first opportunity. Calvino had the picture—he was the one who'd corrupted Josh, led him down the path of temptation.

As Josh moaned on Nero's sofa on the Lower East Side, Calvino stared at him, thinking no one would have mistaken Josh for a highly paid corporate lawyer. Take him out of the office, away from his papers, and put him in the street with people who understand the flow chart of violence, life in the back alleys, and life on yachts like the *Last Money*, and Josh was lost. Josh had been right about one thing—he had no hand to play. He'd never had a hand to play except in his deluded mind.

"You've run out of options," said Calvino.

"Is that supposed to be a pun?"

Calvino picked up his phone. "I'm phoning the Colonel. He'll want to hear this."

The reaction from Josh was immediate and intense. "No fucking way I'm talking to anyone else. Not tonight. Not until I get it straightened out with Tess."

He lifted himself off the sofa, balanced himself on his good foot, and hobbled to the coat rack.

"Where the fuck do you think you're going?"

"Home."

"Where's that, Josh?"

Josh put one arm through a sleeve of his jacket and struggled to thread his other arm through the other sleeve. He was framed in the doorway, his weight off the injured foot.

"Thanks for getting me out of there tonight. When I got in that Caddy outside Sammy's that night, we were two, three blocks away and I said to the guy driving, 'This is fucking nuts. Take me back. I don't want to do this.' And I saw his eyes in the rear-view mirror. Hard, mean fucking eyes. You know what he said? Nothing."

Nothing had worked out according to plan. Calvino cracked a smile looking at his busted up friend. "It was your idea to hire the zombie woman at Sammy's," said Calvino.

Josh bit his lip, looking thoughtful. "She acted as a diversion."

"You fooled me."

"I didn't have a lot of choice, Vinny," he said, heading to the door "Phone you tomorrow."

"Nero knows a doctor. I can send him around."

"Thanks, Vinny. I'll get back to you on that."

Calvino stood next to him as Josh opened the door looking like a perfect match for the zombie who had barfed the vodka at Sammy's.

"Andrei's gonna know you've been busted out. Men like him have a large reserve of people to call on. Just so you know."

"He's not going to do anything."

"Yeah?"

"Because I'm going to give him what he wants."

"I never got the coins, Josh."

"You're lying."

"I know that. You know that. But Andrei doesn't."

"You won't help me out?

"Let me go with you. I'll get Falcon to come around and some men. Throw up some protection. Get Tess to open the safe. Then . . ."

"Then what, Vinny?"

"There is no then, then. You know it. I know it."

Part 5

Deal Breaker

ONE

"He's running," said Colonel Pratt, slipping on his jacket. "Before he goes, I want to talk to him. I think he owes me that much."

CALVINO STARTED PHONING Josh at eight on Thursday morning. The phone rang, but Josh didn't pick up. At nine o'clock Colonel Pratt said, "We should go around to the apartment."

Just then Josh answered the phone. "It's not a good time," he said. Tess screamed at him in the background, calling him a coward, a prick, and a bastard. Judging from the sound of her voice, she was just warming up, getting to the part of her vocabulary that had seen her through her last divorce. Calvino held the phone away from his ear. The Colonel nodded. No further explanation was necessary. Josh had gone from the hands of Russian kidnappers into the hands of one very unhappy woman.

"I talked with Nero, and no problem about a doctor," said Calvino.

"This afternoon. I've got to get my story straight."

"This doctor isn't gonna ask any questions."

"I'm not talking about the doctor."

"Who are you talking about?" asked Calvino.

Over the phone Calvino heard the doorbell in the background.

"I'll get back to you this afternoon. I've got someone at the door."

It'll take more than a month of afternoons before Josh gets his story straight, thought Calvino.

"I'll phone Nero," said Calvino.

Josh had hung up without answering. Calvino continued to hold the phone against his ear, smiling. He thought how Josh must have looked wearing a werewolf mask, stepping in the back of the white Caddy, believing, at each stage, he remained in control. As if at any time, all he had to do was make that T sign with his hands, the way he did as a kid. Time out. But with the Russians, history marched forward relentlessly, and no one ever got a time out. In some corners of the world, kidnappings, like executions, aren't faked. With the Russian brand, as Josh should have known, such things can be reliably counted on as the real McCoy.

Colonel Pratt removed his coat from one of the pegs on the corridor wall and started to put it on.

"*Hiew khow*," he said.

It literally meant hungry for rice. It was the Thai way of saying it was time to eat.

A light snow fell as they walked along Saint Marks. The shops were still closed and gated. Large black garbage bags were piled at the curb. Empty of people, the desolate street was turning white under their feet. They walked into a restaurant on Second Avenue and ordered breakfast. Calvino went over Josh's story from the previous night and the Colonel listened.

After Calvino had finished ordering eggs, bacon, toast, and coffee, Colonel Pratt said, "Steamed rice and green curry."

The waiter said, "Never had anyone order green curry for breakfast before. I'll have to check with the cook."

"You eat what you're used to eating. That's not hard to understand, is it?" asked Calvino.

"It's easy to understand. Just hard to know if the cook will make it at breakfast time."

The Colonel put down the menu. "Change my order. I'll have the same as my friend."

The waiter walked away shaking his head, putting the pen behind his ear.

"*Jai yen*," said Colonel Pratt, suggesting to Calvino in Thai to chill out. "Phone Falcon and send him around to make certain Josh is all right. Have your cousin send his doctor around this afternoon. His foot needs medical attention or he'll lose it.

Calvino had one of those "Why didn't I think of that?" moments of self-loathing. "Falcon said in the car it was better if we weren't seen together for a week or so. Just in case someone might have seen us together. They'd be looking for four men, one of whom was a cripple."

"No one saw us. Everyone was glued to the TV watching the game."

"You can't ever be certain."

The waiter set Calvino's plate of eggs and bacon on the table and walked away.

"They won't be looking for two men with one of them limping."

Calvino said, looking at his food, "Can I get some more coffee over here? And hey, have you gone to Jersey for my friend's breakfast?"

Calvino sat up straight and shrugged his shoulders. "Where was I? Yeah, I was talking about why the department was going to promote you. You know all of this shit backwards and forwards, and Shakespeare, and Herbie Hancock."

"The big bosses have their own way of counting," said Colonel Pratt.

The waiter came with a bowl of rice and green curry and a smug grin.

"Green curry," he said.

Colonel Pratt sniffed at the bowl, an eyebrow raised. "From a can?"

"Get out of here," Calvino said. "Green curry in a can?"

Calvino smelled the bowl.

"Campbell's soup. You think we're fucking tourists?"

The waiter picked up the bowl, lowered his nose, raised his nose, lowered it one more time and turned to the Colonel.

"Try more pepper," said the waiter.

Calvino's cell phone rang, and the waiter took the interruption as a good excuse to slip away from the table, carrying away the bowl of green curry on a tray.

"Falcon," said Calvino, winking at the Colonel. "I'm sitting next to Colonel Pratt, and we're thinking it'd be a good idea if you went uptown and checked on Josh. You got the address? Sorry, didn't hear that. Yeah, what's that supposed to mean?"

He turned, looking at the Colonel.

Closing his phone, Calvino shrugged his shoulders. "He's already been around to see Josh."

"What's going on?" asked Colonel Pratt.

"He said Josh was throwing shirts into a suitcase. Tess was sitting on the bed, crying."

It didn't sound like they were going on a honeymoon.

"Where's he going?" asked Colonel Pratt.

"He wouldn't tell Falcon. Someplace safe. Once he's arrived, he'll phone."

"He's scared."

"Not an unreasonable response."

"Did Falcon ask him about the Rama V collection?"

It had all come down to the nine bullets. Colonel Pratt wanted them. Major Tinakorn and a battalion of Thai brass waited to hear that the coins had been found and were on their way back to Thailand. A committee would have been formed to plan the welcoming ceremony, thought Colonel Pratt. They'd be deciding who would be in the front, second, and third rows, and who would be at the center of the photo.

Calvino started again, as the Colonel's attention drifted off: "Josh said that he wanted to get out of town for a few days. Clear his head. He said he wasn't doing anything for anybody until he got some space to think. He said everyone was telling him to do this, do that, and it was time he reclaimed some control in his life. He needs to figure out what he should do."

"He's running," said Colonel Pratt, slipping on his jacket. "Before he goes, I want to talk to him. I think he owes me that much."

Calvino was no longer hungry.

He phoned Nero. "Cancel the doctor. I'll tell you about it later. Thanks, Nero."

He closed his phone and called for the bill.

"We're out of here," he said to the Colonel, who was already on his feet.

The Russians who held Josh hadn't treated him with tender loving care. When his rescuers had busted in, Josh was a slice of pizza away from losing more toes. The Colonel was right, thought Calvino; Josh was running away from a string of unpaid debts—one of them owed to Falcon, the Colonel, and himself. It was a question of priorities. No man redeems a personal debt before first settling up with the three men who got him out of a hostage situation alive. And nearly got him out in one piece.

Outside the restaurant Calvino stopped the Colonel. "You haven't eaten."

"After I talk to Josh."

A taxi pulled to the curb. Colonel Pratt climbed in the back and slid over to the far window. Calvino got in, closed the door, and gave the driver Tess Reynolds's apartment address at East 81st and Second.

The doorman wore a North Korean general's hat tipped forward on his head. He recognized Calvino from a couple of days before. As he opened the door to Calvino and Colonel Pratt, he raised three fingers and touched the bill of his hat in a salute. With the man's gecko eyes, Calvino half-expected him to flick his tongue to test the air.

Colonel Pratt removed his gloves and unwrapped a long brown scarf from around his neck. He looked cold. The wind from outside blew in as people came and went. Calvino turned down the collar on his leather jacket and looked around the lobby. The narrow space was crammed with uniforms—emergency services, cops, and forensics, all of them talking at the same time, sometimes to each other, sometimes into their phones; others waited, one foot against the wall, arms folded; others shook hands, shook heads, and shook the snow off their boots as they walked in from outside. The doorman looked cold as he closed the door. He had worked more in one shift than a normal week.

"What's going on here?" asked Calvino.

A detective an elbow away turned around and asked, "Remind me, who are you two again?"

"Friends of Josh and Tess," said Calvino, the Colonel nodding.

"Is that right? Friends? That's good. I've got a few things to ask you about."

The tone of the detective's voice said these things were going to be bad. Cops on duty never came up to talk to someone unless they wanted something. None of the cops in the lobby looked like they were soliciting for charity.

"You'd be Calvino, and you'd be the Thai police colonel," he said, as if he'd been expecting them.

The Colonel nodded at the detective and exchanged a look with Calvino, the look of a man who's cracked his adversary's coded number.

Josh was in the sitting room, face down on the floor, a .22-caliber five-shot revolver clutched in his right hand. A black carry-on roller, locked and ready, was pushed against a chair. A copy of *Time Magazine*, creased and folded, lay on top.

"That your friend?" asked the cop who had taken the lift to the second floor with them and escorted them into the apartment. The cop looked at Calvino and then the Colonel.

Both nodded as the cop scratched the side of his cheek. "Can you be a little more specific? Give me his name. How you know him, when you saw him last, and any reason why he might have killed his girlfriend before killing himself."

A forensics expert walked out of the bedroom, shutting the door behind her.

"We're pretty much finished up," she said to the cop. "You can bag the bodies any time."

"Can you ID the woman?" asked the cop, looking at Calvino.

He gestured to both men for them to follow as he opened the bedroom door. Tess's body sprawled face up across the bed, legs curled at the knee, a small hole with black, torn flesh along the edges between her open green eyes. Her red silk top was buttoned, and black satin trousers in early winter in New York said she wasn't traveling anywhere outside the apartment. Calvino looked for a suitcase; there wasn't one.

"You recognize her?"

Calvino stared at the face. "Tess Reynolds. They were going to get married."

"And you were going to be best man," said Falcon, who appeared in the door.

Both Colonel Pratt and Calvino turned and saw the Russian, hands in his pockets, coming to the end of the bed, turning his head one way and then the other. A senior NYPD officer came in and whispered to Falcon, who nodded. The officer left.

"They're writing it up as a murder-suicide. They've already run a GSR field test and Josh tested positive for firing a gun. All they needed was someone who knew them to make an ID."

"Josh didn't kill himself," said Calvino. "If there was ever a man who wanted to live, it was Josh Levy."

Both Falcon and the Colonel knew as well as he did that Josh had fired the Smith and Wesson at one of the dead Russians. Of course he had residue on his hands, but the problem was explaining it.

"Neighbors heard them screaming. Heard her, anyway. The cops were here to settle them down. Tess had called 911. Nothing was stolen. And. . ." Falcon looked around and motioned for Calvino and the Colonel to come in closer. "The forensics guy got the safe combination from her hard disk. It took him less than five minutes to find it. Americans can be very stupid. No coins inside. Cash, jewels, usual papers."

"He said the coins were in Tess's bedroom safe," said Calvino.

"There's only one safe. I saw what was inside. I saw it with my own eyes. This isn't Moscow or Bangkok. The police here don't loot wrongful death scenes. Even if they had a chance, why would they go for coins and leave the cash and diamonds? They'd have gone for the cash. But I'm thinking too much like a Russian," said Falcon.

"What would Andrei have gone after?"

Falcon grinned, scratching his three-day stubble. "Of course, the coins."

"Why are you grinning?"

"Andrei's got an alibi for the hours around the probable time of death. As I said, Mr. Levy and the woman had gotten into a fight. A neighbor said he heard him slapping her around. Mr. Levy was under considerable stress. She

264

pissed him off. He finds the gun. He shoots her. Then he sees what's happened. It soaks in. He has no way out. And he's right; there isn't one. So he marches back into the living room, sits on the sofa, and shoots himself." Falcon made his hand into a gun and put it to his temple. "Happens every day, somewhere. Sure, Bangkok, too. Sure."

"You know how the residue got on Josh's hand," said Calvino, pulling him off to the side. "You were there. So was I. So was the Colonel."

Falcon lit a cigarette, narrowed his eyes as the smoke rose, and slowly released the smoke from his nostrils. "But you weren't here."

Falcon was one of the last people who'd talked to Josh. Josh had phoned Falcon after the cops called by the neighbors ended the fighting and brokered a ceasefire agreement. Falcon told him to pack a case and get out of there. One of the investigating cops found Falcon's number on Josh's cell phone call log. Twenty minutes later, Falcon was on the scene. As an ex-NYPD homicide officer, Falcon had a reputation—good and bad, ugly and sad, helpful and bull-headed. The senior officer ran a background check on Falcon's record. Executive summary: Falcon read a crime scene better than any man who has ever worked for the department and made everyone who worked with him miserable and angry. There had been no real choice short of telling the cops the alternative explanation for the residue on Josh's hands, and no one was willing to make that confession to save Josh Levy's reputation.

He was dead, after all.

Inside his head, Calvino heard Corey Hart singing "Never Surrender," one of those buried relics of the '80s slamming back into consciousness. Things hadn't changed in all of those years. Everybody still wanted to knock you down. You were supposed to stay down, roll over, and go

265

along with the program. People almost always surrendered in the end and joined the herd. Josh was no fanatic or true believer with an eye to martyrdom. What was worth dying for, once he understood that the game had been rigged from the start?

TWO

Twentieth anniversary of the fall of the Berlin Wall

COLONEL PRATT, WEARING dark business suit under a heavy overcoat, walked into the Thai embassy. They had been expecting him. He was waved inside and taken upstairs to the ambassador's office. He removed his coat and an official took it. He went into an open space where a podium, chairs, and a table had been set up. At the far end of the room, near the window, Andrei and Major Tinakorn, Chanya, and the ambassador were talking. Seated at a table opposite the group, several journalists waited along with a TV crew. Colonel Pratt had been the last to arrive. He had come on a flight that had been delayed leaving New York.

Chanya broke ranks, crossed the room, and *waied* him. Leading him straight to the ambassador, she introduced Colonel Pratt, mentioning his connection with General Yosaporn.

"The General is a great man," said the ambassador.

Major Tinakorn smiled and *waied* the Colonel. Andrei stepped forward, looking uncertain whether to extend his hand. Colonel Pratt extended his hand to Andrei. The Russian's mouth formed an O like a fish coming to the surface. The O reshaped itself into a hint of a smile. The Colonel withdrew his hand, letting his arm drop to his side.

"The weather delayed all flights out of New York," said Chanya. "We are so glad you were able to get out."

But they hadn't gathered to talk about the weather.

On the wooden stand set up on the ambassador's desk were the Rama V nine gold bullet collection; the letter from Rama V to Nicholas II was framed and set beside the dark blue velvet box. Beside the box were the Thai flag and an old photograph of the two monarchs. One of the aides led Colonel Pratt off to the side. From where he stood, he felt like a victim looking at a lineup, only no one had given him the opportunity to point his finger at Andrei. Once the Colonel had been sidelined, Major Tinakorn motioned to the journalists and TV crew. They stirred, adjusted pens, lenses, and tripods and slowly put down their coffee cups.

The ambassador waited until the TV producer signaled him. The ceremony started with a history of Rama V's journey to Russia and the long friendship between the Thai and Russian people. And how Rama V had valued that relationship and wished to preserve that special connection in the memory of both peoples with a commemorative set of coins.

"After the Russian revolution, the coins had disappeared and were thought to be lost. They might have vanished, but they remained in the memory of all Thai citizens. When they reappeared, our hearts were filled with joy. Shortly after they returned to Thailand, they were lost to us again, and our hearts were sad with this new loss. Now a great friend of Thailand has restored them. Professor Dr. Andrei, who was born in Russia, has earned the admiration of all Thais for helping us."

As diplomatic speeches go, it was shorter than expected. The journalists taped the ambassador's words. The TV cameras recorded the moment. The ambassador asked Andrei to say a few words.

"I can't improve upon the presentation of the ambassador," Andrei said. "I want to thank him and the embassy staff. Major Tinakorn, who is responsible for the security of this rare collection, will see that it is preserved for all Thais. Our two great countries have a historical link that will always remain, making us brothers and sisters. It is the twentieth anniversary of the fall of the Berlin Wall. That was the start of a new day. The return of these coins to Thailand is also an historic moment. One day soon, I hope to return to Thailand and see the Rama V collection in its rightful place."

Editing reality required men willing to conveniently ignore uncomfortable details.

Major Tinakorn said a few words. He explained the procedure to ensure the security of the coins, including the measures to transport them to Thailand. The Major had his moment before the cameras. He'd worn his uniform for the occasion. It gave him an official look. Colonel Pratt could have passed for one of the journalists in his suit. The embassy had flown him to Washington not so much as a reward but as a punishment. Colonel Pratt watched from the back row while the others smiled in front of the cameras, claiming the honor and the glory.

Thai culture is set up like the human immune system. Outsiders, viruses, are detected, marginalized, and eliminated. Looking at Andrei, Colonel Pratt thought of the Thai phrase for the immune system—it was *poom koom kan*. Literally it translated as "protective status," and every foreign investor fought hard to win it. To be accepted by the immune system as part of the Thai body was to erase the alien status. Andrei had stood in the embassy with officials as evidence that he'd won the coveted status.

Colonel Pratt was glad that Calvino hadn't been invited to the function. Of course, he understood that from the embassy's point of view, there would have been no reason to do so. Calvino had already triggered the Thai immune system that repels invaders. He was an outsider, someone to keep at a distance. It was better that Calvino had stayed in New York, hanging out with his cousin Nero and other family members. That was his protective status.

"Just ask Andrei a couple of questions for me," Calvino had said, before the Colonel had left for the airport.

"I may not get the chance."

Calvino lowered his eyes as if he had a headache coming on. "Colonel, make the chance. When exactly does Josh, in between popping Tess and himself, get the coins to him? That's one. And two, tell him he's still three cards short of a full house."

Andrei's speech deflected the authenticity problem with three of the bullet coins saying a police specialist would brief them on the details. No one else raised the subject. But they had a candidate detailed for the job—conveying bad news had been assigned to Colonel Pratt. After the little ceremony ended, he found out why they'd flown him down from New York. They'd let the Russian raise the problem.

After the Colonel had been pointed out to the others in the room, the journalists were informed that there would be a Q&A period and Colonel Pratt was available to answer questions about his investigation into the missing bullets.

When drug dealers unleash attack dogs, ears flat against their heads, showing teeth, the normal reaction is to either shoot them or run. Colonel Pratt looked out at the press and decided he had no choice but to stand his ground. The snarling and barking started immediately. Colonel Pratt calmly explained the status of the investigation into the missing coins. Calvino had told him about Josh Levy's confession, which had been fortunate; otherwise, the Colonel would have been embarrassed to hear it for the first time at the embassy. The fact was he had no solid information, only hearsay. But that didn't matter; he'd been chosen to field questions from the press.

How long would the investigation take?

He didn't know.

Were the missing coins in Thailand or America?

He wasn't certain.

Did he have a theory about the criminals behind the theft?

He said that all possibilities were under investigation. As it was a continuing investigation, he wasn't at liberty to speculate which theory would prevail. In other words, the Colonel had been detailed the job of handling the press, to say all of the official, vague, meaningless statements, like weaving bamboo cages without saying how the cages would be used. As he spoke, the Colonel thought that even to himself he sounded like an evasive, stone-walling, ass-covering machine—the kind of cop that made a viewer want to punch their fist through the TV screen.

"You did well," whispered Chanya, after he moved away from the podium.

"I was terrible," he said.

"There's a private meeting room upstairs. I've arranged for you to discuss the case with Andrei."

Colonel Pratt had phoned her on the way to Washington and asked whether she could assist in making those arrangements. He had felt from her tone that it was impossible. Now she stood next to him, smiling, having accomplished the impossible.

After the journalists cleared out, Colonel Pratt followed Chanya and Andrei upstairs into a conference room. Andrei's two bodyguards, with black suits, thin lips, and eroded smiles, sat against the wall looking bored. They came to attention when Andrei stepped into the room. The two black-suited men stared at the Colonel, sizing him up.

"My dear Colonel, I suspect you want to ask me some questions," Andrei said with a long sigh. "Thank you, Khun Chanya, for your help."

Colonel Pratt couldn't help admiring a man who walked into another country's embassy and commanded its resources and personnel. And parked his bodyguards in a conference room. He'd become part of the immune system, and the Colonel the outsider. Chanya excused herself on the grounds of another appointment. She and the Colonel exchanged perfunctory *wais*.

Once the door was closed and they were alone—not counting the two bodyguards—Andrei leaned forward, his fingers splayed on the polished table with a fresh-cut orchid in a blue Chinese bowl. The Colonel thought it must have cost a fortune to ship in fresh orchids during an American winter.

Andrei didn't waste any time getting started. "During the Russian Revolution the Red Army didn't loot the Hermitage. This is the place of great treasure in Saint Petersburg. The czars had collected the best paintings, sculptures, coins, and manuscripts. Lenin said, 'Leave every object of art, each item, on display. We want the working classes to see exactly what their exploiters have accumulated from their forced labor. He wanted the peasants to file through the Hermitage and see with their own eyes the sheer scope and magnitude of the objects of great and rare beauty, all bought with their sweat and blood. It is good to preserve the past. It is our mirror. We look, but we don't see ourselves when we walk through the Hermitage. We see the other Russians who had been hidden from sight. That was what Lenin wished. So there was no looting. This is why it remains a mystery about who would have stolen the Rama V collection nearly a hundred years ago. As to Josh Levy, he remains a mystery and an open book. Which would you prefer to discuss first?"

That was Andrei's opening. Starting with one dead man—Lenin and his pact with the devil, the Hermitage—he'd proceeded to establish his innocence, his lack of knowledge, and his absence of responsibility for whoever had taken the collection on the journey from Bangkok to New York over the last month. He'd ended with another dead man, Josh Levy, pointing his finger upward, holding it in that position and smiling.

"Do you believe that Mr. Levy killed Ms. Reynolds and then shot himself?"

"That's for the experts to decide. Though I understand that is what the police say. In the circumstances, it is difficult to disagree with their conclusion."

"When was the last time you spoke with Mr. Levy?"

Andrei eased himself into the heavily padded leather chair, an executive chair, and leaned back. He said something in Russian, and one of the bodyguards opened a briefcase and pulled out a diary. The bodyguard handed it to Andrei, who leafed through the pages.

He stopped, put on his glasses, and read: " 'Sammy's restaurant.' It was Halloween night. We were there to celebrate his impending marriage."

"The night he was grabbed in New York," said Colonel Pratt.

"So it appeared."

"Appeared?"

"He seemed upset that evening. He had some kind of injury. His face bruised and cut. I thought he'd been assaulted. I personally think Mr. Levy was having second thoughts about the woman he planned to marry and decided to disappear."

"You knew that Mr. Levy had placed the Rama V collection in Ms. Reynolds's bedroom safe," said Colonel Pratt.

"Did I really, Colonel? Or is this a conjecture?"

Colonel Pratt had no proof. What he had was Vincent Calvino's second-hand account of what Josh Levy had told him. The Colonel had been drinking coffee at the pizza place off Astor Place and Saint Marks. He should have stayed in the apartment and listened, he told himself. At the time Josh Levy wasn't saying a word. He'd clammed up, and the only way for the clam to open is when the cop leaves the room. He'd left the apartment. Andrei was right—having left the room that night, the Colonel now had only bluff and second-guessing, and a fragile hope that Andrei would be trapped into admitting something that only the killer could have known.

"You admit that Mr. Levy had the coins?"

"Yes, of course he had them. I asked him to bring them. I worked very hard to find and have them delivered to the Thai authorities. I know their importance."

"I thought you'd asked Mr. Levy to acquire coins for your grandson."

"That had been my original intention. You have children, don't you, Colonel?"

Andrei stared at him from no more than a couple of feet away. Cold, hard eyes asking about his children.

"How did that original intention change?"

"Once I learnt what had happened in Bangkok with the procurement, I felt that I had no choice but to intervene. Mr. Levy was my personal lawyer. Mr. Maxim was my business associate. I trusted both of these men. And behind my back, they got themselves into a secret scheme. If you are going to conspire to extort money, you should never hold a national treasure to ransom. That is a dangerous game."

"Why would Mr. Levy have been involved with your business associate in Bangkok? Didn't you send him to Bangkok to meet Maxim?"

"Mr. Levy was a trained lawyer. Experienced. I sent him to go over a contract with Mr. Saytev." Andrei had gone formal, using Maxim's family name.

"What are you saying? They ended up doing business together?"

Andrei nodded. "And once I found what they were up to, I demanded that Mr. Levy hand over the coins. He refused. Next, he tried to extort shares and cash from me. The woman he killed also wanted me to pay her money. Imagine that."

"What did you do?"

"I refused to pay."

"But you convinced Mr. Levy to give you the coins."

Andrei shook his head. "He never gave them to me." The look of surprise on the Colonel's face forced a smile. Andrei enjoyed the Colonel's discomfort; the sight gave the Russian a second wind. "Did someone say Mr. Levy gave me the coins?"

Colonel Pratt, like Calvino, had made a number of assumptions, and one of them was that Josh had handed over the coins to Andrei as a last-ditch effort to put the whole affair behind him.

"You told a group of journalists that you delivered the coins."

"Indeed I did. But I never said Mr. Levy gave them to me."

"Who did?"

"One of Mr. Levy's partners at the law firm, Ben Harris. He's a tax partner. Josh used the office messenger service to send the coins to Mr. Harris. He phoned Mr. Harris and told them to see they were given to me. Mr. Harris did what he'd been asked."

"When did this happen?"

"You'll have to ask Mr. Harris. I have no knowledge. Or you might ask your friend, Mr. Calvino, who seems to have been somehow involved."

Calvino's name hovered in the air between the two men.

"Vincent was Mr. Levy's close friend."

"Men do things for their close friends, wouldn't you agree?"

"Theft isn't something Vincent would do for anybody," said Colonel Pratt, wishing almost immediately he hadn't said it. Dragging Calvino into the discussion was Andrei's way of laying down a smokescreen; both men knew it.

"You asked Mr. Levy for scans of all nine bullets."

"Because I didn't believe he'd be that foolish. I wanted verification. And when I checked the coins with a specialist at the Hermitage I was told three of the coins were different from the originals. Very tiny differences, just as with a fingerprint, where one whorl sets one man apart from another. The same with bullet coins."

"You knew that Mr. Levy had been kidnapped by Russians," said Colonel Pratt.

Andrei shrugged, "You are making an assumption again about what I knew and didn't know. If Mr. Levy was kidnapped, why wasn't it reported to the New York police? Why would only a Thai cop in America have such knowledge?"

"Mr. Levy said you offered him a job. But he had to resign from his law firm."

"Ambition is the great danger—not capitalism or communism or radical Islam. Ambition is unhealthy; it does strange things to a man. Ambition is often accompanied by degeneracy and corruption. From the fall of Rome it has destroyed empires and men. When ambition is blocked, desperation sets in. Desperate men commit unpredictable and outrageous acts."

The last Facebook message sent by Tess Reynolds, written a couple of hours before the police found her body, had been a smiley face and the words, "Feeling better already." Those words and the icon for happiness didn't square with the crazed, desperate woman that Andrei had described.

The Colonel decided to return to Tess's mental state later.

Andrei hadn't denied that he'd made a job offer to Josh Levy. But he hadn't admitted it either.

"You offered him a job?" asked Colonel Pratt.

"I seriously considered it. The devil of ambition wouldn't leave him. That wasn't good enough. He was obsessed about buying a house in East Hampton. He needed three and half million dollars. Imagine that. He approached me to become my personal lawyer. Next thing, he demands that kind of money. His ambition didn't stop with the house in the Hamptons. Josh gave me a list of preconditions— this amount of money, so many shares, and on and on. I'm thinking, this is mad. I need a lawyer to hire a lawyer. When he used the coins as a weapon, I said to myself enough is enough."

"Why a weapon?"

"He was no longer the man I knew. He was angry and unreasonable. I should have seen it sooner. He wasn't the same Josh Levy I had worked with. His ambition had got the best of him, and he had the misfortune of having a beautiful but ambitious woman pushing him. It came as no surprise to me that he'd committed criminal acts. Josh no longer had any shame. Like a trapped animal, he'd do whatever he had to in order to free himself, even if it meant biting off his own leg."

It was as if Andrei had covered a blackboard with white-chalked equations, line after line, and the equations came to one proof—he was a hero who'd been duped by two trusted men. Like two failed algorithms, they had to be replaced before the formula could be improved and taken to the next level. According to Andrei, Josh had confessed to Ben Harris his role in the extortion, Maxim Saytev's role, and how everything had gone wrong and destroyed his life.

"Was I surprised he shot himself?" The Russian shrugged, turned his head to the side, looked his interrogator in the eyes, and said, "Such a man is a surprise even to himself."

Colonel Pratt wrote it down, read it, and analyzed it, but he had no idea what Andrei meant.

Chanya slipped back into the conference room and stood behind Andrei.

"Your car for the airport is waiting downstairs, Colonel Pratt."

Andrei sighed, "Perhaps we can continue our discussion another time."

"I'd like that," said Colonel Pratt, rising from the table.

The embassy had booked the Colonel's return flight to New York. They were keeping him on a short time leash—giving him enough time to take the heat for the missing coins, arranging a limited time window to interview Andrei, as he had requested, and then shutting him down. The time had come to send him away. Out of sight, he could be forgotten or shuffled into the realm of another department's problem.

In the downstairs lobby Chanya seemed relieved; the worst of her assignment was nearly over.

"You handled the press very well today," she said.

"I handled them about the same as the interview with Andrei," he said. "It was a disappointment."

"You don't seem to like Mr. Andrei. May I ask why?"

He slipped on his coat and looked out at the snow, wondering if the flight would be delayed. "Are you familiar with William Shakespeare?"

"I know you are something of a scholar of Shakespeare."

"He wrote in a play titled *Henry VI*, 'These days are dangerous: virtue is choked with foul ambition.'"

"Is this a hint about Andrei or someone else?"

"You should ask Mr. Andrei about ambition. He's something of an expert."

"Please give General Yosaporn my regards," she said. "Tell him that my father misses him."

The Colonel buttoned his coat. Accepting her parting *wai*, he left her question hanging as the frigid air from the open door enveloped him. She watched the Colonel approach the limo waiting at the curb. He didn't glance back. In front of him the embassy sloped down to the Potomac. He got in the car and it headed up the hill. They'd finished with him, and he'd finished with the embassy. He thought about how Andrei had managed to place an exhibit in a possible murder case in the custody of an embassy. It was no longer possible for a prosecutor or court to have access. Exhibit A was now on Thai territory in Washington, D.C.

General Yosaporn would understand if he had to delay passing along Chanya's greetings.

THREE

Shaarey Pardes Accabonac Grove Cemetery, East Hampton—
Tuesday, November 10

"You come up with anything on the gun?" asked Calvino.

THE NAKED BRANCHES of trees lining both sides of the lane touched like bony fingers. Members of the family and friends gathered around the freshly dug graves at Shaarey Pardes off the Old Stone Road and listened to a number of people speak about Josh Levy. During the levayah procession, part of the Jewish funeral, Calvino had seen his ex-wife. The sight of her reminded him of the Thai expression *pee lawk*—haunted by a ghost, or the shock of someone from the past unexpectedly turning up. An ex-wife was a common *pee lawk* experience for *farang*. They hadn't had time to exchange words. That happened after the last eulogy, as the mourners gathered around the grave. A shovel was passed around. Calvino pointed the tip upwards and passed it to Ingram, who stood next to him. They stood next to the grave as it was being filled.

"Come out to East Hampton," said Ingram. "I've bought a beach house. I know that Josh would have wanted you to come and see it."

"Josh mentioned you were interested but had to wait eighteen months to cash out some stock option."

"In the digital world, eighteen months happens in eight days." He handed Calvino a business card. "Let me know when you want to come out and stay."

Calvino looked at Ingram's card. "Yeah, I'll let you know."

As Ingram left, Calvino looked up in time to see his ex-wife, Janet, and her husband walk toward him, crossing the lawn carefully so as not to step on a grave.

Charlie Hellerman, Janet's husband, stared at his shoes, damp from the grass as he walked next to her. To judge from his body language, Charlie wasn't looking forward to meeting Calvino. When he did glance up and meet Calvino's eye, it was only for a brief moment, and then he looked away. He had a desk job at the printers' union, and the look was one Calvino figured Charlie had used on management representatives. Charlie looked as tired and as obsolete as the technology he represented. As Janet and Charlie came closer, Calvino remembered a much younger version of this woman, though he'd never met Charlie, a soft-gutted middle-aged man beside an overweight wife with too much makeup, her nervous hands clutching his arm a little too firmly.

"Hi, Vinny. It's been a long time," Janet said, fiddling with the sleeve on Charlie's coat.

"Charlie," her husband said, extending his hand. "Heard a lot about you."

Calvino smiled, thinking he'd like a tape of those conversations.

"It's so terrible about Josh," she said, sighing and shaking her head.

Janet had known Josh since the old days in Brooklyn.

"A tragedy," said Charlie.

"Did you know Josh?" asked Calvino.

Charlie shook his head. "But I heard a lot of good things about him."

Janet hadn't been in touch with Josh for years. Funerals brought out of the woodwork faces that people half-remembered, faces from the past, with a past, and a sad awareness that death brings home the long-standing disconnection.

Janet dabbed her eyes with a fresh handkerchief that Charlie had fished from his jacket pocket.

"I can't believe Josh could do this," she said.

Calvino wanted to say, "What if he didn't?" But the cemetery wasn't the place, and with people filing past, it wasn't the time, and the woman asking the question, an ex-wife, wasn't the right person to start such a conversation with.

When Calvino didn't reply, a silence drifted between them, one of those junctures when two people either say everything that has been left unsaid between them or say nothing. It'd been more than twenty years since they'd seen each other. Long enough for the emotions to drain, but not long enough to examine the dry gully of memories scattered like debris from an ancient storm.

"I heard you'd come back to New York," she said, as Charlie looked on, nodding.

"Josh asked me to be his best man."

"Like he was your best man at our wedding," she said.

Calvino glanced at his watch. "I've gotta go, Janet. I fly back to Thailand tomorrow night."

"Always on the run, Vinny. Never the right time." Sucking a lemon.

"Thailand," said Charlie, touching Janet's hand. "People bust their ass to get into America. Can't think why anyone born here would wanna live elsewhere. But that's just me talking."

"You're right, Charlie. Just you talking."

Calvino walked back to the road, turned, and looked back at the cemetery, collar around his ears, thinking about what Colonel Pratt had said.

"You have to accept what your friend has done. Andrei is right. Ambition had undone him. 'Dreams indeed are ambition,' " he'd said, quoting *Hamlet*.

"It's hard for you to understand. Money fell into your hands. An inheritance. You had no intention of finding that money; it happened that money found you. Josh Levy worked for his. He wanted more than he could make. You're different. All of the years I've known you, you've been highly motivated, but it was never about money. Maxim Saytev and Levy are the kind of men whose heads are turned by money. You never hungered for a yacht or a house in the Hamptons. You're not the kind of man who can understand that hunger."

When Calvino opened the door to Nero's apartment at Astor Place, Falcon and Colonel Pratt were sitting in the living room. He'd interrupted their conversation. Papers were spread out on the coffee table. More papers were stacked in small piles on the floor; on top of one pile was a photograph of Josh Levy's body. Taking off his coat and hanging it on a peg, Calvino walked into the kitchen and poured himself a cup of coffee.

"The rabbi said God works in mysterious ways. I saw Janet," said Calvino, coming out with the coffee mug steaming. "But I didn't see Andrei. The law firm drafted a couple of lawyers and sent them along. Ben Harris was there. Ingram and Williams and their wives were at the cemetery, and other people from the city and the Hamptons. Harris wore a yarmulke that almost covered his bald spot. It took ten years off his age."

Neither the Colonel nor Falcon said anything. They weren't interested in the funeral. Calvino sat down across from Falcon, who sat on the sofa smoking.

"You come up with anything on the gun?" asked Calvino. He had their attention.

"Forensics ran tests on the gun," Falcon said, shifting through the papers on the coffee table. He pulled a document out of a file.

"Use of a silencer inconclusive," said Calvino, sipping coffee from the mug.

"That's why professionals love a .22 caliber bullet," said Falcon. "No grooves to trace back to the gun. And it's very difficult to know if a silencer was used."

He shrugged as if it were a mystery beyond his ability to solve.

"At close range the .22 gets the job done."

That much Falcon knew.

"You want to see the autopsy report?" asked Falcon, holding it up.

"A hollow-point .22 round scrambles the brain into an omelet," said Calvino.

"Have you eaten?" asked Colonel Pratt.

"A slice of pizza downstairs. Chicken and Caesar salad," said Calvino. "Did you find anything inside Tess's apartment?"

Falcon lit a cigarette. "CCTV tapes showed people coming in and out, all of them accounted for—other tenants, friends of tenants, and a couple of uniformed FedEx delivery guys."

"One of the FedEx guys couldn't be traced back," said Colonel Pratt.

"What do you think, Falcon?"

The Russian sighed, exhaling a perfect smoke ring. "He could have been in the wrong building. A new guy gets the wrong address. Or it could have been a professional dressed up like a FedEx delivery man. Goes in, gets Tess to open the safe. Sits Levy down and gets him to write out a note—'Dear Ben, Immediately notify Andrei that you have the coins. Deliver them to him.'—and sign it. Gets him to sign the FedEx delivery form. Excuses himself, asks the woman to show him the bathroom. She takes him into the bedroom. Sits her on the bed, shoots her. Goes back into the living room. Levy is sitting on the couch, looking at the coins.

284

The gunman goes up and shoots him in the head, takes the gun, puts it in Levy's hand. Packs up the coins and leaves. CCTV tape shows him exiting the elevator and going out the door. Here's a copy of Levy's handwritten note."

He handed it across to Calvino, who got out of his chair, walked to a lamp, and held the copy under the lamp.

"How did Ben get the coins?" asked Calvino, returning the photocopy to Falcon. "Was he in on it?"

Falcon shrugged, smoke flushing out of his nose like a dragon.

"Maybe, maybe not. Chances are the hit man disappeared inside a van that he'd parked around the corner and changed his clothes. Then he drove over to the closest FedEx depot in the neighborhood and dropped it into the box. No one saw him."

"Or Josh Levy killed Tess Reynolds and himself," said Colonel Pratt.

"You know why I think that is bullshit?"

Both men looked at him as he reached over and picked up the photocopy.

"See that little drawing next to his signature?"

"So what?" asked Falcon.

"You don't have fucking poison ivy in Russia?"

"Yes," said Falcon.

"What's it mean, Vincent?" asked Colonel Pratt.

"When we were kids one summer our parents sent us to the same camp upstate, to get a couple of ten-years-olds out of their hair. The first day, the counselors gave all of the kids an orientation about what to do and not to do and what to avoid, and we got a lecture about poison ivy. Stay away from the shit. Third day, Josh says let's go down to the river. He wanted to swim. He said he knew a shortcut, but he was winging it. We went this way, then that way. I said let's go back to the main path. He said no and headed off alone through a field of poison ivy. By the time he dragged himself back to camp, he was scratching his arms, legs, and balls. He had a bad case. Later when he'd find himself doing something he knew was stupid, going overland when he should circle back, fucking up by doing something he shouldn't do, he would say that he had a poison ivy moment. And I'm saying, he drew the leaf of a poison ivy plant because he knew I'd see it for what it was. Josh was sending a message."

Colonel Pratt adjusted his glasses and studied the photocopy of Josh's note and the small doodle beside the signature.

"It's not enough," he said, laying down the paper.

"The Colonel's right," said Falcon. "You see poison ivy. It could be anything. Whatever it is, there's not enough evidence to upset the murder-suicide report."

"Andrei gets away with a double murder," said Calvino.

"Ah, to be brave and angry like the young," said Colonel Pratt. "Such an attitude befits a young man, but in an old one makes him a raging King Lear."

"Shakespeare," said Calvino. "I don't wanna hear of Shakespeare."

"It's not Shakespeare. It's me talking, Vincent."

"The powerful get away with multiple murders," said Falcon. He shrugged his shoulders. "The police do what they can. And if I were still on the force, I'd get on to the next case, one with some evidence I can use in court and not get laughed at."

Calvino watched Falcon stub his cigarette into an overflowing ashtray on the coffee table.

"Janet reminded me of something after the funeral."

Both men said nothing, waiting for him to continue.

"Josh was best man at our wedding. I understand why *that* marriage died. And I understand why Josh died. I can't do anything about the death of the marriage. But I can do something about Josh's memory."

Part 6

Last Money

ONE

Bangkok, Soi Cowboy—Christmas Week

What are the chances of a krathong reaching the sea when released in the Chao Phraya River?

THE TRAFFIC IN front of Queen Sirikit Center was backed up on the bridge over Rama IV Road. Calvino sat alone in his sitting room, pouring himself a drink, watching the cars inch forward. In the distance were Lake Ratchada and a large tract of land owned by the Tobacco Monopoly. No traffic jams on the pathway around the lake. He watched a cyclist lazily circle the lake, passing a couple of joggers who'd slowed to a trot behind a couple walking with a baby carriage. Two different worlds existing side by side: one congested, frustrated, and angry, the other leisurely, relaxed, and centered.

He thought about standing in the cemetery at Josh's service. Janet in tears, her husband red-faced and anxious, and Ingram holding a shovel and inviting him to his beach house. December was no time to be in the Hamptons, he told himself.

He was back in Bangkok. The NYPD had closed the case and filed it under murder-suicide. Calvino wondered what his chances were of getting justice for Josh. Was there any hope of that happening? He stared down at the lake, dark and still in the night, thinking how the candles illuminated it once a year. With the light came hope, something Calvino was finding in short supply.

He imagined the lake during the annual festival of Loy Krathong when hope was reflected through a hundred points of candlelight. Each banana leaf float carried a small candle and a coin. Not a gold bullet coin, but an ordinary one-baht coin. The celebrants each lit their candle and slipped their *krathong* into the water with a prayer that it would reach the sea, the candle still burning, believing that if it reached the sea, all of their sins from the previous year would be washed away. What are the chances of a *krathong* reaching the sea when released in the Chao Phraya River? Almost zero. But every year millions of Thais perform the ritual of cleansing their sins by buying a *krathong* and placing it in a lake or river, sending it on a journey to the sea. Reaching the goal isn't likely, but just the smallest of possibilities is enough to keep the faith that tomorrow might be a day when multiple sins evaporate, leaving a life unblemished, like the cloudless sky outside Calvino's window.

Calvino had a small flame of hope resting on one last *krathong*. Not exactly a *krathong* but a *ying* who specialized in happy endings for a price.

Her name was Dew. Number 19. She'd been gone from the Soi Cowboy bar for over three months. The night after he'd last seen her, at the outside Soi Cowboy bar, she had vanished. No one knew where she'd gone, but that didn't stop them from guessing—upcountry, Germany, Japan, Hong Kong, England? Each possible location replaced the previous one in the reports he'd gathered. By now the gossip had grown cold. A couple of months out of any bar, a *ying* was nearly forgotten. The nightly stage show moved on as the cast turned over, and the regulars forgot about her one drink at a time.

The weather site on Calvino's computer screen showed the temperature in Bangkok as being twenty-eight Celsius. He should have been outside enjoying the weather, walking around the lake, a patch of health inside the dead lungs of Bangkok, instead of thinking about a missing *ying* or a doomed *krathong*. New York lay paralyzed under a blanket in snow. Using Google Maps' satellite view, he zoomed in on Nero's building opposite Cooper Union. At the end of the building a forest of eight or nine trees was blanketed in snow. On the same website he retraced his path through New York—to the warehouse in Port Elizabeth, to Sammy's restaurant, and uptown to Tess Reynolds's building. He studied each location, finding new details about the surroundings, making notes, and thinking that all the time he'd spent in New York, he'd overlooked so much. You no longer had to be somewhere to get the picture of the place straight in your head. Memory can play a man for a fool, and often does, but when the buildings and roads and cars can be studied without interruption for hours on end, that opens a new door for investigation.

During the six weeks since Calvino had returned, he'd been to the Honda dealership four more times looking at that new Accord. Tanaka loved talking baseball and envied Calvino for being in New York for the World Series. Calvino let it ride—both Tanaka's delusion and his own decision whether to buy the car. He had gone out to the Pattaya Yacht Club and, from a safe distance, taken photographs of the *Last Money* in the marina. For days he trolled the Internet, looking for information on Andrei and his companies, associates, and awards.

Calvino mailed Colonel Pratt a Christmas card on which he had written a quote from Shakespeare's *Richard III*: "You have no cause to hold my friendship doubtful: I never was nor never will be false."

For long stretches of time Calvino, except for drinking green tea with Tanaka, secluded himself inside his condo, occasionally going into his office. He had no desire to sit at his desk, answer the phone, check email, or take on anything that appeared to involve work. At first he had wanted to

291

shut out the world. He couldn't stop thinking about finding Dew. If he could make that happen, then he could move on. It would be over; he wouldn't have done all he could.

Ratana had seen it coming—his withdrawal, his disappearance, his lack of interest in work, his absence of plans.

Colonel Pratt told her, "Vincent's still getting over the loss of his friend. Give him some time."

"He's depressed," Ratana had said.

"He tried to go back home. But it didn't work out the way he thought."

"He's waiting for her, that woman who worked in Soi Cowboy," she had said. "Every day he phones the *mamasan* and asks if she's back or if she's heard anything from her."

A wound in Ratana's heart opened when she talked about Dew.

Colonel Pratt listened to Ratana, his wife, and women in general. In the Colonel's mind, women registered a frequency for signals that most men lacked.

"We all are waiting for something or someone," said the Colonel. "In Vincent's case, I'd be surprised if he has a personal interest in Dew."

"He's trying to put his friend's memory to rest. I know it's been hard on him," said Ratana.

The Colonel told her about Calvino's Christmas card. How he'd gone to the trouble to find the right words to send to a friend. In Thailand the stream of goods, thoughts, dreams, promotions, and the future all circled like a flock of birds, seeking refuge in the rookery of one's friends. Calvino, who'd lost an old friend, had failed to come to terms with his loss. The card had been his way to reach out to the Colonel. It was a gesture, but not the gesture Calvino wanted to make—handing the missing bullet coins to Colonel Pratt. He'd been back six weeks, and each day he woke up and asked himself if this was the day he'd give the coins to the Colonel.

The annual police department promotion list had been delayed again. There had been a great deal of internal wrangling over the composition of the list. The ministers and politicians had been deadlocked, so it became like paper with invisible ink, appearing as one thing under black light, another in blue, red, or yellow light. There was a Christmas tree's worth of colored lights, all flashing different names. Now and again, the Colonel's name appeared, hovered, and dissolved.

Maxim had kept a low profile in Pattaya since the authorities confiscated his Ilyushin Il-76 aircraft at Don Muang Airport, along with thirty-five crates of weapons, and deposited the crew in prison cells. The plane had been charted by one of Maxim's companies. Someone wasn't playing nice. Like the police promotion list, no one was able to make a decision and risk blowback once it had been made. Thailand had become all half-time show, with no sign of the game resuming on the field. The paralysis of the government had become normal. Like a quadriplegic, any movement and communication seemed like a miracle when it happened.

With the arrival of Christmas week, Calvino accepted that his self-imposed isolation had to end. Christmas had long ceased to be a religious holiday. In Bangkok, Christianity had been hollowed out and repackaged into another holiday, a winter festival. Leafing through the *Bangkok Post*, Calvino read an article about an oil concession contract that would be announced by the Cabinet within three days. Chances were the three days would come and go without a decision.

On the social page of the newspaper, he saw a picture of Andrei, who was in Bangkok receiving from the Russian ambassador the Order of Saint Nicholas, something like a knighthood but without the myth of the roundtable. The Colonel had briefed Calvino about Andrei's local connections, how he'd plugged into the network, and the wiring went this way and that, until it was finally lost like a cable in the thick spaghetti tangle of Bangkok's overhead power cables.

"What if Andrei planned from the beginning to deliver the coins to Tinakorn's crowd?" Calvino said to the Colonel. "But he needed some drama. Russians are good at making drama when they need one. He persuades Maxim and Josh to do the grunt work. Then when it looks like the coins are lost forever, he produces them, like pulling a rabbit out of a hat."

"Or it happened the way he said," said Colonel Pratt.

It had been like that between Calvino and the Colonel ever since they'd returned from New York. The Colonel had had enough of Calvino's speculation about Andrei's role in the deaths of Levy and his fiancée. And Calvino had the conviction that Andrei was lying through his capped teeth. Falcon had sided with the Colonel. In New York it had been two against one. In Bangkok it was one against one.

On the glass table surface a golden bullet coin glittered in the overhead light inside its box. Calvino picked out the four-baht gold bullet, sheltered inside a sealed plastic pouch, and felt the weight of it in the palm of his hand. Calvino held the coin tight and then, opening his palm, held it to the light and turned it around as he thought about its history. Rama V had the set struck as a presentation gift to Nicholas II—a man he had called his brother, a man who had run through his own field of poison ivy. The initial press interest in the missing coins had faded. The papers only talked about the restored Rama V gold bullets as if they were a single, complete set. Andrei had achieved his hero status. The coins were no longer being sought. The missing bullets were an embarrassment and therefore forgotten.

Calvino put the bullet coin back in the box. Closing the box, he returned it to its drawer and locked it. Andrei was not only in town but on the society page of the newspaper, wearing a gold sash, holding a glass of champagne, and smiling into the camera. It was the face of a man on top of the world. Calvino wondered how long it would be before Andrei hooked up with Maxim. Unless Andrei had been behind the seizure of the Ilyushin Il-76, Maxim would have been looking for a way to have Andrei help get his crew and plane back. When they finally met, what information about New York would pass between them? He wanted to be the fly on the wall during that conversation.

When Calvino's cell phone rang, he recognized the number immediately.

"Dew come to the bar tonight," said the *mamasan*, her voice as sharp as an elbow in a crowded train.

He'd promised her five thousand baht if her information proved right.

The *mamasan* hadn't been reliable in the past. That wasn't part of her job description, and despite having been kicked up to management, she wasn't that different from the *yings* working the stage, and none of them were about to break a Guinness World Record for dependability. He'd had her calls before and waited at the bar, but Dew hadn't showed. After she'd been wrong five times, Calvino modified the deal—if Dew was a no-show, Calvino drank for free. He would drink just enough to make the bill heavy in her hands. But in her mind the carrot of winning a five thousand baht prize was a better bet than the stick of his bar bill.

Calvino put the phone down on call number six. He had no reason to consider the number six lucky. But he decided to go around if only to see if the *mamasan* would live up to their new bargain. He made a side bet against himself. She'd live up to the deal if it served her interests. Otherwise, she would probably grab onto the old standby English word "misunderstanding," as if it could rear up like a dancing dragon—all drums, bells, and whistles. After all the belching noise she'd stiff him for the bar bill, standing with her hands on her hips, looking like she hadn't had a bowel movement in three days.

"See you tonight. And one of us is going to get paid."

"Thank you, Khun Vinny. Five thousand baht."

TWO

Bangkok, Soi Cowboy—Christmas Week

Bar yings can shuttle between reality and unreality
as if they ran on parallel tracks.

CALVINO WALKED INTO the bar just before seven. He wore a black T-shirt with a sports jacket and jeans. He'd left his .38 police special locked up at the condo. He had no reason to carry a gun.

A couple of things bothered him. The first was Tess's reaction to Dew's phone call. He'd dismissed it at the time as an emotional explosion that any man would have expected in the circumstances from a woman born, raised, and educated in the West. And there was something else: Josh's first instinct in the bar and again later in New York after they'd busted him out of the warehouse—avoiding eye contact, breaking into a sweat, defensive, quick to change the subject. Again, Calvino, at the time, thought Josh's newbie reaction was typical. Guilt, Calvino could understand. But a man needed something to be guilty about. Josh had nothing to be guilty about, so why was he acting guilty?

Calvino kept going over what had happened on his last night with Josh in Soi Cowboy. He had dragged Josh into the bar where Dew, wiggling her ass, blurring Number 19 into the prime number of the universe, had greeted Josh.

"You, *farang*, you don't remember me?"

Josh had said, "Never saw the woman in my life."

Calvino took Josh's statement at face value. Bar *yings* can shuttle between reality and unreality as if they ran on parallel tracks. The *mamasan's* major job is to keep them from derailing. In addition, bar *yings* are notorious for confusing one *farang* with the next, as if they were sacks of rice, and the hardcore *yings* rope in new customers by getting them to believe they've already met before. Once that tiny seed of doubt about a prior intimacy has been planted—and it is a reasonable doubt because the *yings* are interchangeable to the *farangs* as well—the customer stops, takes a second look, takes a chance, and buys a lady drink. Before he's certain they've never met, he has already coughed up the bar fine. Call it the interactive show business model, where cast and audience exchange bodily fluids rather than applause.

Dew was that last *krathong* Calvino planned to launch before finally letting go of the hope to change the way people would remember Josh Levy. The way a man is remembered matters, Calvino told himself.

When Calvino walked into the bar, it was way too early for the curtain to go up on the show. For one thing, no one had shut off the daytime lighting system. A couple of dozen *yings* sat on benches, using the mirrors to put on lipstick, eyeliner, makeup, and lotion on their body and legs. Casual, eating pieces of chicken, sticky rice, *som tam*, and fish paste, they looked like village girls on a picnic. Calvino sat on a stool. No one was in any hurry to serve him. He figured the *mamasan* must've put the word out to go easy on serving him as she might get stuck with the bill.

He had arrived early because he feared a couple of things might happen if he rolled in around nine or ten. Dew was a hot dancer and was usually bar fined early in the evening. He didn't want to take the chance that once again she'd vanish for a couple of months. Call it the road tour—a member of the cast goes international or disappears to play in the provinces.

Calvino studied the faces of the *yings* seated on benches around the bar. For the moment it seemed as if the cast were seated among the audience. None of them showed any interest in Calvino. They saw no irony. It just wasn't showtime yet, and their brains were grinding through a hundred offstage problems. Mentally, Calvino marked them off, one by one, as not being Dew. He'd first seen her in neon. Back at the condo it had been low lighting. The next morning she'd disappeared without his ever getting a clear look at her. She'd been a blur of motion, bolting out the door as she slipped the two thousand baht into her handbag. Could he really remember her? Scanning the faces, he wondered if she might already be there but, without makeup, incognito.

Soon someone would switch the lighting from day to night mode—a muted, bluesy, sexy neon. Neon would convert the dancers' skin into a perfect honey tone. The daytime lights were a series of overhead rows of fluorescent tubes, and their clinical glow highlighted every imperfection, every patch of cellulite, and every scar from child-bearing, surgery, accidents, and fights.

More *yings* filed past, fresh from the street, strutting in like leading actresses. None of them was Dew. The new *yings* flopped down on vacant benches and applied their makeup, knowing all other eyes were on these stragglers, who were the bar superstars. Sitting without a drink, Calvino saw the first wave of *yings* stand up, stretch in their bikinis, step into their ten-dollar high heels, and wobble toward the stage. It was as if, backstage, the assistant director had told the cast that the audience was seated. Break a leg.

Finally a drink arrived, along with the chit cup and white paper bill stuffed inside. Just then the neon came on and the fluorescent lights switched off. Neon light painted the bodies in a smooth flow, covering the signs of age and violence or bad luck. The neon glow softened everything it touched; soon it would drive lust and desire through lizard-brained pathways.

Fifteen minutes later the *mamasan* walked into the bar smiling like she'd won the lottery. One of the *yings* dancing onstage stopped and pointed at the door. The *yings* whose dance shift had ended, now re-colonizing the benches, automatically looked in the same direction. Dew followed the *mamasan* into the bar, waving like a film star. A couple of the *yings* ran down the aisle and hugged her. But the *mamasan* cut Dew's victory run short and stuffed a piece of paper into Calvino's chit cup. He pulled it out and read the bill for five thousand baht.

Pointing at the cup and at Dew, he said, "Add her bar fine."

Dew shrugged. "You remember me?"

"Like a book from beginning to end. A short book."

"Where we go?"

"My place."

She remembered but it hadn't stopped Dew from pulling a face.

"*Hiew khow,*" she moaned, rubbing her belly.

The beast of hunger lurked behind her eyes.

He remembered another reason for arriving early: there was no need to wait until the *ying* changed out of her bikini and into her street clothes. It was the same satisfaction as heating up instant noodles.

Calvino turned his car into the parking lot of a supermarket on Soi 16. It housed a restaurant and was close to his condo. Not a place to linger over a meal; more of a food pit stop on the way to the big race. The name of the restaurant translated as Cheap and Good. It was nothing more than a long bar counter lined with stools, along with a few tables alongside the supermarket.

Calvino signaled a passing waitress for a table. The waitress returned a moment later and handed out menus and waited until they had ordered. Calvino ordered wonton soup, and Dew pointed at the *pad thai*, *som tam*, and pork chop before closing the menu. Some *yings* ate like a racehorse but performed like a sloth. Some ate like a sloth and performed like a thoroughbred. Dew was a thoroughbred in both areas. He might not have remembered her face until she'd walked into the bar, but he could never have forgotten a thoroughbred who'd run the race and come to the starting gate with her own supply of spurs and whips.

He waited until Dew ate half of the *pad thai*, pushed the plate away, and picked at the *som tam*, leaving the pork chop untouched. She looked up, smiling.

"*Mamasan* say you ask about Dew every day," she said, stopping to finish a glass of water.

She refilled her glass, looking around at the people at the other tables, including a couple of lone males at the bar. Always working the room.

"You want something else?" he asked.

She nodded. "*Im laew*," Dew said.

"You remember the first night we met?"

She smiled. "Long time ago."

"I was with my friend, Khun Josh. You remember the guy? Bald-headed and a little shorter than me. An American."

She sighed, running a fork over the cold pork chop. He wasn't getting through to her. She was bored.

"We go your condo now," she said—the five words translated as "Let's get it over with."

Eat, work, play, sleep were the four stages of a bar *ying's* day. Stage one was done—stomach full. Dew started to rise from her chair.

Calvino reached over and pulled her down. "Let's talk it over first."

Dew pulled a pack of cigarettes out of her handbag. A waitress came over and told her that she couldn't smoke in the restaurant. She put the cigarettes away and pouted.

"Want a cigarette," she said.

"A couple of quick questions. Then we go."

"The night we met, you said that you recognized Josh. I thought it was bullshit."

Her mouth narrowed, flatlined like a hospital monitor, to register the lack of feeling she had for Calvino or anyone else—at least until she had a cigarette.

"Not bullshit. Dew never talk bullshit. Dew always talk truth. You believe me?"

It was the old bar *ying* line, always ending with the same question. When people lie for a profession, it's nearly impossible to figure out how much of what they say is true.

"I believe you, sweetheart."

"Your friend jealous you," she said.

"Josh, jealous of me?"

She nodded. "He say you his best friend. When he come back to Thailand?"

"Next life," he said.

She laughed, "Don't joke Dew. When he come back?"

"He's dead. He died in America last month. It was sudden."

He watched as her eyes opened wide and her jaw dropped.

"Oh my God," she said in perfect English. "Heart attack? I think he very old."

"Heart stopped."

"Sorry for his family."

Certain attitudes can be faked—appearing to be attracted to a customer, pretending to be happy, interested, and sexy—but bar *yings* had little experience faking remorse. It was the closest thing to a guarantee they'd tell the truth. Death did

302

that; it closed the books on old promises and opened a set of new ones with the memory of the living restored.

"How'd you meet him?"

"Dew want cigarette. Can't think," she said, talking about herself in the third-person.

Calvino pulled out his wallet and opened it to display two inches' worth of thousand-baht notes. He waited until her eyes had passed over the thickness of that edge before pulling one out and putting it in the chit cup.

"Two thousand inside has Dew's name on it. Those notes want to come out and hug Dew, but first she has to tell them where she met Khun Josh."

He started to remove another two notes from his wallet.

"On a boat."

He gave her one thousand baht.

"Where was this boat?"

"Pattaya."

He held out the note, just out of reach. As he glanced at the money, he remembered crossing the street in front of Sammy's in New York and handing out money to the gangbangers for information about the men who'd grabbed Josh. That same cash magic worked with street people in Bangkok, who had a wealth of experience in the value of what people came into the night to buy and sell.

"Were there other people on the boat?"

"Russians. My friend and two other girls, but I don't remember their names."

"It was a party."

She nodded, looking at the bank note.

"Overnight?"

"Two nights."

"Josh took you to Pattaya?"

"I go with my friend. Meet him on the boat."

The waitress brought back the change. Calvino left a tip and got up from his chair. He drove Dew back to his condo.

She kicked off her shoes and skipped through the dining area and into the sitting room. There she opened one of the glass doors, walked out onto the verandah, and stared down at the traffic.

"I remember you now," she said, looking over her shoulder.

He walked out onto the verandah and stood with his hands on the railing. The lake beyond was black; a ring of lights around the outer perimeter outlined its dark void.

He'd been remembered by a *ying* for the view from his condo balcony. There were worse things to be remembered for, Calvino thought. He smiled, thinking that his *krathong* might just have reached the open sea. They went back inside and Dew headed for the kitchen, opened the fridge and, uncorking a bottle of white wine, poured herself a glass. Then she lit a cigarette and, holding the wine glass by the stem, padded back into the sitting room, where she sat in a chair, drinking and smoking. And looking like a million dollars.

Calvino sat in front of a laptop.

"Do you remember the Russian's name?"

She held the glass by the stem and sipped the white wine, tilting her head like a lady. The neurons were firing blanks in the name department. He decided that she could use some help. He typed Maxim's full name into Google and clicked on images. On the first page were photos of a thirty-something Russian man in a gold sweatshirt pulled over a white T-shirt, with a large gold chain looping across his barrel-like chest. His forehead was round and sunburnt, as if the eyebrows had been scorched. His eyes squinted into slits as he raised a glass of vodka and saluted the photographer. Calvino turned the screen around on the table.

"Was this one of the men on the boat?"

She leaned forward and looked at the screen.

"Everyone called him Khun Stev."

When he didn't reach for his wallet to reward her answer, she sat back, folding her legs up, smoking and looking bored.

"We go bedroom now?"

She was on the fast track to get the show over and back to the bar. In the two months since he'd met her, Dew had mastered the stagecraft. There was fun and there was work. She stared at Calvino. He was work. He removed his wallet and set it next to his computer.

"If you tell me about the two nights on the boat, you get another two thousand baht and you can go."

"Can."

The response was a little too eager.

"You don't leave anything out."

"Give me four thousand."

"That's a lot for a boat story with no happy ending."

She registered a half-smile; every working *ying* knew a happy ending was what a punter paid for. What she'd come to appreciate, though, was that happy endings were far more complicated than she'd ever imagined, and men were simply never happy.

"I promise your friend not to tell you."

"He's dead."

She thought about the logic of promises ending on death. Hawk-eyed, Dew watched him like a rabbit in an open field. He slowly removed the notes from his wallet, one by one. He stopped and looked up.

"Three thousand baht plus the two I already gave you at the restaurant makes five. That's how much I gave to your *mamasan*. She worked hard to bring you back. Time now for you to go to work, Dew."

THREE

Pattaya, Chonburi Province—Wednesday, September 9

"Som's a Jpeg," Dew whispered to Josh.

IT STARTED AFTER a Russian pimp named Victor recruited Dew's friend. Over a period of ten years, Victor had run a string of beautiful women for Russian expats. He'd been introduced to Maxim, who found him a useful supplier of pretties suitable to entertain guests on his 110-foot yacht, the *Last Money*, which the crew also referred to as *Easy Money*, *Fast Money*, or *Stupid Money*. The *Last Money*, when not at sea with pretties, was anchored at the Pattaya Yacht Club. One day, Victor received his usual call from Maxim.

"I want some stunning young women, superstars."

This was his usual grocery list. Victor trolled the bar selecting the best on offer. Maxim set a budget high enough to ensure that these yacht ornaments would burnish his reputation in front of his important associates.

Not every *ying* Victor recruited came from a bar or a lounge.

For instance, Victor spotted Taya walking down Beach Road. She'd wandered out alone. An Englishman had bar-fined her out of a Soi Cowboy bar and taken her to Pattaya that evening. The next day he'd made the mistake of parking her alone in a small room in a low-rent hotel near the beach. The Englishman had left to go drinking with friends. Taya got bored and went out for food, dressed in a tank top, shorts, and heels. Victor had opened the door of his SUV and offered her a ride. He had a small brown moustache, brown eyes, and bags under his eyes like he'd not slept in years. But he wasn't ugly or vile. He looked fit enough for a middle-aged *farang*, with soft-looking hands and an easy smile. She said that her hotel was just across the road. He offered her a ride anyway. After she closed the door, he headed for the marina.

"You like boats?"

Taya nodded. "Like."

"Ever been on a big boat?"

She shook her head. He parked the SUV in the marina and pointed out the *Last Money* in the distance. It was hard to miss; it was the largest boat moored in the marina.

Taya smiled. "That boat?"

Then Victor explained to her the terms of the package. She'd never seen anything like the *Last Money*. It was a ship, not a boat.

"Seven thousand a night, two-night minimum," he said.

She asked if she could bring a friend from the bar.

"Only if she is catwalk beautiful. Otherwise, sorry, friend or no friend, she doesn't get on the yacht. Understand?"

Victor had his reputation to consider.

"I go on boat now?"

"Tomorrow."

"Why tomorrow?"

"Because tonight you stay with me."

She had things back at the hotel. Victor asked what they were. The inventory was the usual collection of clothes, toilet articles, and makeup that would fit in a bag big enough for two hamsters.

"I buy everything new. You don't go back to your room."

"I call my friend," Taya said.

"Phone her. Is your friend in Pattaya?"

"She will be soon." As she waited for Dew to answer, Taya wondered if Victor was paying seven thousand for her to stay with him. He had a shiny new SUV, looked rich, and promised a budget to buy her a new set of road clothes and accessories, but he didn't act like he owned the yacht. He acted like a big shot, but she had the idea that his boss was on the boat. Bosses paid more.

Dew paid her own bar fine and took the bus from Ekamai Station, arriving in Pattaya at nine in the evening. Victor drove Taya to the bus station to meet her. He smiled as he watched her wave at Taya and walk in that confident, slow stride, all slender hips in motion, moving toward the SUV. Dew had long dark hair falling over her shoulders, beneath her short skirt, tapered legs like a supermodel, and a face that his boss would like aboard the *Last Money*.

"Superstar," he said, slamming the heel of one hand on the steering wheel.

She climbed into the back and leaned forward, extending her hand.

Victor reached back and shook her hand.

"My name is Dew."

"You like water, Dew?"

"I like man with a water heart," she said, winking at Taya.

A water heart signaled a secret wish that the empathy sluice gate would open, showering the person on the other side with money.

"You'll have to settle for a yacht heart." He smiled.

Taya and Dew exchanged perplexed looks and shrugged, their faces caught in the expression that meant "Crazy *farang*. Who knows what the fuck they're talking about?" On the ride to the marina Taya explained in Thai the financial package. She'd hinted about the money on the phone, sufficient information for Dew to pay her own bar fine—an uncommon practice—and take off for Pattaya, all on the word of a friend.

Victor had his own orientation program. No flirting with, wooing, seducing, or talking to the crew. The yacht's eight-member crew were off limits—not even eye contact was allowed. As for the big boss and his guest—there would be only one guest, an American—flirting, kissing, wooing, teasing (playfully done), and easing into the bed was in the job description. They understood the necessity of acting out passionate orgasms and romantic feelings, which for an instant created the "girlfriend" experience.

Victor explained the difference between the girlfriend and whore experiences. He told them that at night they were to stay below deck, and anyone caught topside would have a problem. Being in a yacht at sea, no one wanted a problem. During the day they could move around on the top deck, relax, enjoy themselves. But at night they were ordered to stay below deck unless requested by the big boss or his special guest—and someone would come to bring them up. No photographs allowed. No phone calls. Victor said they had to give him their cell phones, and once the yacht returned to Pattaya, they'd be given back. Nothing they saw or heard on the yacht could leave the yacht. No gossip about the big boss or his friend.

Victor stared at each of them. "This is important. Thai girls like to talk too much. It's dangerous for them when I find out. And I know many people. Victor always finds out. Believe me, you don't want my big bosses to get angry with Victor. Once a long time ago a *ying* go back to her bar and talk too much, and later she disappeared. No one could ever find her."

Dew and Taya got the picture.

A member of the crew greeted them on arrival with a bottle of champagne. They tried not to smile. Victor took them below deck. On the right was the engine room. They looked inside at the 18,500 horsepower engines, red and polished and silent. Down the lower deck corridor, Victor walked ahead and opened a door. He stepped into the master cabin and gestured at the bed and head. Taya stuck her head in and smiled. He closed the yacht door, turned to his right, and walked two steps, opening another yacht door. Dew peered inside the guest cabin. The cabins had varnished, triple-planked mahogany paneling with cream-colored furnishings and matching trim.

Having changed into her bikini, Taya emerged from the master cabin first and walked into Dew's cabin without knocking. Dew turned around, fastening her bikini top.

They hugged. "This is a rich *farang*," said Taya. "How much you think boat cost?"

"More than a million baht," said Dew.

Sticking his head into the guest cabin, Victor said, "*Last Money* costs sixty times that amount just to operate. The diesel fuel tanks hold 32,000 gallons. It costs more than two million baht to fill it."

Neither *ying* had any frame of reference for how much fuel that was or how anyone could spend that kind of money to fill up a boat, but they liked the idea that the big boss with that kind of money had invited them aboard.

Taya and Dew climbed up to the top deck, padding barefoot over the floorboards of the cockpit. Spotting a Jacuzzi amidships, they raced to it and eased in up to their necks. Their fingers, splayed, pushed through white lotus petals, sending them in tiny swirls on the water's surface. They drank champagne and waited for someone to tell them what to do. Victor stayed behind, and they wondered who would take Victor's place.

Two other *yings* showed up a half-hour later. Neither Dew nor Taya had set eyes on the new *yings* before. They were tall and slender like models, with silky white skin and thin arms, and were perfumed sweet enough to foul the satellite navigation system. The four eyed each other like gladiators inside the Roman Coliseum. Victor assigned each of the newcomers to one of the cabins. Daeng shared with Taya and Som with Dew. Divide and conquer. If Victor's intention onshore had been to scare the *yings*, he'd not quite succeeded. But fear re-emerged like a bad disease once the four *yings* looked each other over.

It took about twenty minutes before they reached a truce; after an hour they were friends. Each understood the situation and had begun to look more like the whore role rather than the girlfriend part. The big boss had hedged his *ying* bets. Or he might have liked variety in his diet. A real gourmet normally didn't eat at buffets. But a sexual gourmet ate anything put in front of him. Even without meeting the big boss, Taya and Dew had a grudging admiration for a *farang* who was rich enough to shell out two million baht for a tank of diesel, along with four beautiful women in a Jacuzzi.

So where was he, Victor's replacement? Or would it be just the big boss and his friend?

Victor didn't tell them why he wasn't staying on the yacht. It wasn't all that necessary because they knew he'd finished his business. He waved from the marina as the yacht got underway. They watched him until he became a dot, and then even the dot disappeared as a tiny line of sand hugged the sky and sea.

The women were on the top deck while Maxim and his guest worked—Taya didn't know what kind of work—in the stateroom below, which featured cream-colored sofas, blue and red striped pillows, a long coffee table, a large LCD screen TV, a stereo system, lamps, and ceiling lighting. When Maxim emerged for dinner, Josh Levy, a step behind, saw the four *yings* splashing water at each other in the Jacuzzi. It was the first time Dew locked eyes with Josh, giving him that hypnotic, swinging-from-the-chrome-pole power stare.

He smiled at her. Her onstage magic—the Thais call it *saneh*—transferred without a bump, adapting almost immediately to life on the top deck of a yacht. She returned her stage smile; it was all working for her. And Josh, during dinner, continued to glance her way. Dew and the other *yings* perched on a couch a few feet away from the dining table. Taya's hair was wet, dripping down her shoulders and back. Dew slowly toweled as the two men ate.

A chef, a small Thai man who hovered near the table, had prepared fresh lobsters, a plate of caviar, smoked salmon, black bread, and a large bowl of pumpkin soup. Maxim had ordered him to make the soup because he loved asking the chef to slowly repeat the Thai word for pumpkin, which sounded roughly like "fuck thong."

Maxim had his eye on Taya and her roommate, Daeng, a Chiang Mai *ying*. He snapped his fingers, and a member of the crew came up and saluted him. Maxim told him to take Taya and Daeng to the master cabin, turn on the air, and close the door. The remaining two *yings* smiled at Josh, who looked over his shoulder to see who they were looking at. It took a moment before it registered they were looking at him. No one had informed him about the sleeping arrangements. He waited, thinking Maxim would say something on the subject. But after a while Josh forgot about it, or figured it wouldn't be a problem.

"Do you like the soup?" Maxim asked.

Josh leaned over his soup, chin dipped like a boxer looking for an opening, his eyes focused on Dew.

"Chef, what's the Thai name of this soup again?"

The chef half-whispered the Thai name as if he were coughing up a frog.

"Fuck what?"

"Fuck thong," said the chef, like a guitar player holding the beat, sneaking a smile at the *yings*.

Maxim pointed at the soup. "You have this kind of soup in New York?"

"It's probably illegal to call a soup by that name." Josh decided to play along with Maxim's word game.

After dinner Josh paired off with Dew and the *ying* named Som, who shadowed them to the guest cabin like a spare tire waiting for Dew to go flat. She was waiting to wheel Dew off the road and jack up Josh and have him running around those hairpin curves on the guest cabin's queen-sized bed.

Som crawled off the bed, pulled a towel around herself, and slipped into the head, where she turned on the shower.

"Som's a Jpeg," Dew whispered to Josh.

Josh furrowed his brow. "A what?"

"A *ying* who prefers to sleep with Japanese customers."

"How computer literate of her," said Josh.

But Dew didn't understand the connection. A Jpeg had nothing to do with computers. It was a code word among the *yings*, a word she assumed everyone knew. Borrowed language is like a corrupted digital file with the pixels rearranged, creating images with overlapping but distinctly different meanings.

She saw from his expression that Josh didn't get it. Plan B was always the same: change the subject.

"I like *farang*," said Dew. "I like you."

"I've never, never slept with two women," he said.

He tried to make a joke about it. He wasn't certain how it worked or what to do. The sound of the shower filled the silence between them. Dew thought he was teasing her. But true or not, it didn't matter, and clearly that was the way he wanted her to play it: innocent. She touched his forehead; he had a thin band of sweat.

Som stepped out of the shower singing, a towel wrapped around her breast. Still singing, she jumped onto the bed. She was also very drunk.

Dew thought about taking a shower but it was risky; it meant leaving Josh alone in the room with Som. If this man sitting next to her on the bed were truly that new to the scene, it was possible that Som would be his first Thai *ying*. The bar *ying* rule of thumb, same for bankers—first priority is not only important but essential. Always be his first Thai girlfriend. There could only be one First One; all the others would blur until they became a collective vagueness like a memory inside an Alzheimer's brain. With a man like Victor or Maxim there was no chance, even if she mattered for a while. Inside their world a *ying* had no chance to join the tenure track. She was on her way out as quickly as she'd gone in. Except for the money, a *ying* in that position saw a dead end, a place where priority was largely irrelevant.

Only Josh seemed different. He wasn't like Maxim or Victor. He was a nice guy.

Dew held her position on the bed, placing a possessive hand on Josh's leg. The two *yings* on the bed exchanged a glance that was all about guarding a perimeter. Josh slipped out of his trousers and unbuttoned his shirt. He was taking it off when there was a knock on the door. He ignored it, dropping the shirt on a chair. Josh was down to his underwear as he climbed into bed. The knock came a second time, only a bit louder, and Som giggled. Josh rolled off the bed and padded barefoot to the door. He opened it a crack and saw one of the Russian crew standing outside. The Russian, who looked like he'd been carved from a slab of bronze, told him that Maxim was waiting for him on the top deck.

"Maxim's request," said the Russian, shifting his eyes to the two *yings* in the bed behind Josh.

"When does he want to meet?"

"Now."

314

The Russian, smelling of brine and oil, pushed his way forward and stepped into the bedroom. Like a large reptile, he showed no emotion, tongue flicking at the air, registering temperature and tasting the fear sweating out of the pores of his prey. His eyes locked on Dew, who huddled together with Som. The two of them were whispering and smiling like teenagers. Som asked why fate had sent a young, handsome man to take away an old, balding guy with spiny legs. They both giggled.

Josh stood in his underwear, belly hanging over the elastic, and raised his hands.

"Sorry girls, but I need to see my friend. I'll be back in a couple of minutes. Don't go away."

He looked back, smiled, and quickly dressed. The Russian stood in the doorway, watching.

As the two men turned to leave, the Russian leaned into the cabin and switched off the lights.

"Boss's orders."

Dew crawled under the sheets and bedspread, hugging a pillow. Som sat beside her in the dark.

"Are you afraid of ghosts?" asked Dew.

Som crawled under the sheets and the two *yings* hugged each other.

Josh ambled behind the Russian, a lanky, tall man—five inches taller than himself—and twenty-five years young, up to the top deck.

The Russian walked aft, stopping at a railing.

"Wait," he said.

He disappeared below deck, leaving Josh alone.

A yacht at sea, Josh thought. But exactly where they were, he had no idea. He looked around but couldn't see anything but the running lights splitting the black sea like yellow tongues. He drew the sea smell into his lungs—wet, languid, easy, like stepping into the big forever. It was pitch dark. Below, the dull ache of the dual engines crept through the silence. The heading was seaward, the speed leisurely. Nothing about the trip spoke of rush or hurry.

When the Russian returned, he said, "Follow me."

Josh graduated from one to two-word sentences.

The summons sent by Maxim had broken the holiday spell. Josh followed the Russian down to the mid-deck, where Maxim sat in a lounge area. The lounge was a huge, enclosed salon.

"Josh, join me," he said. Several lights illuminated the furnishings—two sofas and three stuffed chairs. Enough crystal and art to make it even more obvious that Maxim was inventing a world he wanted others to admire and envy. Josh entered the area looking around like a virgin in a knock shop, not certain he was allowed to touch anything or sit down.

Maxim stretched his arm across the top of the sofa, one leg crossed, cigar smoke curling out of one corner of his mouth. A brandy glass with the bottom third covered in vodka sat in front of him on the table. Maxim made no effort to get up or shake hands.

"What do you think of your two?"

"Is this something about the licensing agreement?" asked Josh, lowering himself into one of the chairs.

Maxim, cigar smoke drifting slowly from each nostril, poured another vodka and handed it to Josh.

"Drink. No licensing agreement discussion tonight. Tonight you relax. First, though, I have a small job for you."

"Yeah?"

Josh took a sip. The idea of work made him feel more comfortable.

"You get to be a witness."

"Happy to. But I didn't bring a pen," Josh said, patting his jacket.

316

He had a top-of-the-line Montblanc that he used for witnessing documents.

"You don't have to sign anything. All you need to use are your two eyes," said Maxim, reaching for his vodka.

The man who had escorted him to Maxim's presence earlier returned with another brandy glass filled with ice and poured vodka to the top, handing it to Josh.

"If I drink this, I'll be blind drunk. And that wouldn't make a good impression on Andrei, getting drunk with someone my boss is doing business with."

He thought that Andrei's name was a perfect shield, only Maxim ignored him, raising his glass to touch his.

"A toast to your new job, and watching out for Andrei's business."

He sipped his vodka and watched Josh drink from his glass.

"And I'd like to toast Andrei. Your boss expects you to get drunk. He'd be surprised if you didn't."

That didn't seem right and it confused Josh. He became less confused as Maxim's toasts proceeded to honor good sailing, beautiful women, and fuck thong soup.

"You don't know how Andrei and me started," said Maxim. "It is a valuable education."

Maxim talked about the old days in Russia and how Andrei had been the one to see his potential. Maxim had financed his first charter plane with money borrowed from Andrei. He had invested in two more business deals with Maxim, and after that they did many more deals together. That made them, in Josh's mind, partners of a sort.

"My uncle was a famous man in Russia, a mathematician, and he won the prize every mathematician wants. Was there ever something you wanted very much and would do anything to get?"

Josh thought about the beach house in East Hampton.

"Andrei never won that prize. My uncle won it. I introduced Andrei to my uncle years ago. He held the award in his hand. He held it like a fucking bible."

When Josh looked at his watch, nearly an hour had passed—long enough for him to become drunk. Vodka, damp and hot in his throat, created an event horizon that swallowed reason. It was late. He had two women in his cabin. So far he hadn't done anything except get almost naked with them. Maybe Maxim was doing him a favor by taking him away from temptation. He hadn't exactly cheated on Tess yet, he told himself. The second brandy glass of vodka had kicked in, knocking against the back of his head like a horse kicking the door in its stable.

The mood changed when two Russian crew members, smelling of cooked cabbage and vodka, frog-marched Wirot through the entryway and into the lounge. Josh sat facing the hatch. He saw the frightened older Thai man with hands and legs tied with nylon rope, his mouth gagged. His eyes, backlit with fear, pleaded with Maxim and the two Russians. Maxim smiled, sipped his vodka, and slowly started to applaud. He was on his feet, hands stretched out, pleading to Josh.

"Let's enjoy the night," Maxim said.

He nodded at the crew, who pulled Wirot, struggling, away from the hatch.

"What's this?"

"It's work. You're on the job for your boss."

Josh's legs wobbled as he climbed to the top deck. Maxim came up behind. They emerged in time to see one of the men drag a long length of heavy chain from a box on the deck. Wirot knelt on the top deck, his head bent forward, his hands tied behind his back. He struggled until he ran out of steam. The men wrapped the chain around his neck and then looped it around his waist. Wirot lifted his head under the weight of the chain and looked at Josh this time as if to say, "Don't at least you have the decency?"

Josh hadn't said a word. He was speechless as Wirot started whimpering under his gag.

"What the fuck are you doing?" asked Josh. The color washed out of his face.

"*Doveryai, no proveryai*," said Maxim.

"Meaning?" asked Josh, his voice wavering as if it were he who was about to be thrown overboard.

"It's Andrei's favorite proverb. Trust but verify. He put you on verification duty. It's how he does business. Andrei hates loose ends and doubt. In simple language, Andrei wants to know if what I tell him is true or bullshit. The trouble with a mathematical mind is it drives a man to cover every bet. My uncle was like this, too. Only he's more brilliant. Don't tell Andrei I said that. He can be quite sensitive about certain matters."

"You aren't going to kill a man."

Horrified, Josh slumped back, shaking his head.

"I am solving a probability problem."

It all depended on how one looked at it. Maxim was removing Wirot as he would pull out a bee's stinger from his hand. He didn't wince as he glanced at the utterly defeated Wirot. Josh waited. He told himself it had to be a test or a joke, something that came from too much vodka. He'd been tapped to be a witness to a murder—it hadn't been in his job description, but he was finding a lot of responsibilities hadn't been spelled out.

Maxim poured another drink. He looked at the sea and smacked his lips. It was the good life. This wasn't murder so much as a business decision, one last banal act of dealing with a loose end. Josh's heart thumping inside his chest and throat seemed ready to burst from his body.

"I don't want to know."

His hands shook; he couldn't stop them.

Maxim nodded at his crew. Three of the big Russian men struggled to lift Wirot, who flopped around like a fish. One of the men pulled a black hood over Wirot's head.

Josh stepped back. Looking over at the stairs that led to the lower decks, he saw Dew's head poke out for a second. He looked over at Maxim and the other Russian who were busy with Wirot. She stuck her head out again and he waved her away. No one else on deck had seen her. But from her vantage point amidships, Dew glimpsed Wirot, a hood over his head, moaning as the crew at the stern lifted him over the side of the top deck.

Maxim had moved to the railing and looked back at Josh. "Come here."

Josh did what he was told. He joined Maxim at the railing, grasping it with both hands to prop himself up.

"Tell Andrei that you saw Maxim clear up the problem. Believe me, he will be pleased."

It was unreal, as if it hadn't really happened. Could someone have tied up and thrown a living person into the open sea? It was an unreal question. He leaned over and looked into the sea. Nothing but a void stretched out, with the cabin lights making buttonholes in the black fabric. The vodka had his mind flipping back and forth between Wirot being thrown overboard and the face of the *ying* who'd been on the bed in his cabin, and who had also witnessed the murder. He studied Maxim. Surely if he'd seen her, he would have done something. Dew would have been one more loose end.

"Who was that man?" asked Josh.

"Wirot. He had the misfortune of outbidding me at the coin auction."

"For a fucking set of coins? I don't fucking believe this. Are you crazy?"

320

Josh was already involved and angry for letting it happen. He couldn't guess the number of counts he'd face in an indictment. They'd hit him for accessory to murder, kidnapping, corrupting the morals of women—and that would be just the first page. On page two they could charge him with grand theft, fraud, conspiracy, and a hundred other things for transporting the murdered man's coins to New York.

"Never cross Andrei. He doesn't play nice. You can go back to your cabin. Your work is done. Now you can play."

Josh had drunk too much, and when he looked at Maxim the nose and mouth blurred, crossed, and doubled-crossed. As Josh entered his guest cabin, he stumbled, moaned, staggered forward, and sat on the bed, massaging his big toe. It was dark and he couldn't find the light switch. He sensed from the lump at one end of the bed that one of them had curled up on the bed, a sheet pulled up to her neck. He could hear her snoring. Not far from where Josh sat, Dew sat with her legs folded up, her chin perched on her knees, watching him.

"It hurt?"

"Yes, it hurts," he said. "Do you know where the light switch is?"

She scooted off the bed, walked over, and flipped the switch. Turning, she resumed her position on the bed as if she were doing yoga.

She watched him run into the head and throw up in the toilet. She heard him brush his teeth, turn off the light, and crawl into bed. She touched his face with the back of her hand.

"You should have stayed in the cabin," he said.

"I get too scared."

"What about your friend?" whispered Josh, pointing at Som lying on her side, snoring.

Som wasn't really her friend.

"Som talk, talk. She get me scared. Ghosts. I think I hear one. I can't stay. So I go find you."

They sat in silence for a long moment.

"You saw what happened on top?"

"I don't know. I am very confused. I see a ghost. Men catch him."

"You know that wasn't a ghost," he said.

"I think ghost now."

"Did you tell Som?"

"No."

"Well, don't. You must promise never to tell anybody. It's important. Do you understand?"

She nodded her head several times.

"Dew not stupid girl. Dew understand."

Josh sighed and turned on his side, leaving Dew in the middle between him and Som. He felt her edge closer until their bodies touched, and she wrapped her arms around his waist, shaking with fear. He'd never had a Thai girl, this wasn't going to be the night for it. He'd just seen a man killed. Making love to a strange woman was as remote to him now as the possibility of swimming to shore and phoning the police. No memory of a first sexual encounter could ever survive what had happened to Wirot. Dew knew from the way that Josh breathed that he was pretending to sleep but that his mind was racing, ticking over, seeing those Russian men throw a man into the sea. He'd been invited aboard to be a witness. She'd been invited to keep the witness happy. Neither invitation was what it had appeared to be on firm land.

As he lay in bed, he told Dew that he was thinking of Tess, wishing she were beside him at that moment. She stroked his face. The words of Breathe's "Hands to Heaven" filtered through his mind. He wanted Tess to hold him in the darkness so he could feel her, taste her. He said he needed Tess to tell him it wasn't his fault, that he'd be okay, and to allow him to disappear into her, praying for forgiveness. Dew had listened until he'd gone quiet, falling asleep in her arms.

Calvino filled in some of the gaps in Dew's story and went over them with her until she raised both hands in surrender.

"*Paw laew,*" she said in Thai. Enough inside her world was never enough when it came to money. Now she wanted to have her money for the story she'd told so she could return to Soi Cowboy and find a customer.

He took out three thousand baht as she watched. She hadn't been lying back in October when she'd said that she knew Josh Levy. It explained why Josh had been so happy to get away from the dance stage and go upstairs. Of all the whorehouses in Bangkok, Calvino had dragged him into the one bar where Josh would encounter the one *ying* he hoped never to see again.

Number 19 had squatted down and leaned out with her hand to Josh, and he had pretended not to know her. She understood why he acted that way. He looked scared and helpless as she bent forward and kissed him softly on the forehead. If she opened her mouth, she could link him to a murder. Calvino wondered if for an instant Josh might have had second thoughts about letting her leave the yacht. But Josh wasn't a criminal. He lacked the natural instinct needed for killing someone. Instead, he acted like a civilian caught under fire in a war zone. "Get me outta here," had been written all over his face.

Josh was tough when it came to fighting over language in a document, but none of that toughness translated into a world where men killed each other. The violence on the yacht would have appalled him. Watching a man being murdered and doing and saying nothing must have rushed back like a hammer blow to the head as Dew called out to him at the bar. Calvino had to hand it to him. He'd held himself together, hadn't blown his composure. He'd pulled it off. Josh had acted like a lost fool of a tourist who was the fish out of water in a Bangkok bar, and Calvino had swallowed the act hook, line, and sinker.

As he put the notes on the glass table, Calvino said, "You haven't been working the bar. Where are you getting money?"

It was a rare bar *ying* who saved for a rainy day; it was a common bar *ying* who kept a list of punters in her cell phone as her umbrella. Getting a square job in the above-board daytime world was as likely for Dew as a hit man going into the business of selling life insurance.

"I have sponsor," she said.

Calvino smiled. "Anyone I might know?"

She shrugged.

"What's his name?" he asked, picking up the notes from the table.

"Victor." She tilted her head and smiled. "No like Russians. My sponsor is Norwegian man. Very good to Dew."

He was glad that Maxim's pimp hadn't managed to keep her on his starting roster. Calvino clicked on a folder icon and a series of images filled the computer monitor. He scrolled through the images, clicked on one, and studied it before turning the monitor around for Dew.

"Have you ever seen this guy?"

She leaned forward, face in the screen, looking at a photograph of Andrei. One of those professional studio jobs with the right lighting and a Photoshop brush to shave ten years off the face and twenty pounds off the body. Her lower lip rolled between her teeth, only to be replaced by her upper lip. She rotated the lip grind as she was deciding what to tell Calvino, never taking her eyes off the money.

She scratched her head. "Maybe," she said.

"He wouldn't be the reason you were in Bangkok?" asked Calvino.

"Maybe," she said.

"*Mamasan* phoned you and said, come to the bar, an old customer wants to see you, and you tell Andrei your mother has a problem and you need to take her to the hospital."

"I go now," she said, holding her hand out for the money.

She had made no connection between the three men—Andrei, Josh, and Maxim. Why should she? Victor had sent her out to a customer who wanted a quality act, who could go to dinner and not look like a hooker. Dew was smart enough to know that each time she opened her mouth in front of a high-rolling client she lost value. He figured she was smart enough to keep a lid on it around the Russians. Let them do all the talking, believing that all their words belonged to the *ying* next to them. The thing with most men was that they had pretty much the same set of stories they told every stranger. Calvino had an idea that stories Andrei told hookers didn't have a lot of original material. He'd have likely tapped into his usual story about his grandchildren. Hookers loved grandchildren stories so long as the grandfathers were rich.

"Andrei has a grandson in New York. Did he tell you about Nicholas? That's the kid's name."

Dew nodded. "He show me picture."

"When are you meeting Andrei?"

She looked at her watch. "I go see him tonight."

"With Maxim and your friend Taya?"

She nodded. The *mamasan* had had enough leverage to pull her out for a lousy five thousand baht. Taya, who had worked at the same bar, would have covered for her. Bar ethics, the code by which both *mamasan* and *yings* live, require that everyone sing from the same primal, mysterious, powerful, and haunting hymn book. Only a heart gone stone cold or one wise to the texture of lies could turn away from a young *ying* pleading her mother's medical emergency.

He handed her the money and added another two thousand baht. She looked at the extra two notes and up again at Calvino.

"If we run into each other again, you don't recognize me," said Calvino. "You pretend you've never seen me in your life. The extra two thousand is a tip."

"Tip" ranked in the top three of the bar *ying's* English vocabulary—tip, taxi fare, and telephone number. She put the money in her handbag and *waied* him.

"You think I am stupid girl?"

"Dew, you are a girl who has figured out how to survive. And I admire that. It shows you are an intelligent woman."

FOUR

Bangkok, Sukhumvit Road—Thursday, December 24

"Man, it's Christmas Eve. What do you want me to do? Decapitate the Statue of Liberty?"

RATANA HADN'T EXPECTED to see Calvino at the office. When he walked through the door carrying a wrapped package, she said, "Hello, stranger."

Before saying hello, he gave a series of instructions as in the old days. At the end of the list was a phone call to McPhail: "And get McPhail on the line. Tell him I've got something important to talk to him about."

She raised an eyebrow; phoning McPhail was a new request. Calvino had always phoned his friends himself, especially McPhail, who could be in a situation that a proper secretary shouldn't have direct knowledge of.

"I'm back to work," he said. "And get Colonel Pratt on the phone. Tell him that things are looking up."

"You are in a good mood."

"It's Christmas Eve. How can you not be in a good mood?"

He had that snap back in his step. She would have been happy enough to know that her boss had come into the office, but coming back with his old attitude was a bonus that she hadn't expected. He handed her the package.

"Feels like a book," she said. "I thought you'd bought John-John a teddy bear."

"Yeah, well. A book is better. He's too old for a teddy bear."

"Last week you said he was the perfect age."

"I should have given it to him then."

She had told John-John to expect a teddy bear from Uncle Vincent. He'd been disappointed. After lunch she'd walk to the Emporium and buy John-John a replacement bear and say it was from Uncle Vincent. She slipped the book into her desk drawer and returned to her Skype chat with a friend in England.

Calvino stood at his office desk, feet spread apart, hands folded behind his back, rocking on his heels as he looked down at the *soi*. Three or four taxi driver louts—same faces every day—squatted at the top of the *soi*, smoking and looking like praying mantises, nudging each other when a tourist passed along Soi 33. He watched as one of them trailed after a tourist, shoving in his face a plastic card with the rows of pictures of girls smiling in ballroom gowns from a massage parlor fishbowl.

When Ratana put through the call from McPhail, Calvino picked up the land-line phone.

"Hey, buddy. Lose your cell phone?" asked McPhail. "Senior moment, right?"

"I need a favor," said Calvino. McPhail lived inside an extended junior moment, thought Calvino.

"Man, it's Christmas Eve. What do you want me to do? Decapitate the Statue of Liberty?"

It was mid-morning and McPhail hadn't wasted time; he'd spent the day so far draining the better part of a fresh bottle of Scotch.

"That's the Christmas spirit. I've checked you into a suite at the Oriental Hotel. I'm paying."

"And I'm listening. Who do I have to kill?"

"Ask for the Gore Vidal suite."

"Okay, then?"

"I'll tell you at lunch. Noon. No more drinking until noon."

"Fuck you."

"You want the work?"

McPhail sighed. "It's fucking Christmas Eve. Only an atheist wouldn't drink on Christmas Eve."

"It's money and sobriety or religion and drink. I leave it entirely up to you."

"Religion and money."

"You're not the Pope."

"I'd like to be." His voice had gone meek. "How much money we talking about?"

"I'll tell you over lunch. Put away the bottle, Ed."

As he put down the phone, he watched the first customer of the day walk toward One Hand Clapping, the massage parlor below his office. The man stopped and looked around, as if he were doing something wrong or being followed. He removed his baseball hat and wiped the sweat from his face. Was he lost, confused, or in an elevated state of high anxiety about the massage? Something about the man reminded him of Josh. Frozen in time, his mind racing through a thousand loops, feeding back a stream of images, desires, and voices; then one of those voices blotted out the others. In Josh's case, he hadn't listened to the right voices whispering inside his head. No question that Josh had the brains, but that hadn't stopped him from getting involved with a man who specialized in the mathematics of fear. Someone who could pull him down and destroy him as easily as a savant reciting Pi decimal places.

The customer below disappeared into the massage parlor.

Ratana buzzed through, alerting him to Colonel Pratt's call.

"Colonel, I need a favor," said Calvino. "You don't happen to know someone who's a member at the Jasmine Park Golf Club? I need someone to sign me in."

"I thought you gave up golf," said Colonel Pratt.

"An early New Year's resolution. Ratana's right; I need to get out. Circulate. Get back in the swing of life," he said.

In New York the Colonel had mentioned the trophy Andrei had won at the Jasmine Park Golf Club.

"Vincent, I'll get you on Parkland Heights. When do you want to play?"

"In the next couple of days. I have to check my calendar. Parkland Heights, I don't like the eighth fairway. Jasmine Park is better. But I need some help getting on the course."

"Your calendar is free. And you are stalking Andrei on the golf course. Does that pretty much sum up the game you intend to play?"

"Ratana, is my calendar free for a game of golf this week?" Calvino said.

"Andrei is a busy man," said the Colonel. "I doubt he's got time for a round of golf."

Ratana stood with her shoulder leaning against the doorway, her jaw dropping.

"Golf?" she asked.

He nodded. "The little white ball and the clubs."

"I know what golf is," said the Colonel.

"I was explaining to Ratana. I know that you know what golf is. Doesn't the General have a couple of buddies who belong to the Jasmine Park Golf Club?"

She remembered. There was no problem with her memory. The last time Calvino had played golf, the manager had phoned the office. He was a sweet Thai man who pleaded with her to promise that Calvino would never play at his golf course again, and she could name her price.

Colonel Pratt was quiet. "That might be a problem."

"I'm not going to do anything to cause a problem."

Even the remote possibility of placing General Yosaporn in a compromising position was unthinkable for the Colonel. And most requests by Calvino requiring the General's intervention set off alarm bells. One of the most important functions of a colonel is to shield his general from foreigners. By their very presence, *farangs* are a problem. The Colonel figured there were likely exceptions, but Calvino wasn't one of them.

"And should you just happen to run into Andrei, you're not going to cause a scene?" asked Colonel Pratt.

"If I wanted to confront him, I'd go to his hotel, stalk him in the lobby. If I see him on the fairway, I'll wave. Other than that, I want a game. Maybe I'll even apply to become a member," said Calvino.

"I'll phone you."

"Colonel."

"Yes."

"Merry Christmas."

After the call Ratana thought about the desperation in the voice of the Thai public relations man who had called those years before saying no worse golfer had ever chewed up more fairway than Vincent Calvino. Certainly five or six years of no golf wouldn't have improved Calvino's game.

"Why not play at a less fancy course?" she said.

"Please book me in Paradise Green Hills in case Colonel Pratt doesn't come through."

"He's always come through for you," she said, amazed that such a statement could be made and for it to be true.

"I've tried to do the same for him."

She blinked, waiting for him to explain.

"Sometimes it is better to leave things alone," she said, going back to her office. "Let Colonel Pratt look out for himself, and you do the same."

"That's not very Thai."

"The world's changing, Vinny. Even in Thailand."

Or Ratana, like a lot of other Thais in Bangkok, was changing, shifting from *mai pen rai*—never mind—to *mai yom rap*—I can't accept it. The easygoing days of extending a helping hand had fallen into long, hard days of fists and clenched jaws. Thousands of red-shirted demonstrators were coming into the streets demanding rights. It was the kind of world where no one could be sure what nerve impulse would rattle through and direct the muscle one way or the other.

Calvino had a well-deserved reputation for hiding his hand. That much Ratana knew. He told her that the less she knew about a case, the better off she was. Ignorance, Calvino believed, was highly underrated as a component of happiness. Not knowing Calvino had something cooking with Andrei and Maxim was a good thing; she wouldn't tense up into a ball of worry over something outside her control. And she wouldn't pass along her fears to Colonel Pratt.

Calvino made his last call of the morning. Mr. Tanaka came on the line and clearly remembered Calvino. He'd stopped into his dealership several afternoons to look at a Honda Accord.

"I was thinking more about the Accord," he said.

"Beautiful car, Mr. Calvino. Have fresh green tea. Come and have a cup. Look at the car."

"I have a better idea. How about we play a game of golf? It would be good to discuss the Accord. I've heard good things about the Jasmine Park Country Club. You wouldn't know someone who's a member?"

Craning his neck, Calvino looked around the corner and saw Ratana busy hammering at the keyboard, eyes glued to the screen, headphones in place.

"You do? That's great. I'll check my schedule and phone you back. Do you have a silver-gray Accord in stock? I thought you might have one."

Even the rats in Washington Square would have agreed that the standards of public health, service, and food at the Lonesome Hawk had seen better days. At the bar two or three faces looked like they'd been squeezed out of a caulking gun and left to dry overnight on scaffolding. No one talked. Heads half-bowed over their beers. The waitresses bunched in a corner, picking at a plate of *som tam* with a ball of sticky rice wedged between their fingers.

Calvino walked past Old George's framed photograph on the wall of ghosts, the display of photos going back decades of men who drank at the bar, told each other lies, grown old, and died. McPhail was in a corner booth with a cup of coffee—real coffee. He'd checked rack rates for an author's suite at the Oriental. He was willing to stop drinking on Christmas Eve to bunk in a room that cost that kind of money. Besides, once he was in the suite, Calvino gone, he'd stretch out, kick back, and order some vintage champagne on Calvino's tab.

"Coffee," said Calvino, as if he'd had some doubt.

"The real stuff Terry sends from Hawaii."

"Terry's coffee is mandatory."

"I hate that word."

"Obligatory."

"Hate that word, too."

"Ratana booked the suite under the name Alex Atwood and Eric Mallory. You're Atwood, who is checking into the suite today. I'm Mallory, checking in tomorrow or the next day."

"I've got to share a room with you?"

"Here's Atwood's passport, California driver's license, Visa credit card, and business card. Says you are a commodities broker in Los Angeles."

"Who are you?"

"Las Vegas event promoter."

"Check in this afternoon. Take a carry-on bag. Once you're inside, keep track of the guest across the hall. I want

333

to know when he comes and goes, and everyone you see him with—women, staff, guests, or deliveries. Note down everything taken into or out of the room—whores, flowers, booze, golf bags, suitcases, briefcases, or live snakes."

"Live snakes?"

"Seeing if you were paying attention. Write it all down. Here are some photos. That's Andrei. That's Maxim. The *ying* is named Dew. Phone me anytime you see any of them leave the room. When Andrei goes out, you follow him. That's why I need you sober. When you drink, the next thing you do is talk to anyone who'll listen. Drunk, the guy you're tailing becomes your new best friend. Your job is to be my eyes. Let me know if he's leaving the hotel or if he's in one of the restaurants or the Bamboo Lounge. Press the hot button if you hear anything about a round of golf."

In his mind's eye McPhail stared at the vintage bottle of champagne, thinking about opening it. He'd only half-heard Calvino.

"Golf?"

It was as if the word had sprouted wings and flown away.

"Andrei's a player."

"No one would ever say that about you," said McPhail.

"You've made your point. Got any other questions?"

McPhail dreaded the idea of standing with his eye against a peephole for hours, waiting to spy on people in the corridor. He sipped his coffee.

"How many days are we talking about?"

Calvino shrugged, held up one, two, and finally three fingers, before folding his hand into a fist.

"You don't know how many days, is what you're saying."

"You've got it. You're on the payroll. I pick up the expenses and put three hundred a day in your pocket, assuming you don't fuck up and start drinking or fall asleep at the door."

"What if I have to take a piss?"

"You've got time to shake it twice."

Calvino pulled McPhail's chits out of the cup, put them together with a thousand baht note, and waved at the barkeeper.

"You want me to go now?"

Calvino nodded. "Now is soon enough."

"When are you checking in?"

"Later, after I finish up some business."

"Where are you going?" asked McPhail, rising from the booth. "It's Christmas Eve. I need to do my shopping."

"Wait until the day after. Everything is half-price," said Calvino.

"The thing with Santa—he's never a day late."

Calvino got his change, stuffed a hundred baht note tip into the chit cup, and walked out with McPhail.

There are precious few places where the rich and powerful criminal classes feel secure enough to relax their guard—on a private yacht, on a Lear jet, and on an exclusive golf course. The first two are nearly impossible to access without the resources available to government intelligence agents. But a private golf club is another matter. With acres of rolling lawns under the open skies, a golf club is an ideal place for deals to be made, money to change hands, and commissions to be wrangled over.

The ears and eyes of an experienced private investigator could easily pierce the world of greens and fairways; it was like sitting on the deck of a yacht at sea, without the risk of exposure. Calvino thought of Wirot disappearing over the side of the *Last Money*. Josh Levy dead too. Ditto Tess Reynolds.

Colonel Pratt had told Calvino about a golf trophy from Jasmine Park in Andrei's New York office. What Calvino hadn't passed along to Colonel Pratt was one tiny piece of information turned up by Calvino's investigation; he'd found that the member who'd signed Andrei in at Jasmine Park that time had been Maxim. Calvino had a feeling the two Russians might have another round to wrap up unfinished business, and this time he wanted to be inside the club.

The day after the authorities released the five-man flight crew and Maxim's plane, McPhail phoned Calvino and told him that Andrei had had a wakeup call at 6:00 a.m. and ordered a limo to take him to Jasmine Park Golf Club in Chonburi. He phoned Calvino a short time later and said a bellboy had come to Andrei's room and left with a set of golf clubs. The bellboy juggled the golf bag. Using his knee to balance it against the wall, he freed his hands to *wai* Andrei and pocket his tip. McPhail got a good look at the black leather golf bag, sealed up, no clubs showing, a platinum chain looped through the zipper lock. Dangling from the chain was a gold medallion.

"What kind of medallion?"

"You want me to go across the hall, knock on his door and ask him?"

"I thought you might have got a look."

"All I saw was some kind of head. It could have been Lenin. It could have been George Washington. I am looking through a peephole, not a telescope."

"Thanks, McPhail. Good job."

"I thought you were staying here in the room."

"Getting lonely?"

"Fuck off, Calvino."

"That's pretty much what I plan to do. Got an early golf match lined up."

With the phone still in one hand, McPhail lit a cigarette with the other. He got up to pull a miniature bottle of whiskey from the fridge and drank straight from the bottle until it was empty. He smacked his lips into the phone, belched, and tossed the empty at a wastebasket beside the sofa. He missed.

Calvino phoned Colonel Pratt, who was in the middle of dinner with his family.

"How did it go with General Yosaporn?" Calvino said.

"He's been busy," said Colonel Pratt. "It is a holiday season."

"It's okay. Don't bother him until after the New Year."

"That's the Christmas present I wanted. Thanks, Vincent. And Merry Christmas."

Next Calvino phoned Tanaka, who answered with an ear-piercing groan, followed by a loud serious of slaps and several masculine grunts and moans, like music notes registering in the upper alto pleasure zone. Tanaka lay face down on a massage table, and on either side of his towel-wrapped body, two *yings* raised their cupped hands, striking up and down at Tanaka's thighs and buttocks like a couple of musicians on barrel drums. In the middle of this concert, Tanaka raised his head and pressed his iPhone to his ear.

"About that game of golf," said Calvino. "First thing tomorrow morning. Tee off at 8:30 a.m. Afterwards, I come around for my Accord."

He never gave Tanaka a chance to protest. The way Tanaka was getting worked over, he didn't have a chance to say that he'd already booked the course, teeing off at 9.00 a.m. When Tanaka phoned back two hours later, he gave Calvino the news, suggesting he'd had to burn some chits to accommodate the request. Tanaka had one more piece of information; Calvino would be playing with three Japanese, two of whom spoke no English.

"No problem," said Calvino.

His success at getting Tanaka to sign him in at Jasmine Park was starting to convert Calvino into a believer in karma.

FIVE

Chonburi Province—December 26

Transire suum pectus mundoque potiri.

CALVINO SLIPPED HIS car into the far end of the parking lot, even though there were empty spaces closer to the clubhouse. The fountains in the lake nearby carried a light mist to the edge of the parking area. It felt refreshing as he crossed to the enormous clubhouse, with a large arched doorway. Along one side was a tennis court, and on the other a swimming pool, the clear blue water catching the early morning sun. Calvino set foot into the most exclusive golf course in Thailand. The feeling was that of a five-star spa, one of those places movie stars and celebrities loved largely for their entry restrictions.

Everything about the clubhouse, including the manicured garden, tropical flowering plants, shrubs, palms, and banana trees, suggested that cost savings had not been an issue during the construction. Reception had three names marked down next to Tanaka's, two of them Japanese and the third Khun Win. He told the receptionist that he was Khun Win. She gave him a double look; the Thai name didn't belong to the *farang* face in front of her.

"Tanaka uses my Thai nickname. You know, the Japanese get confused with *farang* names. I corrected him before. My name's Vincent, I tell Tanaka. He nods and calls me Khun Win."

338

Times and parties change all the time. The reception book was written in number 2 pencil. Calvino looked over her shoulder as she ran her long red fingernail by his name.

Looking at the register, he spotted the names of Maxim and three guests; two Thais and Andrei had been checked off. They were on the course. Or they could still be in the clubhouse. Calvino looked around at the other golfers and staff. The woman at the reception desk looked Calvino up and down as he explained how he and Tanaka were old buddies. He described Tanaka and added that the other men were Japanese. At that point she leaned over, shaking her head, and looked up from the registration book. Avoiding confrontation was a mantra that had begun to be shed in the name of progress and modernity.

She didn't smile as she handed him a locker key, wrote down the number and time, and pointed him to a sofa near the entrance of the locker room.

"You wait for Mr. Tanaka. Club policy."

She'd gone cold ever since Calvino had insisted on the name being wrong.

He sat in a chair, watching golfers coming and going from the locker room, dressed like pimps and smiling like fools. The men had reverted to the baseline of the ninth grade, when hormones rushed like a flash flood through their veins and all the girls were young, pretty, and innocent. Calvino left his golf cart and clubs outside on the pavement. He turned his key over. The number 209 was engraved into the bronze handle.

Fifteen minutes later, Tanaka arrived with his two friends, who with gunfighter speed flashed embossed business cards. Calvino tried to guide them away from the receptionist.

"My friend, Mr. Tanaka," Calvino said.

Tanaka swelled up his chest. "Khun Win's my guest," he said.

That sealed the identity deal with the receptionist, who turned away to answer the phone.

"I've got my business cards in my bag outside."

"You change already?" asked Tanaka, looking impressed.

"I'm ready to tee up," said Calvino, nodding, looking at the two perplexed Japanese guests, who looked on without understanding a single word. "See you outside."

Outside the main entrance he followed the paved walkway past the flower bed of red and pink roses to the area the caddies called Mr. Queue, where they waited for customers.

Calvino watched as Tanaka and his two friends teed off first. That solid whack of driver to ball and the straight arrow flight of the ball down the first fairway was impressive. Three small balls in the distance clustered like eggs in a nest. It was Calvino's turn. Pulling out his driver, he teed up the ball, looked down the fairway, at the ball, at Tanaka, and back at the ball, and swung. He missed it by a foot. The Japanese looked at him, wondering if their eyes had fooled them. Calvino addressed the ball and swung again. His drive landed at the ladies' tee. Walking over to the ladies' tee, Calvino pulled out a nine iron and swung the club. The ball advanced another thirty yards. He thought he could kick the ball farther in a straight line than he could ever hit it with a golf club.

At the end of the first hole, it was pointless to cheat. He scored eighteen strokes including a three putt. Tanaka's two Japanese friends had paced for fifteen minutes after putting out, watching Calvino slowly crisscross the fairway, his caddie panting like a greyhound chasing a mechanical rabbit. One of the caddies already looked sun-crazed at 9:30 a.m., a bad omen.

Calvino could see that Tanaka was losing considerable face, and if he played seventeen more holes like the first one, even if he bought two Accords, Tanaka's reputation could be permanently ruined. Tanaka had put it down to his karma. Like Tiger Woods he had a Thai mother, but Tiger would never have played golf with someone like Calvino. He suffered in silence, accepting the verdict of his destiny.

When Calvino caught up with Tanaka, he pulled him off to the side.

"I hope you don't mind if I go back to the driving range and hit some balls there instead. I'm really rusty. But I can keep playing if quitting the game will inconvenience your friends."

Tanaka looked like he was grateful enough to kiss Calvino. Instead, he took hold of Calvino's hands and shook them, even making a slight bow.

"Please, you will not inconvenience my good friends. We see you later at the clubhouse."

Tanaka's karma had just turned, and he suddenly looked lighter than air.

"You think you could drop the price of that Accord a bit more?"

Tanaka nodded.

"Can. For you, Khun Win, can do."

Calvino smiled, and as his caddie held an umbrella over his head, he turned and walked back to the first tee, wondering whether a hole in one felt as good as this felt.

A few minutes later, his caddie, a twenty-six-year-old working mother of two, returned with a bucket of balls. She stood back and watched him tee up a ball and take out a five iron. Glancing back at the clubhouse, he addressed the ball, hunching his shoulders. He stopped and looked once more in the direction of the clubhouse before swinging the club. The head of the five iron cleared the space of the ball without grazing it. Calvino shoved the club in the bag and pulled out a nine iron before performing the same ritual of looking at the clubhouse, at the ball, and then at the range ahead and trying to establish impact between the club and ball. Soon he was setting a new driving range record for the number of swings it took to empty a bucket of balls. It was the kind of stellar non-performance that a caddie was bound to notice, one she'd find difficult to forget.

Calvino slammed his nine iron in the bag and called the caddie over. He pulled a five-hundred-baht note out and handed it to her. It was an amount above a generous tip for eighteen holes of golf. She'd caddied for one hole and at the driving range sat in a chair with her cap pulled forward. He'd thought she'd be happy, but she wasn't. It was her duty to stay with the member until he reached the clubhouse no matter what. She'd finally found out the outer limits of "what" meant.

"I'm almost there. The clubhouse is right there." He pointed. "That's close enough. Go get something to eat."

She glanced at the note, looked up, thought for a moment, *waied* him, and trundled off toward the clubhouse. He watched her walk away, shoulders slumped, weary and beaten.

After three hours at the driving range, he knew just when to stop. Maxim, in green trousers, white shirt, and hat, had appeared in the distance, smoking a cigar. Not far behind, Andrei removed his hat, toweled his head, and put his hat back on. A caddie held an umbrella, shading him as he talked to a middle-aged Thai man, medium built, with a round Chinese face, someone whose face looked familiar from the papers or TV. Another Thai man talking into a cell phone trailed them. The two Thais drew even with each other, laughing, as the junior one joked with his caddie. The foursome looked relaxed and in high spirits.

Andrei studied his scorecard, penciling in his final round. He showed it to the two Thais. They laughed, and Andrei nodded his head. It was as if they'd closed a deal. The group walked up the stairs to the clubhouse like one happy family.

To the right of the entrance, the four caddies rested near the group's parked golf carts. In Andrei's foursome there were three black bags. From the driving range, it was hard to tell them apart, like bags on an airport conveyor belt.

Calvino waited a few minutes for Andrei, Maxim, and the others to settle in. Then it was time to run back and get something from a bag. He slipped a nine iron into his bag and, grabbing his golf cart, walked toward the clubhouse. He parked the cart at the clubhouse drop-off point beside the bags from Andrei's party. They had already gone into the clubhouse. He looked over the four caddies from Andrei's group, sizing them up. They had come off the course sweaty, tired, and hungry. They'd been in the sun for nearly five hours. The deal was they'd stay until the golfers appeared for their clubs, then they'd collect their tips and get something to eat and maybe get lucky by joining the queue and getting another round.

Calvino ducked inside the clubhouse restroom, waited a few minutes, and then pushed through the door again and back out into the heat. He peeled some notes off, handing each of the four caddies two hundred baht.

"Your boss said to give each of you two hundred to get something to eat."

Caddies, like good soldiers, when given money and liberty simply don't see the point in questioning the order. Each caddie *waied* Calvino as he handed out the cash. After he finished, they walked away giggling and gossiping until they disappeared around the corner of the clubhouse. Once they'd gone, he checked the golf bags lined up in rows. He found the one with the chain and gold medal McPhail had described on Andrei's golf bag. He looked around; no one was paying him any attention as he lifted the medal and looked at the inscription. It was in Latin, engraved below the head of an ancient bearded man, reading, *Transire suum pectus mundoque potiri.*

343

Calvino understood basic Italian and that was enough to know that this writing was Latin. Understanding it, though, was another matter. Calvino unzipped a side pouch in Andrei's bag and looked around, as his hand slipped three plastic envelopes inside. He kept his eyes fixed on the door as he zipped the pouch up again. He had no idea why terrorists hadn't figured out that the softest targets in the world are the unattended golf bags of the generals, politicians, and businessmen who are normally ringed with layers of security, but who think nothing of casually leaving their golf bags unattended.

It's a funny old world, he thought. Why would a Russian mathematician have a medal with a Greek or Roman head and Latin writing? And display it as an ornament on his golf bag? Andrei must have had his reasons. It didn't matter to Calvino except that it identified Andrei's bag and allowed Calvino to do his business.

Business it was. If Calvino had to guess, the two Thais had something to do with the offshore oil concession still hanging in the air. Calvino moved to one of the other bags, unzipped the back pocket, and caught a glimpse of a thick wedge of hundred dollar bills. A caddie looked his way and he smiled. Dropping his golf glove, he picked it up and waved. On the way up with the glove, he used his left hand to close the pocket.

Calvino pulled his cart and golf clubs out to the parking area, unlocked the car trunk, and put his golf bag inside. As he looked back, he saw Tanaka and his party with their caddies approaching the clubhouse. They looked pleased with themselves in a stoic samurai kind of way. Tanaka led them up the stairs to the clubhouse.

Calvino got into his car and drove. Cutting his engine, he glided beneath the shade of a large Bo tree and parked.

In golf every motion must be perfectly coordinated. One small shift of weight the wrong way, and the ball will sail out of bounds. And it's difficult to recover a life, or a ball, sliced into a lake. He pulled a pair of binoculars from the glove compartment and focused on the entrance to the clubhouse.

Andrei's hotel limo pulled out of the front row. Rather than stopping at the front entrance, it swung around the circular drive, passed through the parking lot, and exited without a passenger. A few minutes later, Andrei, Maxim, and the two Thais walked out as a group. They climbed into a cream-colored SUV, the kind with the slider door, LCD TV, a couple of plush leather benches, and an icebox filled with ice and mixers. Calvino wrote down the license number. He focused the binoculars on a Thai dressed in a blue safari suit, who was putting Andrei and Maxim's golf bags in the back.

He turned the binoculars on the two well-heeled Thai men who'd been part of the foursome. He watched them walk to their cars. An attendant lifted a set of golf bags into the back of a BMW and pocketed his tip, while another attendant loaded another set of clubs into the trunk of a Benz. The Benz still had the red dealer's plate. Calvino took down the numbers. He guessed that they belonged to the two Thai guests inside the SUV. Once the SUV pulled out, Calvino followed, staying fifty meters back, careful not to get stuck behind slow-moving eighteen-wheelers as the SUV passed them on the way to Pattaya.

Calvino tailed the SUV to the Pattaya Yacht Club. He got out of his car and found a bench near the marina, where he sat with a book and waited. After an hour, Maxim led Andrei and the Thais to the *Last Money*, moored at the far end of the marina. He saw Dew and several other *yings* in bright dresses, their shoulders naked, eyes hidden behind sunglasses, trailing behind the men like the hind legs of an elephant. As the yacht left the marina, Calvino had a decision to make. What would the yacht's destination be?

The chances were Maxim liked the vanity injection of sailing up to the front door of the Oriental Hotel. The power trip had worked on Josh Levy, when he'd stayed at the hotel. Calvino thought Maxim was the kind of man whose ego needs repeated feeding.

Rising from the bench, he thought about what Dew had told him about the night Wirot was thrown overboard. He wondered how she was handling returning to the scene of Wirot's murder with the men who'd killed him. She was back to the place where she'd slept with a man who had witnessed the murder, and he'd ended up dead. What could be going through her head? Money was the likely answer. But she wasn't alone in choosing a life in the dreamscape warmed by the heat that cash generates. The golf bags loaded with cash had been stowed in the BMW and the Benz and were on their way to a place of safety and secrecy—filling that pot of gold at the end of a politician's rainbow.

Moving from an exclusive private golf club to a private yacht to a hotel that catered to private wealthy clients completed a circle that allowed money to be concealed at each stage. If he kept his speed at 130 kilometers an hour, Calvino could return to the Oriental Hotel and let himself into McPhail's room before Andrei returned on the *Last Money*. He pulled onto the expressway and settled back for the hour and a half drive. It gave him time to think of where to find a weakness to break in that closed circle. Calvino had one or two ideas. An axe wouldn't do the job. He'd need a blowtorch and a welder's mask.

SIX

Rise above yourself and grasp the world.

CALVINO OPENED HIS laptop on the coffee table and logged onto the hotel's Wi-Fi connection. McPhail stayed at the door, looking through the peephole.

"No sign of him," said McPhail. "How was your game?"

"I shot an eighteen."

McPhail looked back at Calvino, who was reading text on the computer screen.

"What have you been drinking?"

"I only played one hole," said Calvino, looking up, smiling.

"What's par on that hole?"

"Three."

McPhail shook his head and looked back from the door.

"What's your handicap? Two hundred?"

"Give or take twenty strokes. I couldn't concentrate. I was thinking about the medal you described on Andrei's golf bag."

"Are you blaming your score on me because I saw Lenin's head on his golf bag?"

Calvino was happy with the multiple strokes on the first hole; if he had shot anything reasonable, he wouldn't have had a sufficiently good reason to excuse himself from the round of golf. McPhail walked away from the door and poured himself a glass of water, holding it up for Calvino to examine.

"It's Archimedes' head, not Lenin's," said Calvino, looking up from the screen.

"It looked like Lenin."

"That image is engraved on the Fields Medal."

"A golf trophy."

Calvino's eyes narrowed.

"No, it's a big deal award for a mathematician who is under forty and a certifiable genius."

Calvino read to McPhail the translation of the Latin inscription, *Transire suum pectus mundoque potiri*—To rise above oneself and grasp the world. A code of conduct adopted by bishops, scholars, generals, dictators, and assorted scumbags.

McPhail shuffled from the door and sat down opposite Calvino. "What's it doing on a golf bag? Is Andrei one of those genius golfers?"

The thought made Calvino laugh. McPhail had raised a good question.

"I've read through the Fields Medal winners list. Andrei's name doesn't appear. The last Russian to win was named Grigori Perelman and he declined the medal. So what's Andrei doing with one?"

The last Russian winner before Perelman was Maxim's uncle, who'd accepted the prize.

"Why don't you ask him if you can have one for your golf bag? Next time you shoot 210 for a round, you can claim you're a genius," said McPhail, who went back to the door with the glass of water and pressed his eye against the peephole. "Your genius is coming down the hallway with a friend and a couple of babes."

The Thai men who had played with Andrei and Maxim must have left the hotel, thought Calvino. They'd had their little boat ride on the *Last Money*, docked, had a drink or two on the terrace, and gone back to clean the cash out of their golf bags.

Calvino moved quickly to the door and pushed McPhail to the side in time to see a bellboy carrying the leather bag with the Fields Medal swinging from side to side on the zipper. Fucking phony, thought Calvino. The man who'd killed Josh and Tess should have been a real Fields Medal winner and not just the owner of a counterfeit copy hanging from a zipper on his golf bag. What you see, Calvino thought, isn't always a reliable indicator of what you get.

The two Thais hadn't left the hotel. They showed up at the door to Andrei's suite a few minutes later. They laughed and joked as the floor concierge lightly knocked on the door. The concierge acted deferentially to the Thai men. Maxim opened the door and invited them in. The concierge closed the door but, before he left, bent down and dropped a wad of paper, nudging it against the door. When the paper fell over, someone had left the room. It was an old hotel tradition that reminded rich people they were being watched over.

Calvino walked back to the sofa, paced back to the door, and looked at McPhail. "Go ask him about the medal," said McPhail.

"I've got a better idea."

He phoned Colonel Pratt. In the background Calvino heard Miles Davis playing. The Colonel was in his den, reading and listening to jazz. The predictability of friends was one of life's great comforts.

"How was your golf game?" asked Colonel Pratt.

"Improving. I'm sitting in a suite at the Oriental Hotel. Come and join me."

"It's after nine."

Calvino was aware that it was late. Colonel Pratt's response came as no surprise.

"It can't wait. Bring a couple of your colleagues. To cover your ass."

It was as if the line had gone dead, dropping out. Calvino couldn't hear the Colonel breathing, and that happened when he held his breath, waiting until he was forced to come up for air.

"Give me a hint what this is about, Vincent."

"Three missing gold bullets."

There was a gasp, a beat. Colonel Pratt collected his thoughts the best he could. When he reviewed those thoughts, one question stood out among all the others.

"Do you have the bullets?"

"No, but I know who does. And he's nearby."

After the call ended, he pocketed his cell phone, went into the bathroom, and used McPhail's razor to shave. Calvino splashed his face and looked into the mirror. What he saw staring back looked like one of the men at the Lonesome Hawk who hung on through the afternoon drinking until the bar closed. He stared at a face in serious need of a neon makeover. He had to go with what he had. He dried his face with a towel and splashed on McPhail's aftershave. He came out of the bathroom pulling on his jacket.

"Where you going?"

"To ask Andrei where I can buy one of those knock-off genius medals."

"Hey, buddy. Get one for me, too."

One of Maxim's *yings* opened the door to the suite. She looked surprised to see Calvino standing there. She'd expected a room service delivery, but instead of a waiter and a cart, she found Vincent Calvino stepping into the living room of the suite. Maxim was the first to look up.

He did a double take and nudged Andrei, who had an arm wrapped around Dew. She clutched a large brown teddy bear wedged like a chaperone between the Russian and herself. Andrei clocked him with eyes set back under puffy bags. Andrei's pudding-like face frowned. The two Thais didn't like what they saw in Andrei's clouded face. They were on their feet and out the door faster than a couple of hookers with text-message directions to their next appointment.

Calvino walked over and sat in an overstuffed chair, stretching his hands out on the winged arms.

"I hope it wasn't because of me that your friends left."

Dew avoided eye contact with him. The spunky pole dancer appeared to shrink inside her teddy bear. She was good, thought Calvino.

"Why are you here?" asked Andrei, trying to control his anger.

"I heard you were in town. And I saw your sidekick's boat tied up at the dock, and I wondered if you were having a party. I thought I'd drop in and see if there's anything you need. You want me to go and bring those two guys back?"

Leaning forward, Calvino pulled an apple from a fruit plate and sank his teeth in it.

Andrei said something in Russian. Maxim got to his feet, pulled Calvino out of the chair, and patted him down. He turned and looked at Andrei and spoke in Russian, telling him Calvino wasn't armed.

"Mr. Calvino, why don't we make an appointment for another day?"

"But I'm already at your party. Are you saying you want me to go?"

Maxim set his jaw as if he was going to throw a punch. "That's exactly what he wants."

Calvino nodded, tilted his head to the side, and smiled at Maxim. "Maxim, congratulations on getting your plane and crew back. That must have cost more than filling the tank of the *Last Money*."

Maxim raised his fist, but before it smashed the target, Andrei called him off.

"We are civilized men. There's no need for violence."

"I remember you saying something like that in New York."

Andrei shrugged and poured wine in his glass. He kissed Dew on the cheek and told her to go into the bedroom with the other two *yings* and close the door. Even Dew's bar *ying* English comprehension was good enough to understand she was in a room of *farangs* who had no problem beating up and drowning people who got in their way. Hookers and high rollers are like Siamese twins who share the same heart, lungs, and brain.

After the *yings* closed the bedroom door behind them, Calvino took another bite out of the apple.

"In New York there was something I didn't understand. If you thought I had the coins, what were you doing fucking around with Josh? Why not jump me? Cut out the middle man."

Andrei drank his wine and studied Calvino. He nodded for Maxim, who was in an ugly mood with his *ying* in the bedroom, to sit down in a chair within easy intimidation distance from Calvino.

"No one would grab you in New York, Mr. Calvino. That would have been counterproductive. Perhaps it would start a war with the Italians. No one wants to start such a war. Especially when there were other means available. You stayed with your cousin Nero. That message wasn't lost. Josh was the one who suggested that we fake his kidnapping. He probably left that piece of information out of his explanation."

"Josh wanted to back out."

Andrei grinned like a man witnessing an execution.

"You can't stuff a butterfly back into a cocoon," said Andrei, obviously pleased with his turn of phrase. "Mr. Levy had no special baggage attached. New York lawyers are as common as Franklin Delano Roosevelt on a dime."

"Josh told me how Maxim, with a little help, dropped Wirot over the side of his boat. How he buried him in the deep, blue sea."

Calvino played the bluff with no expression. He glanced at a putter, a glass, and half a dozen golf balls on the floor near his chair, evidence that Andrei or Maxim had been practicing putting.

"Interesting. But isn't this the word of a dead man?"

Andrei said something in Russian to Maxim, who had a mad dog look as he paced behind Calvino's chair.

"Calling his yacht a boat is insulting."

"Hey, Maxim, I'm sorry if I in any way injured your manhood."

Maxim had had enough. He took a wild, emotional swing, tipping forward a little off-balance. Diving forward, Calvino grabbed the putter from the floor, rolled over, and came up swinging the club, catching Maxim across the bridge of his nose. The Russian fell into a plate of fruit, scattering apples, oranges, and a mango across the floor. The plate shattered and pieces showered the room. Calvino stood holding the club, wondering if he needed a second putt. But it looked like Maxim, though on his knees, hadn't had enough.

"Stay down, Maxim," he said.

But Maxim came up fighting. Calvino took a half swing with the putter, balled with enough force to break the Russian's nose. Blood sprayed across the table, sofa, and carpet. Andrei went to great lengths to keep himself several degrees removed from the scene of actual violence. The surface deniability was important. But Calvino figured that in terms of the six degrees of separation game, Andrei was the Russian equivalent of Kevin Bacon, linking the players to business-inspired violence.

Inside his suite there was no degree of separation. Andrei was face to face with the blood oozing from Maxim's wound. He looked like he might be sick. Calvino could see that he didn't have the stomach for it. A cold formula was one thing, but when the thing spouted blood, the formula became largely irrelevant.

"A double putt for a par. If only I could do that on the golf course," said Calvino.

"Please leave," said Andrei, the words sticking in his throat.

Calvino's cell phone rang and he slowly switched the golf club to his left hand. "Hold on a minute."

"Get out!" said Andrei. The "please" had vanished as Andrei's anger overcame his shock at the violence.

Calvino held up the hand with the golf club.

"I'll stay for awhile. I like your party so far. Order another fruit plate. Maxim and I are warming up."

Calvino slowly pulled his phone out of his jacket.

"No man does this to my partner and lives," said Andrei.

"I thought your motto was no violence. My mistake. Colonel Pratt, Andrei was just asking about you. I am in Khun Andrei's room. It doesn't have a number. It's the Somerset Maugham suite."

He handed the phone to Andrei.

"The Colonel wants to talk to you."

"Please come immediately. I want you to remove Mr. Calvino. He's assaulted my associate. Yes, I would like to press charges."

Colonel Pratt and two non-uniformed officers arrived with the concierge in minutes. The concierge had already alerted the front desk about a reported fight inside the Somerset Maugham suite. The concierge, a small man in a white uniform, looked worried. There was a tense moment as everyone stood in the suite, looking at each other, deciding what to do next. Maxim had a bloodied towel over his nose, covering his mouth. He lay sprawled like a wounded animal on the sofa, his head on a pillow and Dew's stuffed teddy bear, resting over his forehead. The bedroom door had opened far enough to show three sets of *ying* eyes staring out.

Andrei, his arm outstretched, pointed a finger at Calvino.

"He's been stalking me. In Bangkok and New York. Please arrest this man for assault," he said.

Colonel Pratt smiled, thinking the Russian had seen too many movies. The Colonel walked over and checked on Maxim, who moaned, his face already ballooned up. Colonel Pratt glanced over at Calvino.

"Did you do this?" asked Colonel Pratt.

"Maxim tried to grab the last apple on the fruit plate and things got out of hand. He's not hurt much. There's a lot of blood in the nose. A three-iron-sized nose. He might have a quarter of his blood in that snout. It's pretty much diluted with vodka."

Colonel Pratt held up his hand.

"Vincent, stop. This is serious. You hit him."

Maxim sat up on the sofa, lowering the teddy bear from his face.

"I kill you," he said.

The police exchanged a knowing smile. They'd heard that phrase used many times but this was the first time a Russian holding a blood soaked teddy bear had issued the threat. Maxim's lower lip trembled as he started to go after Calvino.

"Actually, it's 'I *will* kill you,' " said Calvino. "Making death threats in a foreign language is a challenge."

One of the cops pushed Maxim back on the sofa.

"Josh said you partied hard," said Calvino. "He said you liked cocaine, and he said that you kept a stash of the pure stuff on your yacht. When I saw your boat parked outside, I thought you might be having a party. We'd met at this hotel before and gone to dinner. I thought we were friends. I wanted to tell you what had happened to Josh in New York. You two were close, so I thought you'd want to know. I thought we could share a little blow. That's about it."

"Bullshit," said Maxim.

"That's Russian for I agree," said Calvino.

Maxim didn't find the remark funny and again tried to go for Calvino. Again he was restrained by one of the cops.

"What made you think Maxim would stash coke inside a friend's golf bag?" asked one of the cops.

Calvino kept an eye on Maxim, waiting for him to break free. But most of the fight had gone out of him.

"Andrei's a bigwig. No one inspects the golf bag of a *poo yai*. It's like diplomatic immunity, only without going to a government office and meetings."

Calvino's arguments were full of holes.

Andrei shook his head. "This is foolish. My evening is ruined. Take him out of my room. Immediately."

"It was self-defense. He tried to throw one of those Russian sleeper locks on me."

Andrei intervened again, trying to take control of the situation. "The attack was unprovoked."

The Colonel was in an awkward position. The nightmare of the usual "he said, she said" exchange, with one of the participants a long-time friend and the other a very important person. Normal procedure before arresting someone for assault required an investigation into who had instigated the violence. But this wasn't a normal case, and normal procedure wouldn't be good enough for Andrei. He expected, because of his position, that his word should be the final one.

The Colonel thought Andrei would have a good point. The Thai Embassy in Washington, D.C., had honored him. Andrei was the toast of the town. He was entitled to respect. He was entitled to having the book thrown at Calvino.

In a game of chess Andrei's move had resulted, in his mind, in a clear checkmate to Calvino's position. The game was over. All that remained was for the Colonel and his men to take Calvino away. That left Colonel Pratt with a couple of options. Play it safe, play by the book, remove Calvino from the room immediately, limit the damage, and leave Andrei and Maxim and their powerful friends to continue their own game. Or he could, as a police officer, conduct a routine search. If he did, and if Calvino proved to have given a false statement, the damage from the search of Andrei's room would blow back, not only on the Colonel, but on the reputations and careers of the other two officers in the room.

In New York he'd been in Andrei's office off Union Square, and he remembered Andrei's veiled warning, "Mr. Calvino has lived in Thailand for too long."

In the Colonel's judgment it came down to a simple question—had Calvino changed into a man he could no longer trust? He remembered the Shakespeare quote Calvino had hand-written on the Christmas card. Shakespeare had also written, "Most friendship is feigning, most loving mere folly." His two colleagues waited for the Colonel's decision. He glanced at Calvino, who stood between the two police officers, who by their posture had already given their silent vote.

In Calvino's own words, he said he'd come to the suite to party and consume cocaine. He admitted to assaulting a man.

"I am phoning a friend who will remind you of your duty as a police officer," said Andrei.

He poured more wine in his glass and picked up the telephone.

The Colonel looked on as Andrei sipped his wine, his upper lip curling in disgust at Calvino. A distinguished man, his bearing filled with authority and power, waited. Andrei had powerful friends in Thailand. The kind of men who could have the Colonel transferred to the Burmese border on twenty-four hours' notice. What did the Colonel have? He glanced at Calvino, who stood with his hands in his pockets. The Colonel knelt beside Maxim.

"Do you wish to press charges?"

The Russian blinked, his head turned slightly, as he looked to Andrei, who nodded his head.

"Please remove him and keep him away," said Andrei. "He attacked my friend."

Colonel Pratt rose to his feet, standing over the Russian on the couch. Calvino thought the Colonel was about to ask him further questions.

"He promised to share some drugs. He changed his mind," said Calvino.

"He's crazy. Colonel, I have a minister on the line and he wishes to talk to you," said Andrei.

He handed the phone to Colonel Pratt. They spoke in Thai, and then Colonel Pratt hung up the phone rather than giving it back to Andrei.

"That settles it," said Andrei. "Goodbye, Mr. Calvino."

"You said something about drugs?" he asked Calvino.

"The cocaine inside the golf bag."

Andrei laughed. "Calvino, you are only making things worse for yourself."

"Maxim told Josh that's the safest place to hide coke."

"You play golf, Mr. Andrei?" one of the officers asked politely.

"Yes, I play golf."

He glared at Calvino.

"Do you have your golf bag?"

He looked around the room.

"It's in the bedroom."

"Do you mind if we have a look?"

Andrei showed them into the bedroom. The three *yings* escaped into the bathroom. The leather bag was on a bench at the foot of the large bed.

He pointed at the bag.

"Please, be my guest."

The cops pulled the black leather golf bag off the bench and into the living room area, where there was better light. They pulled out the woods, looking at the shafts, and then the irons, turning them over. Finishing the inspection of each club, they set it on the carpet. After the clubs were all taken out, they unzipped half a dozen pockets, taking out gloves, tees, golf balls, socks, a pair of spiked golf shoes. No drugs. Only golf gear lay on the carpet. But they hadn't quite finished.

"Isn't that the Fields Medal?" asked Calvino, looking at the chain and medal hanging from a side pocket. "That's got to be a first. A man wins a Fields Medal and hooks it to his golf bag?"

The series of questions caught Andrei by surprise.

"It is a reproduction."

"That's strange. Who would reproduce the Fields Medal?" asked Calvino.

The cop pulled out the first plastic envelope with the four-baht gold bullet. He opened it, looked inside, smiled, and handed it to Colonel Pratt. Andrei watched as the Colonel removed two more plastic bags, each holding a single gold bullet.

"The medal is a good fake," said Calvino, as he watched Andrei meet Colonel Pratt's eyes. "Even the Latin inscription looks real. *Transire suum pectus mundoque potiri.* To rise above oneself and grasp the world. But the Latin kind of tells your story, Andrei. Maybe you grasped too far."

It was like seeing the reaction of a Russian general who had witnessed an airbrush erasing him from the photograph of VIPs in the review stand inside Red Square. One minute he was a hero in the history books, the next moment he'd vanished, a non-entity whose name was whispered among the brave few who remembered the untouched photo. Both the Colonel and Andrei understood exactly what would flow from that moment. The immune system would kick in. The intruder would be recognized and targeted. The power had shifted. Andrei's bullying confidence and the threats of friends in high places were swallowed up in the Latin phrase. All of his words about ambition, honor, glory, history, and heritage suddenly failed him. He stood speechless before the Colonel.

"The gold bullets look familiar," said Colonel Pratt. "Could they be the missing Rama V bullets?"

"I have no knowledge of these coins."

The last plastic envelope removed from the golf bag contained a name card. A picture of a yacht inserted in the upper right-hand corner of the card. A telephone number and an email address. The name: Maxim Saytev.

Colonel Pratt took the card from one of the officers and showed it to Andrei. "Your friend?"

Andrei stared at Maxim, who sat on the couch, his eyes puffy, looking out through slits at the blurry world. Andrei was aware that his smooth circulation throughout the system was about to end. He eyed Maxim in the way an executioner stares at a condemned man. Maxim dropped his gaze and stared at the floor like a teenager, blindsided as if he'd been caught by his mother reading a porno magazine.

There was nothing for Andrei to say. The three police officers had witnessed the gold bullets pulled from Andrei's golf bag. A fake medal and three genuine missing coins had cleared his throat of words.

"Perhaps there's a way I can make a contribution to settle these matters?" asked Andrei. "Nothing has to leave this room if we can agree."

Colonel Pratt remembered Andrei at the embassy. It was his day in the sun. Andrei was prepared to pay to prevent that sun from setting. In the Colonel's eyes all he saw were a cold darkness. He had his answer before the Colonel confirmed his suspicion.

"I am afraid that is out of the question. If you want to phone your friend the minister again, please do so."

Andrei declined to phone in the Colonel's presence.

"Please take Mr. Calvino and leave."

"What about the assault charges?"

"Andrei, sorry about the drugs," said Calvino. "Maxim was clean. But he should have told you about the coins. I'm certain he'll explain everything later. Won't you, Maxim?"

Andrei swallowed hard and glared at Calvino.

"Goodbye, Mr. Calvino."

"I'll let Nero know you were a good sport. Not to start any wars," said Calvino. "One final thing. Exactly how much were you going to offer as a payoff?"

Andrei stared at him. It wasn't the look of a man who was throwing his weight around, barking orders; it was the look of a man who at the moment of victory looked down and saw the hilt of a sword sticking out of his guts, a thrust that had come from a direction he hadn't expected. In a day the minister wouldn't be taking Andrei's calls. No one would be taking his calls.

SEVEN

"It never came up." Calvino looked straight ahead as he said it.

MEN AS BIG as Andrei were like American banks too big to fail. Men like him skated above the law, and even when caught red-handed they had the resources to wait out the storm. They were too smart, careful, connected. The most that ever happened to men like Andrei was someone inflicted on him a minor set back or brushed a few strokes of disgrace against his name. But over time no one of substance would remember his involvement. The world moved too fast and Andrei kept one step ahead. Like a virus, he'd reinvent himself and find another entry point. There was always another time, another immune system to compromise.

The government announced that the oil concession had been granted to one of the large international companies. Andrei's company and name weren't mentioned. His campaign for the oil concession had been quietly dropped. At the Ministry of Finance Museum, Andrei's name was removed without explanation from the exhibit of the Rama V gold bullet set. Andrei became a non-entity in Thailand, vanishing from the histories, a name no one wished to mention, and a name no one wished to have lodged in the collective memory.

Maxim also vanished. His yacht, the *Last Money*, remained in the marina at the Pattaya Yacht Club. But the Russian was rumored to have returned to Moscow. There were occasional unconfirmed sightings of him in Kabul, Somalia, Kenya, and the Philippines. No one searched for him. A man needs friends before a search is launched. Maxim had associates, but no friends.

None of the setbacks to Andrei's plans had brought Josh Levy back. Falcon said the NYPD hadn't found any reason to reopen the case.

Colonel Pratt said, "We know, Vincent. Karma will take care of the rest."

Good old karma. Waiting until the next life to see what kind of lizard, bird, or ant a murderer came back as wasn't an immediately satisfying alternative to revenge.

"You proved your loyalty to a friend," said Colonel Pratt.

It was left open whether the Colonel meant Josh. What Calvino had left were memories of Josh. As a ten-year-old kid, Josh with poison ivy on his thighs and balls, crying like a baby. Josh had taken a shortcut to the lake. At ten he hadn't learned the lesson of how shortcuts can turn deadly. He grasped at the world, but things hadn't worked out the way he'd wanted. No one had told him that, when he grew into a man, evil of men like Andrei would never be apparent until the promise of safe passage through a field of poison ivy was broken.

Ratana and Manee were members of a tai chi group that met each Wednesday in Benjasiri Park on Sukhumvit Road. There were thirty or so people in the group. Barefoot, they moved to the music from a boom box to the side of the instructor, a young Thai in baggy white trousers and a loose, long-sleeved cotton shirt. Calvino sat next to Colonel Pratt on the bench. John-John sat between the two men, playing a video game on his mother's iPhone.

The Colonel folded up his copy of the *Matichon* newspaper.

"Where are you going?" asked Calvino.

"I have an appointment."

"Now?"

He nodded. "I need to settle something."

The Colonel's manner increased the mystery.

"Colonel Pratt, you don't do vague well."

"It's Wirot's family. I promised to look in on them."

"What are you going to tell them?"

"The truth. That Wirot was lost at sea. That he's dead."

It was the right thing. He watched as the Colonel walked away, carrying his newspaper. Colonel Pratt climbed into a taxi and it pulled into traffic. The Colonel was going on a journey of compassion. Being dead was a bad state of affairs, but leaving a family who had no idea whether a man was dead or alive was to condemn them to the living dead. That was no way to leave people, hanging in limbo, not knowing, wondering whether that man would come through the door any day.

Twenty minutes later, the tai chi class ended and Manee and Ratana walked up to the bench.

"Colonel Pratt's off to see Wirot's widow," Calvino said.

Manee nodded as if she knew already.

"Did he tell you that his promotion was announced?"

A wide smile lit up her face. It was as if she'd received a gold star, one that let her float a few feet off the ground.

"It never came up." Calvino looked straight ahead as he said it.

Calvino walked Ratana and John-John past the small lake at Benjasiri Park. For an instant he thought he saw a *krathong* floating on the surface, but it was the light playing tricks. He stopped for a second look and the image was gone. Ratana saw him staring at the water.

"You see something?"

"Do you believe what they say about a *krathong* reaching the sea and washing away all sins?"

"Of course," she said. "I am Thai. We believe."

It was good to believe in something, so why not a *krathong* made from a banana leaf, set afloat with a single candle and a prayer that it would reach the sea? Colonel Pratt was like that *krathong* sailing to Wirot's family, giving them the greatest gift of all—peace of mind.

Later on the second floor of the Emporium parking lot, Calvino pointed his key chain at the new silver-gray Honda Accord and the taillights flashed.

As they got into the car, Ratana fastened her seat belt and said, "Did you tell Colonel Pratt about the discount Tanaka gave you on the Accord?"

Calvino started the engine and adjusted his rear-view mirror.

"It didn't come up."

"That's what you said to Manee," said Ratana.

The things that didn't come up between men never ceased to amaze Ratana, and the next day when she phoned Manee, the Colonel's wife agreed. Men simply live in a different world from women. They are connected to the world of women by a web of mutual obligation and genuine affection. Women promise a safe refuge after they fail to grasp the brass ring. Women know that such men never stop reaching and failing, leaving a trail of disappointment and broken promises. No matter that the lesson never sticks or that the price of reaching too far is higher each time. And every time it is paid, some small part of the man dies before her eyes.

ACKNOWLEDGMENTS

During the process of writing a book I rely on many others for research, editing and advice. For *9 Gold Bullets*, I owe gratitude to a number of friends and colleagues for sharing their expertise, advice and comments.

My advance readers provided useful and insightful comments and suggestions, which helped greatly in the writing process. Charles Mchugh, Les Rose, Richard Diran, and Phillip Laskaris took the time to read and comment on earlier drafts of the manuscript. Their advice was invaluable. Without their assistance, *9 Gold Bullets* would have been a lesser book. Thanks, guys.

In researching the history of Thai coins, two of the leading numismatists in Thailand—Ron Cristal and Jan Aamli—kindly introduced me to the world of Thai coin collecting, auctions and collectors and opened a window overlooking the history of Thai gold bullet coins.

Many thanks to Martin Townsend for his excellent copy edit work on the manuscript.

Bridget Wagner, my literary agent at Sagalyn Literary Agency, does what very few agents do these days: she not only read but offered extensive comments that improved the book in many small and large ways.

Busakorn Suriyasarn reviewed the manuscript, providing her usual insights into Thai culture and language, and double checking that the Thai aspects in the story are true to life.

PRAISE FOR THE VINCENT CALVINO P.I. SERIES

One of "100 Eyes of Mystery Scene Era" in the 100th issue of *Mystery Scene Magazine*

"Vincent Calvino is one of the most notable detectives of modern crime literature."
—Harmut Wilmes, *Kölnische Rundschau* (Germany)

"This series belongs on every Asian crime list."
—*Booklist*

"Moore's Vincent Calvino novels are crisp, atmospheric entertainments set in a noirish Bangkok."
—*Guardian*

"Vincent Calvino is a terrific character who could only have been drafted into action by a terrific writer."
—T. Jefferson Parker

"Think Dashiell Hammett in Bangkok."
—*San Francisco Chronicle*

"Moore's flashy style successfully captures the dizzying contradictions in [Bangkok's] vertiginous landscape."
—Marilyn Stasio, *The New York Times Book Review*

"Moore reveals the seething stew of wealth, corruption, cultural clashes, poverty and lust that is modern Bangkok.... All will appreciate the raw passion that drives the action."
—*Publishers Weekly*

"A vivid sense of place ... The city of Bangkok, with its chaos and mystery, is almost another character. Recommended."
—*Library Journal*

"A worthy example of a serial character, Vincent Calvino is human and convincing." —*Thriller Magazine* (Italy)

"It's about time everyone discovered Bangkok PI Vincent Calvino." —*The Globe and Mail*

"Every big city has its fictional detective; and Bangkok's is Vincent Calvino." —*Bangkok 101*

"To paraphrase Graham Greene in another context, Moore is our man in Bangkok." —*Bangkok Post*

"Vincent Calvino is at once in the finest tradition of the lone private detective and a complete original."
—Matt Beynon Rees, author of *The Samaritan's Secret*

"Moore comprehends the local mindset as well as the Thais themselves, perhaps even more so for he tirelessly analyses their mores, beliefs, superstitions, attitudes, actions."
—*Bangkok Post*

"It's easy to see why Moore's books are popular: While seasoned with a spicy mixture of humor and realism, they stand out as model studies in East-West encounters, as satisfying for their cultural insights as they are for their hardboiled action."
—Mark Schreiber, *The Japan Times*

"Chris Moore's series of private-eye tales set in the full mysterious splendor of bubbling Bangkok, Thailand, remind us anew of how much meaning we miss out on when we don't worship true artists. Underneath Bangkok society is a deeply encrusted demiworld of hope, despair, corruption and courage that Moore . . . paints with maestrolike Dickensian strokes." —Thomas Plate, *The Seattle Times*

"Moore's work recalls the international 'entertainments' of Graham Greene or John le Carré, but the hard-bitten worldview and the cynical, bruised idealism of his battered hero is right out of Chandler. Intelligent and articulate, Moore offers a rich, passionate and original take on the private eye game."
—Kevin Burton Smith, *January Magazine*

"Calvino is a wonderful private detective figure! Consistent action, masterful language . . . and Anglo-Saxon humor at its best." —*Deutschland Radio*

"The Calvino series is distinctive and wonderful, not to be missed, and I'm pleased to see that it is finally becoming better known in the States."
—Cameron Hughes, *The Rap Sheet*

"Moore is a genuine novelist who just happens to employ the conventions of the thriller genre. His real interests are believable human behavior and way cultures cross-pollinate and sometimes clash. This is real prose, not Raymond Chandler stuff, and his motives are as close to art as to entertainment. Read him."
—Douglas Fetherling, *Ottawa Citizen*

"Relishing another Christopher Moore novel is like receiving essential nutrients for a healthier, safe in Thailand. Insights into the human condition of expat existence, which underpin his thriller plots, can though, be painful to swallow. They reveal us to ourselves painfully clearly but as balanced as a sweet and sour Thai dish."
—Richard Ravensdale, *Pattaya People*

SPIRIT HOUSE
First in the series
Heaven Lake Press (2004) ISBN 974-92389-3-1

The Bangkok police already have a confession by a nineteen-year-old drug addict who has admitted to the murder of a British computer wizard, Ben Hoadly. From the bruises on his face shown at the press conference, it is clear that the young suspect had some help from the police in the making of his confession. The case is wrapped up. Only there are some loose ends that the police and just about everyone else are happy to overlook.

The search for the killer of Ben Hoadley plunges Calvino into the dark side of Bangkok, where professional hit men have orders to stop him. From the world of thinner addicts, dope dealers, fortunetellers, and high-class call girls, Calvino peels away the mystery surrounding the death of the English ex-public schoolboy who had a lot of dubious friends.

"Well-written, tough and bloody."
—Bernard Knight, *Tangled Web* (UK)

"A thinking man's Philip Marlowe, Calvino is a cynic on the surface but a romantic at heart. Calvino . . . found himself in Bangkok—the end of the world—for a whole host of bizarre foreigners unwilling, unable, or uninterested in going home."
—*The Daily Yomiuri*

"Good, that there are still real crime writers. Christopher G. Moore's [*Spirit House*] is colorful and crafty."
—*Hessischer Rundfunk* (Germany)

ASIA HAND
Second in the series
Heaven Lake Press (2000) ISBN 974-87171-2-7

Bangkok—the Year of the Monkey. Calvino's Chinese New Year celebration is interrupted by a call to Lumpini Park Lake, where Thai cops have just fished the body of a *farang* cameraman. CNN is running dramatic footage of several Burmese soldiers on the Thai border executing students.

Calvino follows the trail of the dead man to a feature film crew where he hits the wall of silence. On the other side of that wall, Calvino and Colonel Pratt discover and elite film unit of old Asia Hands with connections to influential people in Southeast Asia. They find themselves matched against a set of *farangs* conditioned for urban survival and willing to go for a knock-out punch.

"Highly recommended to readers of hard-boiled detective fiction" —*Booklist*

"Asia Hand is the kind of novel that grabs you and never lets go." —*The Times of India*

"Skillfully crafted, addictive ride through one of the planet's most raw and vivid cities. Moore and Calvino define the dark pungent cocktail that is Asian noir."
—Eliot Pattison, author of the "*Inspector Shan*" series

"Moore's hard-boiled, noir plots and style place him hands-down as one of the top current crime writers."
—Tom McLaren, *Gallup Journey*

ZERO HOUR IN PHNOM PENH
Third in the series
Heaven Lake Press (2005) ISBN 974-93035-9-8
Winner of 2004 German Critics Award for Crime Fiction (Deutscher Krimi Preis) for best international crime fiction and 2007 Premier Special Director's Award Semana Negra (Spain)

In the early 1990s, at the end of the devastating civil war UN peacekeeping forces try to keep the lid on the violence. Gunfire can still be heard nightly in Phnom Penh, where Vietnamese prostitutes try to hook UN peacekeepers from the balcony of the Lido Bar.

Calvino traces leads on a missing *farang* from Bangkok to war-torn Cambodia, through the Russian market, hospitals, nightclubs, news briefings, and UNTAC headquarters. Calvino's buddy, Colonel Pratt, knows something that Calvino does not: the missing man is connected with the jewels stolen from the Saudi royal family. Calvino quickly finds out that he is not the only one looking for the missing *farang*.

"Political, courageous and perhaps Moore's most important work." —*CrimiCouch.de*

"A bursting, high adventure . . . Extremely gripping . . . A morality portrait with no illusion."
—Ulrich Noller, *Westdeutscher Rundfunk*

"Fast-paced and entertaining. Even outside of his Bangkok comfort zone, Moore shows he is one of the best chroniclers of the expat diaspora." —*The Daily Yomiuri*

"A work of art." —*Deutsche Well Buchipp*, Bonn

COMFORT ZONE
Fourth in the series
Heaven Lake Press (2001) ISBN 974-87754-9-6

Twenty years after the end of the Vietnam War, Vietnam is opening to the outside world. There is a smell of fast money in the air and poverty in the streets. Business is booming and in austere Ho Chi Minh City a new generation of foreigners have arrived to make money and not war. Against the backdrop of Vietnam's economic miracle, *Comfort Zone* reveals a taut, compelling story of a divided people still not reconciled with their past and unsure of their future.

Calvino is hired by an ex-special forces veteran, whose younger brother uncovers corruption and fraud in the emerging business world in which his clients are dealing. But before Calvino even leaves Bangkok, there have already been two murders, one in Saigon and one in Bangkok.

"Calvino digs, discovering layers of intrigue. He's stalked by hired killers and falls in love with a Hanoi girl. Can he trust her? The reader is hooked."
—*NTUC Lifestyle* (Singapore)

"Moore hits home with more of everything in *Comfort Zone*. There is a balanced mix of story-line, narrative, wisdom, knowledge as well as love, sex, and murder."
—*Thailand Times*

"Like a Japanese gardener who captures the land and the sky and recreates it in the backyard, Moore's genius is in portraying the Southeast Asian heartscape behind the tourist industry hotel gloss."
—*The Daily Yomiuri*

THE BIG WEIRD
Fifth in the series
Heaven Lake Press (2008) ISBN 978-974-8418-42-1

A beautiful American blond is found dead with a large bullet hole in her head in the house of her ex-boyfriend. A famous Hollywood screenwriter hires Calvino to investigate her death. Everyone except Calvino's client believes Samantha McNeal has committed suicide.

In the early days of the Internet, Sam ran with a young and wild expat crowd in Bangkok: a Net-savvy pornographer, a Thai hooker plotting to hit it big in cyberspace, an angry feminist with an agenda, a starving writer-cum-scam artist, a Hollywoord legend with a severe case of The Sickness. As Calvino slides into a world where people are dead serious about sex, money and fame, he unearths a hedonistic community where the ritual of death is the ultimate high.

"An excellent read, charming, amusing, insightful, complex, localized yet startlingly universal in its themes."
—*Guide of Bangkok*

"Highly entertaining." —*Bangkok Post*

"A good read, fast-paced and laced with so many of the locales so familiar to the expat denizens of Bangkok."
—*Art of Living* (Thailand)

"Like a noisy, late-night Thai restaurant, Moore serves up tongue-burning spices that swallow up the literature of Generation X and cyberpsace as if they were merely sticky rice." —*The Daily Yomiuri*

COLD HIT
Sixth in the series
Heaven Lake Press (2004) ISBN 974-920104-1-7

Five foreigners have died in Bangkok. Were they drug overdose victims or victims of a serial killer? Calvino believes the evidence points to a serial killer who stalks tourists in Bangkok. The Thai police, including Calvino's best friend and buddy Colonel Pratt, don't buy his theory.

Calvino teams up with an LAPD officer on a bodyguard assignment. Hidden forces pull them through swank shopping malls, rundown hotels, Klong Toey slum, and the Bangkok bars as they try to keep their man and themselves alive. As Calvino learns more about the bodies being shipped back to America, the secret of the serial killer is revealed.

"The story is plausible and riveting to the end."
—*The Japan Times*

"Tight, intricate plotting, wickedly astute . . . *Cold Hit* will have you variously gasping, chuckling, nodding, tut-tutting, ohyesing, and grinding your teeth throughout its 330 pages."
—*Guide of Bangkok*

"The plot is equally tricky, brilliantly devised, and clear. One of the best crime fiction in the first half of the year."
—*Ultimo Biedlefeld* (Germany)

"Moore depicts the city from below. He shows its dirt, its inner conflicts, its cruelty, its devotion. Hard, cruel, comical and good."
—*Readme.de*

MINOR WIFE
Seventh in the series
Heaven Lake Press (2004) ISBN 974-92126-5-7

A contemporary murder set in Bangkok—a neighbor and friend, a young ex-hooker turned artist, is found dead by an American millionaire's minor wife. Her rich expat husband hires Calvino to investigate. While searching for the killer in exclusive clubs and not-so-exclusive bars of Bangkok, Calvino discovers that a minor wife—*mia noi*—has everything to do with a woman's status. From illegal cock fighting matches to elite Bangkok golf clubs, Calvino finds himself caught in the crossfire as he closes in on the murderer.

"The thriller moves in those convoluted circles within which Thai life and society takes place. Moore's knowledge of these gives insights into many aspects of the cultural mores . . . unknown to the expat population. Great writing, great story and a great read."
—*Pattaya Mail*

"What distinguishes Christopher G. Moore from other foreign authors setting their stories in the Land of Smiles is how much more he understands its mystique, the psyche of its populace and the futility of its round residents trying to fit into its square holes."
—*Bangkok Post*

"Moore pursues in even greater detail in *Minor Wife* the changing social roles of Thai women (changing, but not always quickly or for the better) and their relations among themselves and across class lines and other barriers."
—*Vancouver Sun*

PATTAYA 24/7
Eighth in the series
Heaven Lake Press (2008) ISBN 978-974-8418-41-4

Inside a secluded, lush estate located on the edge of Pattaya, an eccentric Englishman's gardener is found hanged. Calvino has been hired to investigate. He finds himself pulled deep into the shadows of the war against drugs, into the empire of a local warlord with the trail leading to a terrorist who has caused Code Orange alerts to flash across the screen of American intelligence.

In a story packed with twists and turns, Calvino traces the links from the gardener's past to the door of men with power and influence who have everything to lose if the mystery of the gardener's death is solved.

"Original, provocative, and rich with details and insights into the underworld of Thai police, provincial gangsters, hit squads, and terrorists."
—Pieke Bierman, award-wining author of *Violetta*

"Intelligent and articulate, Moore offers a rich, passionate and original take on the private-eye game, fans of the genre should definitely investigate, and fans of foreign intrigue will definitely enjoy."
—Kevin Burton Smith, *January Magazine*

"A cast of memorably eccentric figures in an exotic Southeast Asian backdrop."
—*The Japan Times*

"The best in the Calvino series . . . The story is compelling."
—*Bangkok Post*

THE RISK OF INFIDELITY INDEX
Ninth in the series
Heaven Lake Press (2007) ISBN 974-88168-7-6

Major political demonstrations are rocking Bangkok. Chaos and fear sweep through the Thai and expatriate communities. Calvino steps into the political firestorm as he investigates a drug piracy operation. The piracy is traced to a powerful business interest protected by important political connections. A nineteen-year-old Thai woman and a middle-age lawyer end up dead on the same evening. Both are connected to Calvino's investigation. The dead lawyer's law firm denies any knowledge of the case. Calvino is left in the cold. Approached by a group of expat housewives—rattled by *The Risk of Infidelity Index* that ranks Bangkok number one for available sexual temptations—to investigate their husbands, Calvino discovers the alliance of forces blocking his effort to disclose the secret pirate drug investigation.

"A hard-boiled, street-smart, often hilarious pursuit of a double murderer."
—*San Francisco Chronicle*

"There's plenty of violent action . . . Memorable low-life characters . . . The real star of the book is Bangkok."
—*Telegraph* (London)

"Taut, spooky, intelligent, and beautifully written."
—T. Jefferson Parker

"A complex, intelligent novel."
—*Publishers' Weekly*

"The darkly raffish Bangkok milieu is a treat."
—*Kirkus Review*

PAYING BACK JACK
Tenth in the series
Heaven Lake Press (2009) ISBN 978-974-312-920-9

In *Paying Back Jack*, Calvino agrees to follow the 'minor wife' of a Thai politician and report on her movements. His client is Rick Casey, a shady American whose life has been darkened by the unsolved murder of his idealistic son. It seems to be a simple surveillance job, but soon Calvino is entangled in a dangerous web of political allegiance and a reckless quest for revenge.

And, unknown to our man in Bangkok, in an anonymous tower in the center of the city, a two-man sniper team awaits its shot, a shot that will change everything. *Paying Back Jack* is classic Christopher G. Moore: densely-woven, eye-opening, and riveting.

"Crisp, atmospheric . . . Calvino's cynical humour oils the wheels nicely, while the cubist plotting keeps us guessing."
—*Guardian*

"The best Calvino yet . . . There are many wheels within wheels turning in this excellent thriller."
—*The Globe and Mail*

"A rich panorama of east meets west. This time round Calvino is drawn into the murky world of private prisons, political assassination and UN officialdom . . . Whether you try it for the exotic setting, the hard-boiled hero or the intrigue and action, you won't be disappointed. And you'll be back for more!." —*Chris Bilkey, Crime Buzz*

"Moore clearly has no fear that his gloriously corrupt Bangkok will ever run dry." —*Kirkus Review*

THE CORRUPTIONIST
Eleventh in the series
Heaven Lake Press (2010) ISBN 978-616-90393-3-4

Set during the recent turbulent times in Thailand, the 11th novel in the Calvino series centers around the street demonstrations and occupations of Government House in Bangkok.

Hired by an American businessman, Calvino finds himself caught in the middle of a family conflict over a Chinese corporate takeover. This is no ordinary deal. Calvino and his client are up against powerful forces set to seize much more than a family business. As the bodies accumulate while he navigates Thailand's business-political landmines, Calvino becomes increasingly entangled in a secret deal made by men who will stop at nothing—and no one—standing in their way but Calvino refuses to step aside.

The Corruptionist captures with precision the undercurrents enveloping Bangkok, revealing multiple layers of betrayal and deception.

"Politics has a role in the series, more so now than earlier ... Thought-provoking columnists don't do it better."
—*Bangkok Post*

"Moore's understanding of the dynamics of Thai society has always impressed, but considering current events, the timing of his latest [*The Corruptionist*] is absolutely amazing."
—*The Japan Times*

"Very believable ... Another riveting read from Christopher G. Moore and one you should not miss."
—*Pattaya Mail*

Mick Elmore © 2009

Canadian Christopher G. Moore is the creator of the award winning Vincent Calvino Private Eye series and the author of the Land of Smiles Trilogy.

In his former life, he studied at Oxford University and taught law at the University of British Columbia. He wrote radio plays for the CBC and NHK before his first novel was published in New York in 1985, when he promptly left his tenured academic job for an uncertain writing career, leaving his colleagues thinking he was not quite right in the head.

His journey from Canada to Thailand, his adopted home, included some time in Japan in the early 1980s and four years in New York in the late 1980s.

In 1988, he came to Thailand to harvest materials to write a book. The visit was meant to be temporary. More than twenty years on and 22 novels later, he is still in Bangkok and far from having exhausted the rich Southeast Asian literary materials.

His novels have so far appeared in a dozen languages.

For more information about the author and his books, visit his website: www.cgmoore.com. He also blogs at International Crime Authors: Reality Check: www. internationalcrimeauthors.com.

9 786167 503011